Charles Travis teaches at Tilburg University, The Netherlands. Formerly Associate Professor at the University of Calgary, Canada, he has also held visiting positions at the University of California at San Diego and at Tel Aviv University. His previous publications include *Saying and Understanding* (1975), *The True and the False* (1981) and, with Jay Rosenberg, *Readings in the Philosophy of Language* (1971), as well as numerous articles on philosophy of language and philosophy of mind.

Contributors

Charles Travis
Gilles Fauconnier
Deirdre Wilson
Dan Sperber
Ruth Kempson
Adam Morton
Martin Davies
John Campbell
S D Guttenplan
Simon Blackburn
Crispin Wright

Meaning and Interpretation

Meaning and Interpretation

EDITED BY
Charles Travis

Basil Blackwell

© Basil Blackwell 1986

First published 1986

Basil Blackwell Ltd
108 Cowley Road, Oxford OX4 1JF, UK

Basil Blackwell Inc.
432 Park Avenue South, Suite 1505,
New York, NY 10016, USA

All rights reserved. Except for the quotation of short passages for the purposes of criticism and review, no part of this publication may be reproduced, stored in a retrieval system, or transmitted, in any form or by any means, electronic, mechanical, photocopying, recording or otherwise, without the prior permission of the publisher.

British Library Cataloguing in Publication Data

Meaning and interpretation.
  1. Semantics (Philosophy)
  I. Title
  149'.946   B820

ISBN 0–631–14644–X

Library of Congress Cataloging in Publication Data

Meaning and interpretation.
  Bibliography; p.
  Includes index.
  1. Semantics (Philosophy)—Addresses, essays, lectures. 2. Meaning (Philosophy)—Addresses, essays, lectures. I. Travis, Charles, 1943–
B840.M45 1986   121'.68   85–26708
ISBN 0–631–14644–X

Typeset by Photographics, Honiton, Devon
Printed in Great Britain by Page Bros, Norwich

Contents

Preface　　　　　　　　　　　　　　　　　　　　　　　vii
Introduction　　*Charles Travis*　　　　　　　　　　　　1

Part I　Words in Language and Use

1　Roles and connecting paths　　　　　　　　　　　　19
　　Gilles Fauconnier
2　Inference and implicature　　　　　　　　　　　　　45
　　Deirdre Wilson and Dan Sperber
3　Ambiguity and the semantics–pragmatics distinction　77
　　Ruth Kempson
4　Domains of discourse and common-sense metaphysics　105
　　Adam Morton

Part II　Structure in Language and Thought

5　Tacit knowledge, and the structure of thought and
　　language　　　　　　　　　　　　　　　　　　　　127
　　Martin Davies
6　Conceptual structure　　　　　　　　　　　　　　　159
　　John Campbell

Part III　Content and Truth

7　Meaning and metaphysics　　　　　　　　　　　　　177
　　S. D. Guttenplan
8　How can we tell whether a commitment has a
　　truth condition?　　　　　　　　　　　　　　　　201
　　Simon Blackburn

| 9 | Facts about truth bearing and content
Charles Travis | 233 |
| 10 | Rule-following, meaning and constructivism
Crispin Wright | 271 |

Index 299

Preface

Between October 6 and 9 1982 a conference was held at Tilburg University in the Netherlands, under the sponsorship of the university and the Dutch Ministry of Science and Education, with the title 'The psychological content of logic'. As it happened, the participants had less to say directly about the announced topic than they did about another: the sorts of things to which logic must be taken to apply if that topic is to be discussed at all, those things in which we deal in thinking and talking and which bear the sort of content that permits standing in inferential relations. The emphasis was on the relation of such things to discourse and to the sentences of a language out of which discourses are constructed. This book does not reproduce what occurred at that conference. Rather it is a result of a long process which began there, aided and abetted by the opportunity that the conference provided for intensive and pleasant exchange of ideas on some central topics in the area. As editor, I am grateful to the university and to the ministry for providing that opportunity.

Charles Travis

Introduction

Charles Travis

Consider a theory whose aim is to say, for a given language, what each of its expressions means. Call it a semantics of that language. What might be required of such a theory before it was allowed that it accomplished its aim or did so in an optimal way? There are some current commonplaces about this. But commonplaces sometimes fail to be true. This volume examines, from a variety of perspectives, ways in which such failure *might* come about. Thoughts about expectations for a semantics often flow from one or another conception of what it is to say what words mean – or what they say or said. Such often rests in turn on a conception of what it is for words to mean (or say or have said) such-and-such. Sometimes this is an idea of what would bring about that they do so. But more often it is an idea of what properties words would have in virtue of doing so. It is conceptions of the last sort which are primarily under scrutiny here.

Among expectations for a semantics, we may distinguish between substantive and formal ones. A substantive expectation concerns what a theory must say – what information it must provide – about each expression within its scope. A formal expectation concerns the way in which it must provide this information – for example, how it must exhibit relations between the information it provides for one expression and that which it supplies for others. A natural idea along the latter lines, for example, would be that if an expression E and another E' differ in meaning, then a semantics should provide distinct representations or specifications of what each means. If E may mean more than one thing, this would mean that the semantics should provide distinct representations of each of these things. Such would be a requirement on the explicitness of the representations the semantics provided. And the 'ifs' here might plausibly be strengthened by adding 'only ifs'. Note that such requirements leave it open what information the theory might provide for each expression within its scope. In fact, it has been claimed (though the case is not completely clear) that a theory might satisfy the above without saying anything about what any expression means.

Another idea that has seemed natural to many is that the theory should show or describe how the meaning of an expression is 'constructed from' or determined by the meanings of its parts, wherever and to the extent that such is the case. The idea might be that if a semantics fails to do this for some expression E, then there is something about what E means which that semantics has left out of account. Part of being as described in 'split-level house', for example, is being as described in 'house', whereas part of being as described in 'Chinese parsley' is not being as described in 'parsley'. The contrast, it might be thought, points to a fact one would have to know in order to know what 'split-level house' means, and a fact that one would not know *merely* in virtue of knowing what sorts of things that term describes correctly. It is thus, one might think, a fact which a semantic theory of English must represent.

Another motive for the structural requirement is the fact that speakers of a language effortlessly understand novel sentences if they understand their parts. Satisfying the requirement of representing structure could be taken as a way of representing this important aspect of competence – *if* representing competence is taken to be an aim of semantics. It has been suggested further that someone who lacked this competence thoroughly could not even be said to understand the elements out of which complex expressions are built. Such an idea might be motivated by a thought about language: to know the meaning of a word is to know what contribution it makes to the meanings of wholes in which it appears, for it contributes what it does in virtue of meaning what it does. But the idea may also be motivated by a thought about thought: thinking the things that complexes may express requires having concepts adequate for doing so, which requires, in turn, seeing the thought as structured in an appropriate way. If the idea transfers to *saying* what words mean, then a semantics could not say what a part meant without saying what its contribution was to wholes in which it figured. The idea that it is because of certain fundamental features of our thought that understanding requires understanding structure is explored by John Campbell in his contribution to this book.

The intuitive requirement of 'exhibiting structure' begins to come under pressure when we note that, as set out so far, there is a sense in which it would be satisfied by *any* semantics which achieved its primary aim of saying what the expressions of its language mean. For, given the indefinite number of distinct expressions of a language, any semantics must avail itself of *some* recursive devices in order to specify the meanings of all but a fixed finite set of expressions. But wherever it avails itself of such devices, it does show one way in which the meanings of wholes are constructible from the meanings of parts, given what its recursive devices recognize as proper parts. Understood in this way, exhibiting structure imposes no additional requirement on a semantics beyond that of achieving its primary aim.

Whether the notion of structure can do any work in saying what a semantic theory will be like depends, then, on just how that notion is to be spelled out. Such might be done in a variety of ways. One way would be to suppose that, for any expression, there is some way in which its meaning is to be understood to be constructed from the meanings of its parts, and thus some semantic structure in particular which, in virtue of its meaning what it does, it is properly understood to have. The task of a semantic theory would then be to exhibit just this structure, and not just any way of building meanings of wholes out of meanings of parts. A theory might accomplish this goal by recognizing elements of its language, such as syntactic structures, which had meanings in the sense that words do, and hence which were assigned a semantics by the theory, but whose meaning could only be explicated in terms of the results they produced for wholes in which they occurred, given the meanings of other parts with which they occurred. Such an approach to structure might be viewed as formal, since it proposes to account for structure by imposing a requirement on what information a theory must provide in saying what certain elements of a language (e.g. syntactic structures) mean. Note that this view of semantic structure does not directly touch the actual psychologies of actual recognizably competent speakers of the language in question. How such speakers do understand a given expression is generally a powerful determinant of what it ought to be taken to mean; nevertheless, how someone *does* understand an expression and how it is to be (or is properly) understood are two distinct issues.

Another idea about the structure requirement parallels in certain ways an idea about the substance of a semantics. One might think, and some have said, that what a semantics ought to say about a given expression is no less then all there is to say about what it means or, perhaps, about it in virtue of what it means. Indeed, this thought may provide part of the motivation for the idea that semantics ought to show how meanings are composed. Similarly, one might hold that the structure which a semantics ought to exhibit or specify is 'all the structure there is', or all that would be perceivable for an idealized understander of a given sort. Such might be called a formal notion, since the requirement is that, wherever meanings are constructible in certain ways, they be shown to be constructible in those ways, regardless of the specific information a theory may provide in saying what it is that parts and whole do mean. Both the substantive and the formal notion need further working out. One might question whether either represents a realizable ambition. The formal notion, in any event, gets an elaboration and a defence in Martin Davies's contribution to this book. As befits arguments for a formal expectation of semantics, Davies's arguments presuppose nothing about the particular information that a semantics should supply for each expression.

Let us now turn to requirements on the substance of a semantics. As remarked, such requirements generally flow from one or another conception of what it is for an expression to mean one thing or another. Currently dominant views of semantics flow from one conception in particular, and it is that one that is primarily under scrutiny here. In the case of declarative sentences, the conception might be put like this. The job of such a sentence is to express a thought. For each sentence, there is the thought that it expresses. (Let us ignore such matters as referents and times and places of a speaking). If a sentence meant anything other than what it did, it would express a different thought than the one it does, and, conversely, any sentence which expressed a different thought would mean something different than it did. So expressing such-and-such a thought is individuative of meaning such-and-such. Now thoughts are, world willing, either true or false. Further, if a thought is true in situation S, then, given that Leibniz's law applies, any thought not true in S is not that thought. So, one might think, thoughts are individuated by the conditions under which they would be true, and hence by the condition for their being true. But the condition for the truth of a thought transfers, it would seem, to any sentence which expresses it, and hence to any sentence which means what a sentence which does so means. Hence, for any sentence, there must be some condition C such that a sentence will mean what that one does, just in case it is true under condition C. Which is to suggest that we can say what a sentence means (or at least individuate it) by stating the condition under which it (or the thought it expresses) would be true.

A conception of meaning might be scrutinized in either of two ways. One way is to look at the phenomena. One might examine what distinctions must or can be drawn – not only between one thing and another that words in fact mean, but also between one thing and another that words (especially given ones) might say. One can then ask whether these distinctions mesh with notions such as truth – whether they yield objects which can be ascribed properties such as being true or false. Such an approach presupposes an adequate supply of non-controversial judgements on cases where distinctions need drawing, on what was said in given words, which situations would make given words true, when they would do so, and so on. So the approach is not for one, for example, who sincerely doubts whether there are facts on such matters. The second approach examines the conditions that would have to be met for anything to have the properties assigned to expressions by the conception in question, and/or the conditions for expressions meaning what they in fact do mean. The aim is to see whether anything could have the properties figuring in the conception and, if so, whether having them coincides with what we recognize as an expression's having a definite meaning.

Both approaches are represented in the present volume. Let us begin with a brief consideration of the first. Here it is the phenomena one would actually be describing in a semantics which do not seem to fit the conception, and it is work on building working theories of the phenomena that has convinced a number of people that they do not. The idea is that distinctions which need drawing between one thing and another that an expression may mean do not seem to mesh with those that need drawing between one and another condition for a thought's being true. For on examination, even in the most favourable cases, there seems to be no such thing as 'the thought a sentence expresses'. Rather, any declarative sentence seems capable of expressing any of an indefinite number of distinct thoughts, each on some possible speaking of it or another. It is not immediately clear whether such variation calls for a radical break with the picture of semantics as stating truth conditions, or merely for a minor revision. Such depends, for one thing, on what one takes a paradigm of the variation to be. Some take it to be illustrated by sentences such as

(1) I am hot.

There is an obvious way in which this sentence may express different thoughts on different speakings. The variation seems to depend on who the speaker is and when he speaks. For what a speaker will say in speaking the sentence is, roughly, that he is hot at the time of speaking.

The variation just described depends, it seems, on two identifiable variables in a speaking: who did it, and when. Specify values for those, and you determine the thought expressed. If that is *all* that the variation in (1) comes to, then we may say that what (1) means determines a function in two variables from speakings to thoughts expressed in them in speaking (1). Correspondingly, by specifying this function we may hope to specify what (1) means. If the above is the paradigm of variation in the thought expressed in a sentence, then the picture of stating meanings directly in terms of truth conditions might be replaced with one of stating meanings in terms of functions from identifiable sorts of facts about speakings to truth conditions. And the change may well turn out to look to be more in the letter then in the spirit of the original intuitive idea.

Other paradigms of variation are possible, however. Consider a sentence like the following, for example:

(2) The walls are beige.

Suppose it turns out that, referring to given walls, and spoken at a given time, (2) might express any of various thoughts, with any of various conditions for their truth. Though 'beige' speaks of being beige throughout this variety of things to be said in (2), for each of them there are different things to be understood about what being beige is to come to. (For example, will being *painted* beige do?) Which of these things is said in a given speaking of (2) at a given time will of course be determined, somehow or other, by some further facts about the speaking. But are there *identifiable* factors in a speaking which would make what was said in it one thing or the other? If so, such factors must be quite unlike things such as who the speaker is, or time and place of utterance. But there is also the possibility that there are no such factors at all. For it might be that for any specified set of variables in speakings, we can fix values of those and produce two speakings sharing all those features, but none the less expressing different thoughts. If so, then what (2) means cannot determine a function from speakings to conditions for the truth of what is said in it. We will then have to seek some other way of saying what (2) means, which *may* turn out not to be in terms of truth conditions at all.

The last problem seems sometimes obscured by thinking of functions in extensional terms. For take any set of speakings of (2). In each of them, plausibly, one thing or another (or nothing) was said. Within this set, then, for any set of features which identify a speaking, there is a function from those features to the things said in each speaking. It is just the relevant set of ordered pairs. But surely there is such a thing as all the speakings of (2) there will ever be. Take any set of variables in terms of which those speakings may be identified, and choose a function pairing values of those with the appropriate truth conditions for each speaking in this set.

One trouble with this idea is that it confuses semantics with history. What was wanted was not an account of all the things that ever were (or will be) said in (2), but rather an account of what would be said in (2), given what it means, or of how what it means constrains what is (to be) said in it – an account notably absent in the above way of doing things.

Seeking paradigms of variation in what is said or expressed in given words is one way of approaching the question of what it is for words to mean what they do, or, more colourfully, what meanings do. Intuitively, what a sentence means constrains what can be said in speaking it literally. But, if simple paradigms of variation fail, then we are left wanting to know more about what these constraints are. What relations are there between what words express in use and what they mean? And, given what they mean, what factors determine which things they express on an occasion? Such questions are both non-trivial and important for the questions with which we began. For only with a proper grasp of what meanings do determine can we see what there is to say (truly) in saying what words mean.

The question of constraints is faced, in one way or another, in each of the first four chapters in this volume. Facing the problem directly, several models immediately suggest themselves. A simple idea is this: even if there is no such thing as 'the thought a sentence expresses', there is still, for any sentence, a set of thoughts that it can express. Perhaps these thoughts are not related to the sentence, as on the 'I am hot' model, in such a way as to permit doing semantics in terms of truth conditions. Still, wherever the sentence is used to say something, the thought expressed is constrained to be one or another in the set attached to it by what it means. One can then hope to say what the sentence means by specifying what this set is. Another model, suggested by Fauconnier in one special case, is that what a sentence means determines rules for constructing things that can be said or expressed in speaking it, but does not determine any particular set of such things as 'those things expressible in it'. Rather, what can be constructed according to the rules depends on facts about the world in which speakings of the sentence are to be produced. By varying such things as background knowledge, for example, we can vary not only what a sentence *does* express, but what it *could* express. Of course, as expressed here, the above are somewhat imprecise leading ideas. As Fauconnier suggests, making them precise means working through a great deal of linguistic data.

Issues about constraints on what can be said in given words are only one set of issues about the relations between words and what there is to be said or expressed in them. Another set of issues concerns the relation between the sort of entity that, for example, a sentence is, and the sorts of entities produced on occasion in speaking it. A beginning can be made on these issues in the following way. If the simple truth-conditional idea for semantics fails in the way outlined above, then we know that there are certain properties that sentences do not have. They are not, for example, either true or false, at least not *tout court*. Nor do they impose some one condition for the truth of what is expressed in them wherever such matters need considering. Nor can they be assigned any particular thought as the thought that they express. Now suppose we look at words as spoken on an occasion – as it were, *someone's* words, 'The walls are beige' as opposed to the English words, 'The walls are beige.' Or we might look at a speaking of words, or at that which is said or expressed in speaking them. In what respects, and to what extent, might such things have the properties that, for example, the English words such-and-such lack?

One view on these problems might be suggested by Austin (though it is not *obviously* his view.) In his attack on a Tarskian conception of truth, Austin insisted that sentences were precisely the wrong sorts of things to be either true or false. The suggestion might be that there is some other sort of thing which is the right sort of thing to be either true or false (or perhaps a motley of distinct sorts of things.) One might call such a thing a statement, or, with several contributors to this volume, a proposition. To put things generally, such a thing is produced wherever words are spoken and there is something to be evaluated as true or false. Having decided that it is the right sort of thing to be either true or false, we might then continue and assign it all the properties that we denied to sentences: having a definite condition for its truth, expressing (or perhaps being) one thought in particular, and so on.

The idea might be put like this. Perhaps there are various things which, on occasion, being brown might correctly be taken to come to, and hence various things that might be said to be so of something in the words, 'is brown'. But if we have spoken those words on an occasion, then there is (at most) one of these things which we have said to be so. Hence, there is a definite condition for the truth of what we said, namely, that that be so. Call the thing for whose truth this is a condition a proposition.

Here, however, we may, with Wittgenstein, pose the question whether the problems we have so far discovered are *simply* problems about what *sentences* (or expressions of a language) mean, or whether they are not rather problems about content, or what is expressed in general – problems that would always arise where there were questions of how something was to be understood. The idea might be expressed in this way. Words like 'is brown', we have decided, may make any of various contributions to what is said in speaking them, so that what they describe truly on one occasion of using them they might not describe truly on another. Otherwise put, such words function so that there may be variation from occasion to occasion in the words in which a given object may be described or spoken of truly. But if such is the case for words like 'is brown', then why not also for, as it were, 'the semantic terms of our language' – that is, the words in which we assign content to, or describe proper understandings or correct applications of, *inter alia*, words. In that case, the true descriptions of the proper understandings of given words (or whatever), like the true descriptions of the colour of a given object, might vary from occasion to occasion of giving them. And such variation might extend to specification of what the words are, for example, true of. So the same words which count as being true of a given object or situation, on a given occasion of considering the matter, may fail to do so on another. *Mutatis mutandis* for what words require for their truth.

Once we have recognized 'context involvement' or occasion variability on the level of descriptions of content, the question arises whether we need to distinguish any longer between a variety of distinct sorts of things, such as sentences of a language, propositions and the like, in order to describe the facts about content properly. Wittgenstein's answer to this question was no. If we accept it, then we can, with him, speak simply of 'words' (or, in his terminology, *Sätze*), omitting distinctions between such things as someone's words, or words on an occasion, and words in a language. Of course, the properties correctly assigned to words will then vary from occasion to occasion. We would then be taking a sort of exception to the Austinian remark about sentences given above. On this way of looking at things, sentences are not the wrong sorts of things to be either true or false. It is just that they, like anything, are the wrong sorts of things to be true or false *tout court*. There may be occasions for holding given words, such as 'My suit is brown' true, considering facts of a given use of them – one someone did make, or one we want to make, or both. And there may be occasions for holding these same words false, even though we may take the words to be describing the same situation or suit, whether the facts of one or the other sort about use are different. On Wittgenstein's view, there is no calling a halt to such variation by proliferating technical distinctions.

We now turn to the second way of examining a conception of meaning. It is near to a commonplace that one uses words in conformity with what they mean, or not. If not, then the words are not used properly, or as they are to be, or are to be understood to be. So there seems to be something meaning requires for using words properly, or as they are to be understood to be. Commonplaces end when it comes to saying what sort of requirement this is or could be. On the conception under scrutiny above, the meaning of a declarative sentence, for example, determines which situations or states of affairs it would be true of. It was suggested above that *that* idea is shown wrong by the fact that the meaning of such a sentence is compatible with saying a variety of things in it, each with its own distinct condition for its truth. One conclusion one might draw is that meanings of words in a language are the wrong sorts of things to match up with truth conditions or their near relatives. But whether it is words in a language or utterances or what is said in them or thoughts which get conditions for their truth, there are problems about how anything such as what is envisaged on the above conception could be determined at all, or at least could be determined by any properties that any such entity might have at a given time.

Let us for the moment waive problems about the variety in things that words might be used to say consistent with what they mean. Then, restricting attention again to declarative sentences, the idea is roughly this: some facts which now hold about what the words now mean determine for any situation which might arise in the future whether the words are (or would be) true of that situation – at least in so far as such things are ever determined at all. So for any situation, there is some fact about the meaning of the words which determines whether they are true of it. Further, on the conception, this is a fact which one states in (really) (truly) (actually) stating the meaning of the words. And presumably it is a fact which one grasps in grasping the meaning of the words or, more simply, understanding them. The last two points suggest what may also be part of the conception, namely that there is some fact about what the words mean such that for any situation this fact determines whether the words are true of it. (Though such interchanges of quantifiers also sometimes occur unnoticed in philosophy.)

Anyone with sympathy for the late Wittgenstein is likely to feel that there is *something* wrong with this idea. For how could any 'current' fact about words determine such a thing? It seemed to be a moral of Wittgenstein's philosophy that what facts about meaning determine depends on what those facts are taken to mean, there always being a variety of possible understandings of what they say is to be done with the words in question. So any currently stateable fact about the meaning of a word would seem in some sense to be compatible with various patterns of future applications of it. But though Wittgenstein's remarks contain something intuitively compelling in this vein, it proves an amazingly slippery something when it comes to saying exactly what it is. It is difficult to find facts about use or applications which are actually inconsistent with the letter of the original idea about what meaning determines.

One suggestion might be to take a leaf from the attack on words in a language as bearers of conditions for truth. The idea in that case might be put in the following way. If we understand English words such as 'Snow is white', then, whenever anyone says, 'Snow is white', we have an easy enough time telling whether what he said is true, or at least sorting out what does from what does not count against its truth. At least this seems so whenever we come to consider the matter. And if we did not – if we were, as a rule, totally at a loss as to what to count for or against the truth of the words – then we would not be said to understand them. So it *looks* as if what the words mean (what we know when we can perform in such ways) decides what counts for and against *their* truth, and hence determines some definite truth condition for *them*. What this line of thought overlooks, given the above comments on the variety of things to be said in given words, is that our ability, described above, to deal with what was said manifests itself on occasion. It may thus rely not only on our knowledge of what the words mean *in abstracto*, but also on our ability to perceive what that determines or determined in the particular circumstances in which the words were spoken.

The point is that it is easy to overlook the circumstances in which it is to be seen that facts F determine result R. So too, perhaps, for the idea of 'present' facts determining 'future' applications. Suppose someone now says, 'Snow is white.' Later, confronted with a situation, we can tell whether his words are true of it. So it looks as if there is a fact about his words, on their proper understanding, which determines this. What we may overlook here is that what we are perceiving is what a proper understanding of the words determines *on an occasion of judging something about what they are true of.* Just as what the meaning of words determines depends, *inter alia*, on the circumstances of their speaking, so what an understanding determines may depend on facts of an occasion of considering what it determines. Just as the first dependency produces variation in what there is to be said in given words, so the second may produce variation in what given facts about meanings or proper understandings determine about applications. Such, anyway, is an idea for one approach to the intuitive Wittgensteinian thought.

Another tactic in dealing with the above conception of meaning would be simply to oppose it with another and then arbitrate between the two. An ingenious idea along these lines is presented in Crispin Wright's contribution to this book. Wright suggests conceiving of meaning in analogy with a person's character. People do do things out of character. But nothing a person now does can be out of character for him *simply* in virtue of his past doings. It could conceivably merely show what his real character was all along. Rather, what he does can only count as out of character against a backdrop of overall behaviour, past and – where there is some – future. Similarly, we might conceive of using a word in conformity with its meaning as using it in a way that fits with an overall pattern of uses, both past and future. What it can fail to conform with is the pattern, and not merely those facts determined by happenings up to a given time. Arbitrating between this notion of meaning and that which seems to be embedded in the truth-conditional conception of semantics is – as one would expect – an intricate business, about which Wright presents some most interesting ideas.

On the dominant conception, semantics was supposed to be done in terms of notions of truth and falsity. For these notions marked what was supposed to be the business of semantics: describing relations between words and the world. What the conception presupposed was a match between the properties that could actually be ascribed to words (L–ish words, for a language L) and the properties something would have to have for there to be facts, for example, about its truth or falsity. The need for a match generalizes to any notions in terms of which one proposes to say what words of a language mean, whether those of the dominant conception or those of some alternative one. So far we have concentrated on ways of investigating what properties words have. But where a conception proposes doing semantics in terms of given notions, one might also examine the conception by asking what is required for there to be facts about to what those notions apply. The contributions of Samuel Guttenplan and Simon Blackburn are, for two different sets of notions, interesting examples of how progress might be made from this direction.

This volume aims, then, to contribute in a variety of ways to our understanding of understanding and of understandings. Taken as a whole, it cannot be viewed as incremental on some existing body of knowledge, say, about meanings. Nor, if it raises questions about one conception of semantics, is it unified in offering some other. But diversity here is perhaps a reflection of the fact that treatments of meaning and content are not yet *quite* ready to spin off from philosophy and form their own new science, even if the time is long past (if it was ever present) when such things were a philosopher's exclusive domain. If there are still matters to be worked out about how stating meaning is to be done, then it may be at least a small step to progress to realize that fact. And it would be a bigger one to set out some of these issues clearly. Such is the project of this book.

Part I
Words in Language and Use

1

Roles and connecting paths

Gilles Fauconnier

There is undeniably considerable overlap in the area of semantics and pragmatics between the concerns of linguistics and the concerns of philosophy of language: the same phenomena are often studied and considered important, similar theoretical questions are raised, and the technical frameworks conceived by philosophers and logicians are tested and developed by linguists.

Nevertheless, or perhaps because of the overlap, there is a good deal of equivocation as to the link between philosophical questions related to language use, and the study of language organization *per se*.[1] To put things bluntly: if a philosophical study makes use of linguistic data, it is hard to avoid reading into it some linguistic analysis of those data. Conversely, a linguistic picture of semantic/pragmatic language organization will easily appear permeated with 'philosophical' preconceptions: again, one is likely to read more philosophy into it than there actually is.

Certain areas of language study which perhaps put a greater emphasis on form – syntax and phonology – do not suffer, it would seem, from this particular syndrome. Categories, rules, principles and constraints need no ontological justification: one asks 'What is a noun phrase?', 'What is a filter?', 'What is extrinsic ordering?' in a technical sense, within a theoretical framework.

---

1 It is also hard to avoid having such links built in. For example, if semantics is considered *a priori* to be 'truth conditional' in a narrow sense, linguistic theories of meaning will be, at least conceptually, dependent from the start on philosophical theories of truth.

Simplifying somewhat, the analytical constructs are judged in relation and in proportion to the generalizations they allow. As in other sciences, elegance, universality and considerable empirical data carry weight.

I believe that, analogously, it is possible to point out regularities in the organisation of semantic constructions associated with natural language, without taking a stand on the various corresponding philosophical issues. But it must be acknowledged that those issues, or at least their framing, will not necessarily remain unaffected: philosophy can make no absolute, analysis-independent appeal to language data.

The focus of attention in this chapter is not so much on structure and interpretation as on connections. It is presumably uncontroversial, when expressed in a general and admittedly vague sense, that part of our intellectual activity and capability consists in making, recognizing or exploiting connections, and that there are ways in which language either mirrors or sustains this capacity. Metonymy is a likely example: the name or description of something or someone (*trigger*) can be used in relation to something or someone else (*target*), apparently because a salient link between the two is presupposed, perceived or established in some (or all) situations. A nurse in a hospital might exploit this possibility to address one of her colleagues with (1):

(1) Please take some coffee to *the gastric ulcer* in room 13.

A description of an illness serves to single out a patient. The salient link in that situation is between inmates and their ailments.[2]

---

[2] This particular example was provided by R. Lacy. A detailed and perspicacious study of such 'pragmatic functions' can be found in G. Nunberg, 'The pragmatics of reference', Indiana University Linguistics Club, Bloomington, Ind., 1978, together with many other examples. The generality of the phenomenon and its relevance to generative theory was pointed out in 1971 by A. Borkin, *Problems in Form and Function*, appendix A (Ablex, Norwood, NJ, 1984). Further discussion can be found in G. Fauconnier, *Mental Spaces* (MIT Press, Cambridge, Mass., 1985); and T. Gilchrist, 'Metonymy', unpublished manuscript, UC Berkeley, 1983.

Roles and connecting paths

Notice what happens if (1) is understood, that is what information it conveys: some person b is to be given coffee, and b is afflicted with a gastric ulcer a. Each of these pieces of information can only be recovered if two conditions are met: first, that the addressee is aware of, and willing to use, the salient link between patients and illnesses; and second, that a principle of language allows a description of the trigger (here the illness) to stand for the target (here the patient). It is obvious, and yet non-trivial, that nothing in the structure of sentence (1) provides this information.

Schematically, if we note as $S'(x)$ what sentence S says about x, and as F a salient link between trigger a and target b such as 'illnesses → patients', then $F(a) = b$. And the import of S in cases like (1) amounts to

$$S'(F(a))$$

That is, we are told something simultaneously about a and about its counterpart b (=$F(a)$). Grammatically, $F(a)$ (the stricken patient) is identified by means of a description of a (the ulcer).

Now turn to a different type of connection. By way of example, consider sentences (2) and (3):

(2) In 1940, Jane's husband was still a bachelor.
(3) In 1940, Jane's husband divorced her.

Sentences (2) and (3) are mutually consistent if the same linguistic description, 'Jane's husband', is associated with different individuals. Again this is an obvious, but non-trivial, possibility offered by the language: (2) may be about Rex, Jane's present husband, and (3) may be about Leo, married to Jane back in 1940 but not any more.

Under such an interpretation of (2), the same individual is endowed with two superficially contradictory properties, 'bachelor' and 'Jane's husband'. Of course no contradiction ensues, since the properties are relative to different time domains. One way to relativize properties to domains is to have a semantic construction which keeps them distinct. Informally:

(4)

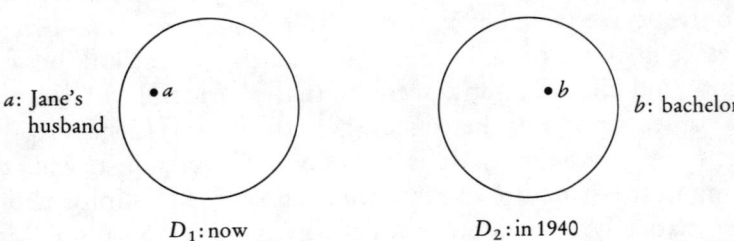

D_1: now D_2: in 1940

Construction (4) may be regarded as abstract: elements a and b both correspond in this case to the real-world referent Rex. Informally again, properties satisfied by a in D_1 correspond to properties of Rex now; properties satisfied by b in D_2 correspond to properties of Rex in 1940. Domains D_1 and D_2 are formally ordinary sets with elements such as a and b, and relations which those elements may satisfy. Elements a and b have no place in the world with respect to which (2) is interpreted, so they are not referents. But one could say, *given* this construction, that a and b both refer to Rex.

There is no *a priori* reason (and why should there be?) to set up a construction like (4) on the basis of sentence (2) or on the basis of the (real) situation referred to by (2). But consider what happens if we do set up (4) as a construction associated with (2). There will be a link between a and b: call it F. Element b (in D_2) is the counterpart of a (in D_1), so that

$$F(a) = b$$

Sentence S has a content S' (1): it yields a property satisfied by b in D_2, but it identifies b by means of a description of a in D_1:

$$S'(b) = S'(F(a))$$

$F(a)$ is identified by the description 'Jane's husband', and this is technically a description applicable to (i.e. satisfied by) a:

(5)

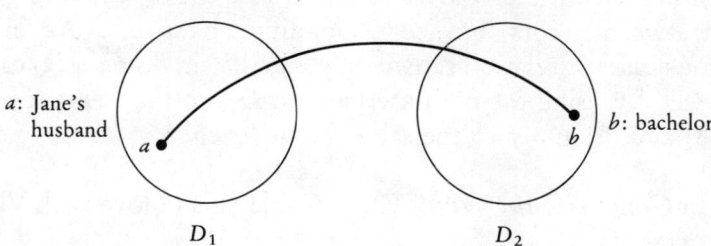

Formally, then, the identity connection in (4) is parallel to the metonymic connection at work in (1). In both cases, target b can be identified by a description of its counterpart a with respect to a connector F. In both cases, the sentence will simultaneously yield properties of a and b, namely $S'(F(a))$ and $S'(b)$. In both cases, the connecting link F is implicit: it is not signalled morphologically or grammatically. This linguistic [3] property of connections has been referred to as the *identification (ID) principle*:

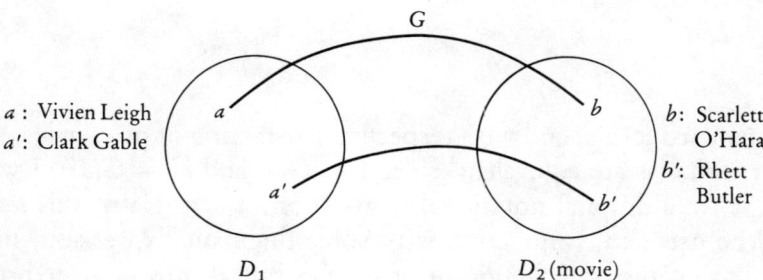

If a and b are linked by a connector F, a's counterpart b may be identified by a description or name satisfied by a. The power of this principle resides in its applicability to connections of very

---

3 As noted by Nunberg, 'The pragmatics of reference', this principle may also apply in cases of ostension. One can point to Elvis Presley at a concert and say: 'That guy should be in your record collection.'

different sorts. Consider the link between actors and the characters they impersonate, for instance Clark Gable/Rhett Butler and Vivien Leigh/Scarlett O'Hara in *Gone with the Wind*. Call G the link between actors and corresponding characters. As in the previous cases, a relation satisfied by b and b' in domain D_2 can be conveyed by using their counterparts in D_1, so that sentences (6), (7), (8) and (9) apply to the same movie 'event':

(6) In *Gone with the Wind*, Clark Gable falls in love with Vivien Leigh.
(7) In *Gone with the Wind*, Clark Gable falls in love with Scarlett O'Hara.
(8) In *Gone with the Wind*, Rhett Butler falls in love with Vivien Leigh.
(9) In *Gone with the Wind*, Rhett Butler falls in love with Scarlett O'Hara.

Using L as a symbol for 'falls in love with', we can write (6), (7), (8) and (9) schematically as (6'), (7'), (8') and (9'):

(6') $L(G(a'), G(a))$
(7') $L(G(a'), b)$
(8') $L(b', G(a'))$
(9') $L(b', b)$

In standard terms, and with respect to satisfaction of properties, all four formulas are equivalent[4] since $b = G(a)$ and $b' = G(a')$. I will adopt an additional notational convention: a formula of this sort will be used, in conjunction with some linguistic expression, not only to express satisfaction of properties but also to indicate how the elements are identified. So, for example, (7') $L(G(a), b')$ and (9') $L(b, b')$ express the same relation between b and b', but the former indicates that b is identified through its counterpart a. It should be borne in mind that $a, b, a', b', \ldots$ are not referents.

What is at issue is the possibility in a sentence, and *a fortiori* in discourse, for properties to be ascribed, not in an absolute sense,

---

[4] 'Equivalence' in this particular sense will be represented later in this chapter by the symbol $\simeq$.

but relative to different domains. Informally, in cases like (2) and (3), someone is Jane's husband (relative to 1940) and is not Jane's husband (relative to 1985). In (7), Clark Gable is in love (*qua* Rhett Butler) and is not in love (*qua* Clark Gable). And if that were all there was to it, one could either just use complex properties ('to be Jane's husband in 1940', 'to play the part of a character in love with Scarlett O'Hara in *Gone with the Wind*', etc.) or speak of the same individual in different domains (or possible worlds, situations, etc.) and of his properties relative to such domains. Furthermore, the apparent generalization about the ID principle applying in all such cases would be lost.

But this approach – cross-domain (or cross-world) identification of the same individual – will not reflect the linguistic situation correctly. One reason is that there may be multiple links between two domains, or multiple counterparts for a single domain element.

Consider the first case, using again, by way of example, reality and film as the two relevant domains. One salient link is G, connecting actors and characters, so that as in (6) and (7) a name or description of an actor may be used to identify the character he plays. Another link, F, will operate if the movie purports to represent something else, say a real historical situation. Suppose for instance it is about the boxer Rocky Marciano, played by Robert de Niro. Suppose further that Rocky Marciano is pictured as having had no children; the speaker, however, is convinced (perhaps correctly) that he (the speaker) is Rocky's son. All of the following sentences are possible:

(10) In the movie, *Rocky Marciano* has no children.
(11) In the movie, *my father* has no children.
(12) In the movie, *Robert de Niro* has no children.

Sentences (11) and (12) both use the ID principle: (11) identifies the character Rocky by way of link F, with a description ('my father') satisfied in the speaker's 'reality', but not in the movie. Sentence (12) identifies the same character by way of link G. And, of course, R. de Niro's son or daughter (if he has one) could use (11) in the same circumstances by appealing to G.

That links *F* and *G* are not differentiated linguistically is confirmed by the use of reflexives; if Rocky Marciano and Robert de Niro are among the spectators watching the boxer on the screen get knocked out, then (13) and (14) are both possible:

(13) Rocky Marciano watched *himself* get knocked out.
(14) Robert de Niro watched *himself* get knocked out.

(15)

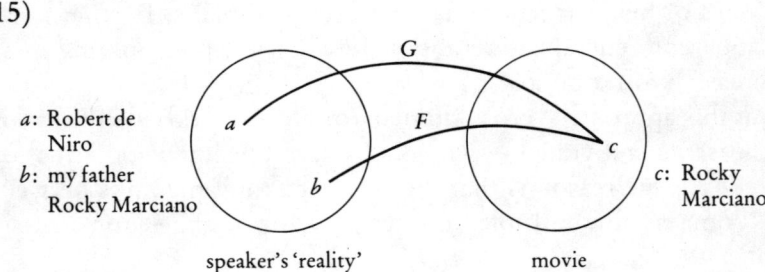

Intuitively, *c* counts as 'identical' to *b* by virtue of link *F*, and 'identical' to *a* by virtue of link *G*. But this does not make *a* and *b* identical: Rocky Marciano and Robert de Niro remain perfectly distinct.

In *Mental Spaces* (henceforth MS)[5] more complex configurations of the form (16) are studied:

(16)

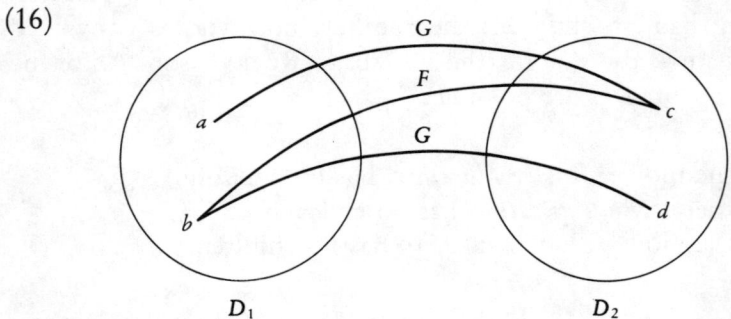

(This is the case where Rocky Marciano also happens to play a small role in the movie: (13) becomes ambiguous, since *c* or *d* could have been knocked out.)

5 Fauconnier, *Mental Spaces*.

In cases like (15) and (16) it is no longer possible to speak about the properties of some individual relative to some domain: b in D_1 has the properties of c in D_2 by link F and the properties of d in D_2 by link G. And different 'individuals' a and b in D_1 have a single counterpart c in D_2. For almost the same reason, complex properties won't do: properties of Rocky Marciano 'in the movie' might be properties satisfied in the model by c or by d (i.e. properties of the 'representation' or the 'character'). They cannot be conflated.

The import of the linguistic data is that properties must be carefully sorted with regard to domains and links. In MS this is done by assuming that between language and world an intermediate construction process takes place to carry out the sorting. Technically, the informal 'domains' mentioned above are 'mental spaces' in the construction process: on a first approximation they are simply sets of elements which can be modified as discourse goes on and which can get linked by connectors (like F and G).

The generality of the linking process and ID principle is non-trivial linguistically: the resulting view is that language has a uniform means of sorting out properties and constructing counterparts when there is a shift of domains. In this respect, although of course not in others, shifts in time or in space from assumed 'reality' to beliefs or hopes, to counterfactuals, to pictures and representations, etc. fall under the same laws.

The mental space constructions are not 'situations' or 'worlds' referred to by expressions. Rather, as suggested by Travis, they correspond to various 'understandings' of a sentence within a context (i.e. given previously constructed space configurations).[6]

What about the philosophical implications? There is no reason to want to draw 'metaphysical' consequences from such constructions. To some extent, language will lead to sorting out properties

---

[6] The space configuration is built up during ongoing discourse. The 'utterance' of some sentence makes a contribution to this configuration by giving instructions for further building. Hence there is no particular configuration, or subconfiguration, corresponding to a sentence (or an utterance). One could view the 'meaning' of an utterance in context as the difference between space configurations before and after it occurs. The 'meaning' of a sentence would be its potential for modifying space configurations.

in this way, with little concern for what the world might 'really' be like. The types of process in question apply equally well to prototype or idealized cases and to metaphorical domains. The 'real' nature of time, space, belief, wishes, counterfactual statements, etc. seems immaterial: the ways in which we can talk about them do not determine what they are, or even for that matter how we conceive of them. Constructions like those suggested should generate no more *a priori* suspicion than grammatical categories, transformations, linguistic levels, etc. They are based on generalizations about language use, not on speculations about what this language refers to (if and when it indeed refers). Needless to say, their adoption needs empirical evidence and scientific consensus of the usual kind. It does not require direct interpretation into some metaphysical system, considered desirable on *a priori* grounds. Yet, as mentioned earlier, it is hard not to read philosophical implications into a semantic analysis. For some, the term 'mental space' is loaded. A frequent question is 'What are mental spaces?' — that is, besides what the model defines them to be. It would be nice to have an answer, but in fact such questions have little content, as can be seen by replacing the term 'mental spaces' by 'electricity', 'complex numbers' or 'magnetic fields', for which we would not think of demanding a theory-independent characterization.

That there might be constructions like (15) and (16), that sort out properties and yield various understandings for sentences in context, is no stranger *per se* than the existence of phonological rules or syntactic derivations. If there is a rationale for the term 'mental space' itself, it will come from linguistic analogies between such constructs and the linguistic treatment of physical space, nicely demonstrated by Lakoff.[7] The term 'mental' is banal. Such constructions, if they take place, will be part of our thought processes; another issue, the possible real-world basis for such constructions (e.g. in terms of evolution, prototypes, analogies, etc.) remains entirely open.

As mentioned above, mental spaces are set up in relation to beliefs and other propositional attitudes, and the ID principle and trigger/target links account for many properties of 'opaque' con-

---

[7] G. Lakoff, *Women, Fire and Dangerous Things* (University of Chicago Press, Chicago, 1985).

texts. If an individual known to the speaker as Ortcutt, and to Ralph as the man on the beach, is believed by Ralph to be a spy, this may be expressed by (17) or by (18):

(17) *Ralph believes* that *the man on the beach* is a spy.
(18) *Ralph believes* that *Ortcutt* is a spy.

In both cases the linguistic expression 'Ralph believes' sets up a mental space B, distinct from the speaker's origin space R. A definite description ('the man on the beach') or a name ('Ortcutt') will point to some trigger element in R or B satisfying the relevant property (name Ortcutt, or man on the beach), and in virtue of the ID principle may identify its target counterpart in B.

(19)

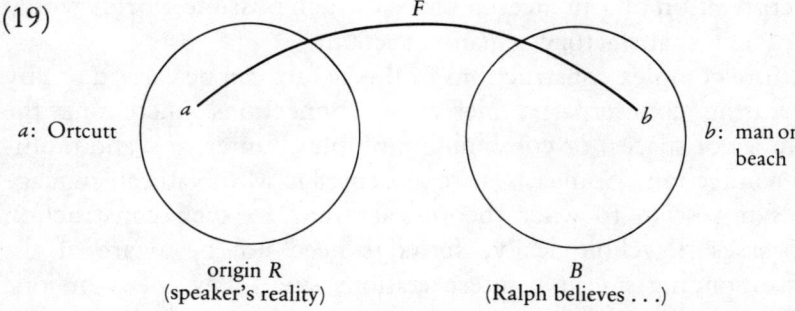

In (17) 'the man on the beach' points to b and identifies it directly (the so-called opaque reading). In (18) 'Ortcutt' points to a and identifies its counterpart ($b = F(a)$) according to ID. With the notation used earlier, (17) and (18) have the form $S'(b)$ and $S'(F(a))$ respectively. They work just like (1), (2), (3), (6), (7), (8) and (9). If Ralph also has beliefs about Ortcutt *qua* Ortcutt, that is if he takes 'Ortcutt' and 'the man on the beach' to be different people while the speaker takes them to be the same, a multiple counterpart situation is set up.

(20)

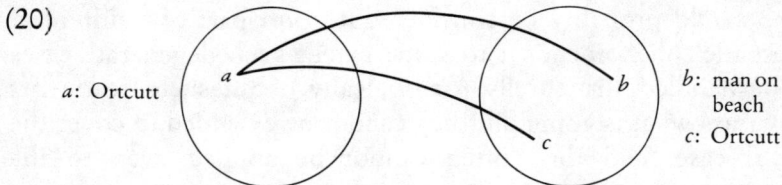

Link F is now one-too-many: $F(a)$ has two possible targets, and (18) has two understandings:

$$S'(F(a)) \simeq S'(b)$$
$$S'(F(a)) \simeq S'(c)$$

In this system the possibility of multiple counterparts is a consequence of simple empirical observation (that (18) is indeed interpretable in both ways). It carries no metaphysical or referential implications, since the spaces are not domains of reference. In particular, there is no reason to interpret such multiple counterpart constructions as violations of possible world uniqueness and rigidity. They do show, however, that direct truth-conditional interpretation of sentences in terms of such possible worlds would not yield a satisfactory semantic account.

More complex constructions of this nature can be carried out by increasing counterparts, increasing connections, increasing the number of spaces, or combining multiple counterparts and multiple connections. Some cases are presented in MS. Natural language does not seem to offer theoretical limits to such construction processes. Psychologically, speakers need not be aware of the corresponding multiple interpretations since they focus on one particular path, usually a more salient one from the point of view of optimization (cf. MS). The multiple (in fact theoretically boundless) possibilities for any given sentence are observed by inducing variation of context.

Notice that the same principles account for the multiplicity of understandings available in discourse and 'simple' cases of ambiguity in a so-called 'neutral' or 'zero' context. The latter are only special ('degenerate') cases of the former, typically those restricted to spaces actually introduced in the sentence itself and involving only one connection. In standard treatments only the degenerate cases are considered (the others are not recognized and, if they were, would probably be considered *a priori* part of a different, 'pragmatic' phenomenon); to some extent such degenerate cases can be handled structurally (or 'logically'). But such treatments really miss what is going on: they cannot be extended to cover the general case, and they often cannot be applied even to the degenerate case.

Roles and connecting paths

The distinction between domains and connections is not complete without another equally important distinction – that between *role* and *value*. In the examples reviewed above, linguistic descriptions (definite, indefinite or names) pick out elements in spaces and their counterparts in other spaces via suitable connections. Such elements were implicitly associated with objects, individuals and so on, but more than that is involved.

Take, by way of example, the following piece of news which appeared in *Le Monde*:

(21) Headline: When the Queen pays a visit to *The Times*.
Text: For the second time in 200 years, *The Times* of London was visited, on Thursday 28 February, by *the queen of England*.

Clearly, under the most salient reading, although Elizabeth II is the sovereign making the second visit, the description 'the queen of England' is not equivalent to 'Elizabeth II'. The news reported is not the same as:

For the second time in 200 years, *The Times* of London was visited, on Thursday, 28 February, by Elizabeth II.

Nor is 'the queen of England' here 'generic' or 'habitual': visiting *The Times* for the second time in 200 years is not a typical property of British sovereigns (or queens).

In the mental space approach, all definite or indefinite descriptions (e.g. 'the queen of England') can pick out *roles*, which are themselves space elements. A role may then take as its *value* another element of the same space, and the connection between a role and a value has the same general properties as other connections mentioned above – metonymy, model/image, actor/character, etc. In particular the ID principle applies, so that a value *a* can be identified by a description of the corresponding role *r*:

Consider (22):

(22) The queen of England has two sons

Sentence (22) is 'true' of Elizabeth, not of the queen of England in general or of a succession of queens of England: the *role* 'queen of England' allows identification of Elizabeth. In contrast to (21), (23) may hold for Elizabeth but not for the queen of England, because the first visit to Canada was before her coronation:

(23) In 19—, the queen of England visited Canada for the second time.

Cases where something holds of a role, but not of the corresponding value, include the following (under one reading):

(24) *The food* in this place gets better all the time.

(This does not imply that a *particular* piece of food improves with age.)

(25) *The Secretary of the UN* changes approximately every ten years.

(26) Last year, *the President* awarded $2 million in prize money. (Context: there was a change of Presidents during the year, say Nixon to Ford: each awarded $1 million. Neither individual has the property of having been President and having awarded $2 million.)

(From *Le Monde*, 5 March 1985, concerning the consumption of coal in Great Britain.)
(27) Worse yet, they might never again burn *the 89 million tonnes of 1980* or even *the 81 million tonnes of 1983*.
(Not to be interpreted as suggesting that 1980s coal should be burnt a second time.)

(28) This is no longer *the leader of the Socialist Party* speaking to you, but *the President of France*.

(Context: the speaker is Mitterrand, who is both leader of the Socialists and President. The statement is not about *who* speaks, but rather in what capacity, i.e. about the relevant role involved.)

The phenomenon illustrated by such examples is widespread.[8] The referential/attributive distinction singled out by philosophers is only one special case of the role/value distinction. And roles need not have values: we can say many things about *the winner* of a contest before anyone actually wins or without anyone ever actually winning. The same goes, *mutatis mutandis*, for 'the food in this restaurant', 'the president', 'the queen of England', etc. In fact, absence of values is often predicated of roles:

(29) In this book   *the tenth chapter* was never written.
                     the preface is missing.
                     we can't find *the plot*.

(30) *The house you designed* was never built.
(Two spaces are involved: the design, in which the role takes a value, and the corresponding material world, where it doesn't.)

Roles are evidently, in one sense, part of our system for structuring the world mentally and collectively; they often depend on shared beliefs, social organization, our own psychological and physiological means of apprehension, and so forth. It does not matter, for linguistic purposes, whether we take a narrow realist view, where roles are outside the 'objective' world, or a 'promiscuous' realist view, where they *exist* on a par with everything else. What matters is the role/value link, that this link falls under the ID principle like other connections, and that, as a result, definite and indefinite descriptions receive multiple understandings.

---

[8] Many interesting examples of role/value ambiguities are given by D. Hofstadter, G. Clossman and M. Meredith, 'Shakespeare's plays weren't written by him, but by someone else of the same name: an essay on intensionality and frame-based knowledge representation systems', Indiana University Linguistics Club, Bloomington, Ind., 1982.

Prototypically, proper names get associated with values, for which identity is a stable property across spaces, while descriptions apply to roles, for which identity (i.e. value) is a variable property. This property of names, exploited in philosophical treatments, is, however, only prototypical, not general. I return to this matter below.

The notion of role is relative, not absolute. If element a is the value of a role b, b itself may be the value of a role c. We can talk here of roles and 'super-roles', or of a hierarchy of roles. A simple example is the description 'head of state'. 'Head of state' is a super-role, which takes for its values roles like 'president', 'queen', 'emperor', 'dictator', etc. These in turn may take particular individuals as their values. Compare (31) and (32):

(31) In France, *the head of state* is elected every seven years.
(32) In France, *the head of state* has been a man for the last 300 years.

Sentence (31) is about the role 'president'. Sentence (32) covers kings and emperors as well. Examples like (31) and (32), although compatible with the role/super-role distinction, could *a priori* be handled in other ways. Decisive evidence is provided by cases like (33):

(Context: in Poldavia there used to be a king and minor officials, including a chancellor. Over the years the monarchy has grown weaker and finally disappeared. During the same period the office of chancellor became more and more important, and 'chancellor' is now the supreme function (head of state).)
(33) In Poldavia, *the head of state* used to be a minor official.

One reading of (33) is that the minor office of chancellor has become the most important. (This reading would be salient, for example, in a dialogue between A and B, where B is trying to find out what function (president, chancellor, prime minister, first secretary, etc.) is currently correlated with heading the state, and A gives him a clue in the form (33).) 'Used to' builds a 'past' space M constrasting with 'present' R. The configuration is (34):

(34)

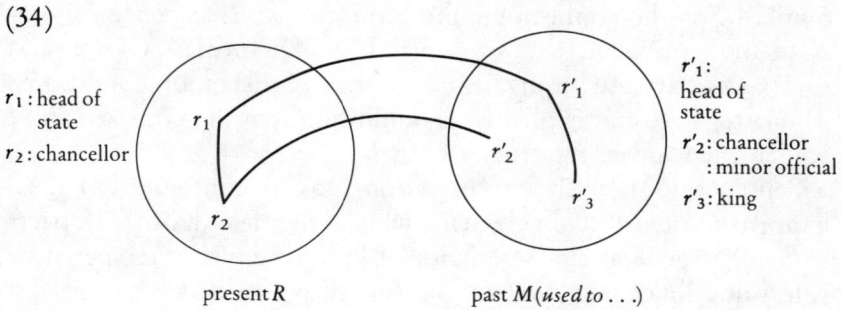

r_1: head of state
r_2: chancellor

r'_1: head of state
r'_2: chancellor : minor official
r'_3: king

Role r_1 (head of state) has a counterpart r'_1 in M. But the two counterparts take values which are not themselves counterparts. Role r'_1 takes r'_3 (the king) as its value, and r_1 takes r_2 (the chancellor) as its value: r_2 and r'_3 are not counterparts. Role r_2 does have a counterpart r'_2 in M, which is not the value of r'_1. Let O stand for the property 'minor official': $O(r'_2)$ holds. In sentence (33), r'_2 is identified by means of a description 'the head of state'. This is accomplished by two successive applications of the ID principle. First, 'the head of state' points to trigger r_1 (super-role); by ID it may identify its value in R, r_2 (the role 'chancellor'). Second, by ID again, it may identify the counterpart of r_2 in space M, namely r'_2.

The required interpretation, $O(r'_2)$, is derived via r_2 and r_1 by two applications of ID:

$$r_1 \longrightarrow r_2 \longrightarrow r'_3$$
description

It is a property of configuration (34) that this linkage is possible, and thus that in the corresponding context (33) will have the reading that yields $O(r'_2)$. More precisely, with the notational conventions introduced earlier, we can write this as

(35) $O(F(r_1(R))$

R is the origin space, in which we find the trigger, role r_1. Quantity $r_1(R)$ is the value of r_1 in space R, in this case another role, r_2.

Symbol F is the connector linking the two spaces; hence $F(r_2) = R'_2$, or equivalently $r'_2 = F(r_1(R))$. Quantities $O(r'_2)$ and $O(F(r_1(R)))$ are thus equivalent in terms of satisfaction conditions. The latter indicates explicitly, in addition, how the target r'_2 in M is identified, given the trigger r_1 in R.

Sentence (33), with interpretation (35) in configuration (34), happens to involve only elements which are roles. In other respects it displays general characteristics of linking: given interspatial or role/value links, a *connecting path* may be formed between elements. When one element on the path serves as trigger, all the other elements are potential targets by successive applications of the ID principle along the links of the path. Given configuration (34), the space builder 'used to' in (33) imposes a target in M. The connecting path from r_1 in (34) is the following:

(36)

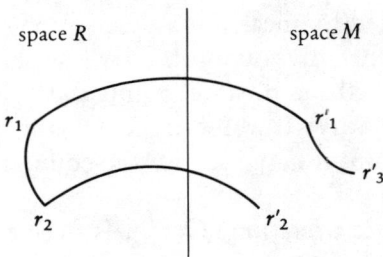

Hence r'_1 and r'_3 are also predicted to be potential targets. Indeed, the corresponding interpretations are possible for (33):

(37) $O(r'_1)$
This would mean that in the past the function of head of state itself was minor, e.g. a token king, with no real power, taking orders from everyone else.

(38) $O(r'_3)$
This means that in the past the function of head of state was exercised by someone occupying a minor position. (This minor position itself could be specific or non-specific, a point which fits

in well with the rest but which I ignore for the sake of simplicity.) So, for instance, the third assistant to the undersecretary (role r'_3) was customarily the head of state, and this office in itself (third assistant ...) was a minor one: $O(r'_3)$. This reading, (38), is compatible with the previous one, (37), but does not entail it: it may be that, although technically a minor official (third assistant ...), the head of state is quite powerful.

As before, we can indicate the links explicitly in our notation:

(37) $O(F(r_1))$
(Property O is satisfied for the counterpart of r_1 in M.)

(38) $O(F(r_1)(M))$
(Property O is satisfied for the value taken by the counterpart of r_1 in M.)

One striking aspect of such constructions is the absence of a theoretical limit on the size of the connecting paths. Consider (33) once again: since the elements involved in configuration (34) are roles, they may all take values.

Let a be the value of r_2 in R: a is the current chancellor, and therefore also head of state, since r_2 is a subrole of r_1. Suppose a proper name goes with a, say 'Ivan'. Value a has a counterpart a' in M. Still taking r_1 as trigger, we can reach a' by way of r_2 and a. The corresponding interpretation is (39):

(39) $O(a') = O(F(r_1(R)(R))$

This says that Ivan, who is now head of state (chancellor: $r_1(R) = r_2$ and $r_2(R) = a$) used to be a minor official ($O(a')$). Clearly, this is also a possible interpretation of (33) – in fact a favoured one.

Now, let u be a value of r'_3 in M, i.e. a person, say Franz-Joseph, who was king (r'_3) and therefore also head of state (r'_1). Value u is also on the connecting path and can be reached from r_1 via r'_1 and r'_3. This yields another interpretation for (33):

(40) $O(u) = O(F(r_1)(M)(M))$

Construction (40) simply attributes the property 'minor official' to Franz-Joseph, independently of his role as king and super-role as head of state. It might be true, for example, if upon becoming king, Franz-Joseph had kept his position as elected assistant to the mayor of his tiny home town.

With values for r_2 and r'_3, the connecting path for (33) now looks as follows:

(41)

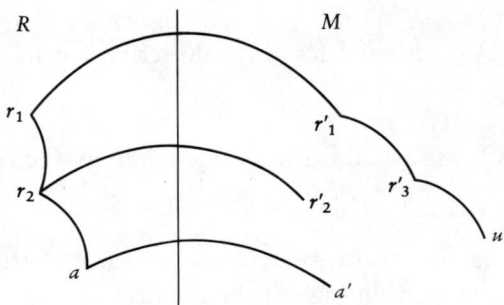

The five elements in M, i.e. r'_1, r'_2, r'_3, a' and u, are all accessible from the trigger r_1. Role r_2 ('the chancellor') could only be a trigger for r'_2 and a' (cf. the interpretations for the sentence 'The chancellor used to be a minor official'). Value a ('Ivan') can only be a trigger for a' (cf. 'Ivan used to be a minor official').

Notice, then, that the connecting path is oriented: one can go from a role to its value, but not conversely. Let us say that if an oriented path goes from a to b ($a \frown b$), b is a successor of a.

The cases examined so far suggest that an element can be a trigger for any of its successors. In other words, by successive applications of the ID principle, one could identify a successor of a, b, by means of a description (or name) of a:

Roles and connecting paths

In (41), r'_1, r'_3 and u are successors of r_1 along one branch of the path; r_2 and r'_2 are successors along another branch, and r_2, a and a' along a third.

However, it turns out that connecting paths cannot be followed blindly. Consider (33) once again. Suppose r'_2 has a value x in M. Value x 'is' Klaus, who used to be chancellor (but of course was not king or head of state, since at the time 'chancellor' was unrelated (r'_2 is not linked to r'_1, r'_3)). There is a connecting path going from r_1 to r_2, to r'_2, and finally to x. Therefore, if paths were unconstrained, x would be accessible from trigger r_1. Sentence (33) would have the interpretation (42):

(42) $O(x) = O(F(r_1(R))(M))$

That is, the sentence 'The head of state used to be a minor official' could be interpreted to mean that Klaus, the former chancellor (who has never been head of state), was a minor official in the past. This interpretation is clearly not available for (33).

Why then is the successive application of the ID principle blocked on this particular route? Consider the connecting path once more, labeling the arrow with F if it represents an interspatial link and with V if it represents a role/value link:

(43)

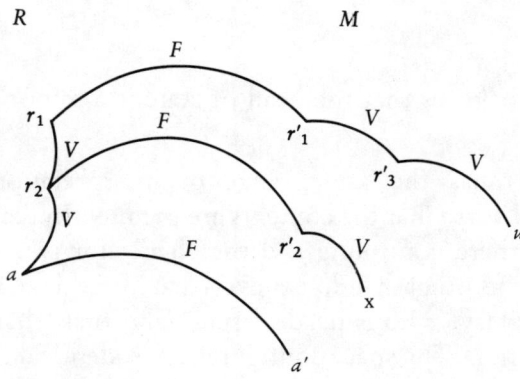

Now consider the links involved in the following various interpretations:

$$
\begin{array}{llllllll}
(35) & r_1 \to & r_2 \to & r'_2 & & & & VF \\
(37) & r_1 \to & r'_1 & & & & & F \\
(38) & r_1 \to & r'_1 \to & r'_3 & & & & FV \\
(39) & r_1 \to & r_2 \to & a \to & a' & & & VVF \\
(40) & r_1 \to & r'_1 \to & r'_3 \to & u & & & FVV \\
*(42) & r_1 \to & r_2 \to & r'_2 \to & x & & & VFV \\
\end{array}
$$

The impossible interpretation, (42), is the only one for which an interspatial link occurs between two role/value links. Why should there be such a prohibition? The following considerations may be relevant. Role/value links are transitive: if a is a value of r_2, and r_2 a value of r_1, then a is a value of r_1 (Ivan is 'head of state' by virtue of being 'chancellor'). As a result, in all the acceptable interpretations ((35), (37) – (40)) the target is identified either by one of its roles or by the role of a counterpart. Only in (42) (path VFV) would the target end up being identified by a role which neither it nor its counterparts has in any space. (Klaus was not, and is not, head of state.)

Example (33) happened to involve two time spaces. Properties of connecting paths do not depend on the type of space involved. Sentence (44) is similar to (33), except that the space introduced is a belief space:

(44) George believes that the head of state is a minor official.

Sentence (44) has the same range of interpretations as (33), providing of course that the contexts are parallel. In reality (i.e. for the speaker) there is no king and the chancellor is head of state. George, on the other hand, believes that there is a king, or an assistant secretary, who is head of state, and that 'chancellor' is a different position. The space configuration is identical to (34), with space M introduced by 'George believes'. All the previous interpretations are available:

(35) $O(r'_2)$
George believes that the office of chancellor (identified by the speaker as 'head of state' is minor.

(37) $O(r'_1)$
George believes that the function of head of state is minor (e.g. for him the king is unimportant).

(38) $O(r'_3)$
George believes that the state is headed by someone with another particular function, say assistant secretary, and that this function is in itself a minor one. Such a reading might make sense if the state is organized like some secret societies: no one knows who the real leader is, but there is another official function (also unknown) which is associated with heading the state. Sentence (44) might then occur in the context of speculation about what this other function is, regardless of who occupies it at the time: is the head of state the admiral of the fleet, the assistant secretary, the third footman at the palace, etc.?

(39) $O(a')$
Although Ivan is actually head of state (according to the speaker), George takes him to be only a minor official.

(40) $O(u)$
George takes Franz–Joseph (instead of Ivan) to be the head of state, and also thinks that Franz–Joseph is a minor official, e.g. assistant mayor of his tiny home town.

As before, reading (42) is blocked:

(42) $O(x)$
If George takes Klaus to be chancellor, and chancellor to be a minor function, and the speaker takes Ivan to be chancellor and head of state, the speaker cannot report George's beliefs using (44).

Such examples underscore the uniformity of identification procedures, over and above the particular connections and spaces involved. They show that a given linguistic expression does not in itself provide a fixed number of readings. Rather, it provides construction possibilities for links and spaces which vary according to what spaces and links are already involved or available in the context.

Semantic explanations of this kind place heavy emphasis on linguistic generalization and maximum empirical adequacy at the 'expense' of *a priori* metaphysical or ontological commitments. Furthermore, they do not assume that there need be any structural correspondence between the way expressions are organized and the 'real' state of affairs which they might be describing. In that sense, they end up not being truth conditional. Space constructions like (35), (37), etc. do not in themselves tell us under what conditions (44) would be true: they indicate only what 'talk about beliefs' is like, how it can be set up and organized. In fact, what is striking about such constructions is precisely that they are not connected to the notion of belief, since they are equally appropriate for other domains, such as time, counterfactuals, images, metaphors, etc.

Now, there is certainly a tendency to assume that truth conditionality is a prerequisite for any serious semantics, not only theoretically, but also methodologically. The 'constructivist' approach defended here does not eliminate classical logical notions: within the spaces themselves it is assumed that relations, satisfaction and, at least partially, inference and implicature operate in a standard way.[9] Furthermore, in the most simple, concrete cases some spaces may be isomorphic to partial models in the truth-conditional, model-theoretic sense. In this prototype case, space elements may correspond directly to objects, and properties 'satisfied' by the elements will correspond directly to properties that hold of the objects in question. Presumably the importance of such prototypes is crucial in the learning processes and in the use we make of mental constructions more generally. Nevertheless,

---

9 Much more needs to be investigated about the internal structuring of spaces. Assuming, as in Lakoff, *Women, Fire and Dangerous Things*, that they are structured by ICMs (idealized cognitive models), the available implicatures will depend on those ICMs. Furthermore, not all logical entailments will hold, only those called in MS 'accessible consequences'.

their characteristics are quite special and not shared by most space constructions.

In the general case, spaces are set up, internally structured, explicitly or implicitly, and linked to one another by various connectors. Utterances will be 'interpreted' – understood – relative to the construction in progress. Properties count as satisfied in some domains and not in others, and properties themselves may have different 'properties' from space to space: glaring but by no means exceptional examples are cases of metaphor or explicit (i.e. asserted) change of meaning.[10]

Undoubtedly, such constructions are used 'as if' they had truth conditions: we present (44) as a true or false statement, but of course there may be no conceivable truth conditions for it, or others of its kind (George believes X), barring considerable and unforeseen progress in the neurological sciences. This is apparently irrelevant with respect to the construction we set up, and with respect to the multiple inferences we feel justified in drawing.[11] These inferences depend on the way in which the notion of belief we use in any particular situation (and the corresponding construction) is assumed to be linked with other notions (and corresponding constructions), e.g. actions, statements, beliefs of others, hopes, etc. There are of course rich arrays of prototypes for such links, and also specific variants in particular situations. What is at issue here is the relation between 'forms of talk' about, say, beliefs and actions, not the actual relation between beliefs and actions, whatever *that* may be. The linguistic evidence suggests that we can study the former without knowing much about the latter.

Be that as it may, another aspect of the relation between expressions of language and meaning needs to be stressed. It is often supposed that if an expression is correlated with more than one understanding, the expression is intrinsically ambiguous, and that some contexts may favour one of the potential interpretations over others. Examples of the kind reviewed above work in a converse fashion: it is the context (e.g. the nature of a connecting

10 E.g. 'Gloria is as sweet as sugar'; 'For Max, roses are blue, because he thinks blue means red.'
11 See C. Travis, 'Are belief ascriptions opaque?', *Proceedings of the Aristotelian Society*, new series, LXXXIV (1983/4).

path) which endows the expression with a certain number of potential interpretations.

The overall view is that an expression specifies some construction to be performed, but that this construction may be underdetermined with respect to the space configuration already set up when the expression occurs: there may be several ways to perform the appropriate construction. For example, the definite description 'head of state' in (44) instructs us to find an element with the property 'head of state', and to identify another element linked to the first by an appropriate connecting path. The number of possibilities will depend on how many spaces we have containing an element 'head of state', and on the length of the connecting paths originating from these elements. There is no theoretical limit on this number but, of course, in each specific configuration it will be finite and even usually very small. The number of readings cannot be a property of the expression *per se*: it results from the possible combinations of the instructions with space configurations.

The standard attribution of ambiguity to expressions is done in isolation, by constructing a minimal context and therefore a minimum space configuration. Since this procedure is standard and reproducible, it creates the illusion that the number of readings is a property of the expression itself. But, in fact, it is a property of the expression in minimal contexts and does not project to the general case.

2
Inference and implicature
Deirdre Wilson and Dan Sperber

Recent accounts of utterance interpretation have tended to downplay the role of deductive reasoning in comprehension. Here are two illustrations from current textbooks on discourse analysis. Brown and Yule say: 'It may be the case that we are capable of drawing a specific conclusion . . . from specific premises . . . via deductive inference, but we are rarely asked to do so in the everyday discourse we encounter. . . . We are more likely to operate with a rather loose form of inferencing.'[1] Similar views are expressed by de Beaugrande and Dressler: 'Humans are evidently capable of intricate reasoning processes that traditional logics cannot explain: jumping to conclusions, pursuing subjective analogies, and even reasoning in the absence of knowledge. . . . The important standard here is not that such a procedure is logically unsound, but rather that the procedures work well enough in everyday affairs.'[2]

The implication of these remarks is that any element of deductive reasoning in the 'loose' or 'unsound' inference processes involved in utterance interpretation can safely be ignored. Our own researches have led us to a quite different conclusion. We do believe that non-demonstrative inference plays a crucial role in utterance interpretation. We also believe, however, that deductive

We are grateful to Rose Maclaran for a number of helpful comments on an earlier version.
1 G. Brown and G. Yule, *Discourse Analysis* (CUP, Cambridge, 1983), p. 33.
2 R. de Beaugrande and W. Dressler, *Introduction to Text Linguistics* (Longman, London, 1981), pp. 93–4.

reasoning makes a crucial contribution to the non-demonstrative inference processes spontaneously used in utterance interpretation. In this chapter we will offer a partial justification of these claims by illustrating the contribution of deductive reasoning to just one aspect of utterance interpretation in which non-demonstrative inference is generally agreed to play a major role: the recovery of implicatures. A fuller justification would deal with other aspects of interpretation – disambiguation, reference assignment, the recovery of illocutionary force and the interpretation of figurative language, for example – and would not merely illustrate the contribution of deductive reasoning to spontaneous non-demonstrative inference processes but would provide a psychologically adequate account of these non-demonstrative inference processes themselves.[3]

THE CALCULABILITY REQUIREMENT ON IMPLICATURES

Grice distinguishes two main types of implicit content or implicature that an utterance can convey.[4] *Conventional implicatures* are determined by particular lexical items or linguistic constructions occurring in the utterance. *Conversational implicatures* follow from general maxims of truthfulness, informativeness, relevance and clarity that speakers are assumed to observe. For Grice, the important difference between conventional and conversational implicature is that the conventional implicatures of an utterance are arbitrarily stipulated, whereas its conversational implicatures should be recoverable by a reasoning process: 'The presence of a conversational implicature must be capable of being worked out; for even if it can in fact be intuitively grasped, unless the intuition is replaceable by an argument, the implicature (if present at all) will not count as a *conversational* implicature: it will be a *conventional* implicature.'[5] Grice regards this calculability requirement as fun-

---

3 This fuller justification is attempted in D. Sperber and D. Wilson, *Relevance: Communication and Cognition* (Basil Blackwell, Oxford, 1986).
4 H. P. Grice, 'Logic and conversation', in *Syntax and Semantics 3: Speech Acts*, eds P. Cole and J. Morgan (Academic Press, New York, 1975), pp. 41–58.
5 Ibid., p. 50.

damental: 'The final test for the presence of a conversational implicature had to be, as far as I could see, a derivation of it. One has to produce an account of how it could have arisen and why it is there. And I am very much opposed to any kind of sloppy use of this philosophical tool in which this condition is not fulfilled.'[6] However, his own account of the derivation process is rather sketchy, and although the idea of conversational implicature has had enormous appeal and been used in an informal way to account for a wide range of pragmatic phenomena, little progress has been made in specifying the exact nature of the inference process by which conversational implicatures are 'worked out'.

Grice suggests that the conversational implicatures of an utterance might be derived by arguments of the following form:[7]

(1) (a) He has said that p.
    (b) There is no reason to suppose that he is not observing the maxims.
    (c) He could not be doing this unless he thought that q.
    (d) He knows (and knows that I know that he knows) that I can see that the supposition that he thinks that q *is* required.
    (e) He had done nothing to stop me thinking that q.
    (f) He intends me to think, or is at least willing to allow me to think, that q.
    (g) And so, he has implicated that q.

It is unclear what sort of argument this is meant to be; it is not even clear which of (1a–g) are meant to be premises and which conclusions. What does seem clear is that (1c), in which the content of the implicature is introduced for the first time, is not directly deducible from (1a–b). Either (1c) is simply an independent premise, or it is meant to be derivable from (1a–b) with the aid of some supplementary premises whose nature has been left unspecified. What (1) really offers is not a method for working out

---

6 H. P. Grice, 'Presupposition and conversational implicature', in *Radical Pragmatics*, ed. P. Cole (Academic Press, New York, 1981), pp. 183–98, at p. 187.
7 Grice, 'Logic and conversation', p. 50.

the content of the propositions that the speaker, in producing an utterance, implicitly commits himself to, but rather a method for working out which of these commitments the speaker *meant*, in Grice's special technical sense.[8] An adequate pragmatic theory should also provide some method of recovering the content of the implicatures themselves: that is, some method of deriving not (1g) but (1c).

It is becoming a commonplace of the pragmatic literature that deductive inference plays little if any role in the recovery of implicatures. Leech says that implicatures are 'probabilistic', and that the process by which they are recovered 'is not a formalized deductive logic, but an informal rational problem-solving strategy'.[9] Levinson says that implicatures 'appear to be quite unlike logical inferences, and cannot be directly modelled in terms of some semantic relation like entailment'.[10] Bach and Harnish say that the form of inference by which implicatures are recovered 'is not deductive but what might be called an inference to a plausible explanation'.[11] Brown and Yule, who as we saw above claim that utterance comprehension rarely involves deductive processes, add that in the recovery of implicatures 'we are more likely to operate with a rather loose form of inferencing.'[12] These remarks can be taken in a number of ways.

In a sense, they follow directly from Grice's characterization of implicature, and some of these authors may be making a purely definitional point. Consider (2b), for example:

(2) (a) *He*: Will you have some coffee?
    (b) *She*: Coffee would keep me awake.

In normal circumstances, the speaker of (2b) would implicate (3):

(3) She won't have any coffee.

8 For discussion, see H. P. Grice, 'Utterer's meaning, sentence meaning and word meaning', *Foundations of Language*, 4 (1968), pp. 1–18.
9 G. N. Leech, *Principles of Pragmatics* (Longman, London, 1983), pp. 30–1.
10 S. C. Levinson, *Pragmatics* (CUP, Cambridge, 1983), pp. 115–16.
11 K. Bach and R. M. Harnish, *Linguistic Communication and Speech Acts* (MIT Press, Cambridge, Mass., 1979), pp. 92–3.
12 Brown and Yule, *Discourse Analysis*, p. 33.

Inference and implicature

Now (3) is not deducible from the content of (2b) alone: (4) is not a contradiction:

(4) Coffee would keep her awake, and she will have some coffee.

Indeed, if (3) *were* deducible from (2b) it would not be an implicature in Grice's sense, since according to him 'the truth of a conversational implicature is not required by the truth of what is said (what is said may be true – what is implicated may be false).'[13] If this is taken as a defining feature of implicature, no implicature will be deducible from the explicit content of an utterance alone.

However, to show that (3) is not directly deducible from (2b) is not to show that deduction plays no significant role in its derivation. Grice himself claims that background knowledge must play a role in the process by which conversational implicatures are 'worked out'. Why should the hearer not simply supply the background assumptions in (5) and use them, together with the content of (2b), to deduce the conclusion in (3)?

(5) (a) She doesn't want to be kept awake.
    (b) She won't have anything that would keep her awake.

We will argue that deduction processes of this type play a central role in the recovery of implicatures. This is not, of course, to tell the whole story about how implicatures are derived. It is also necessary to show how appropriate premises for the deduction process are selected and potential conclusions evaluated: why does the hearer of (2b) supply the background assumptions (5) and accept the conclusion (3) rather than, say, supplying the assumptions (6) and deriving the conclusion (7)?

(6) (a) She wants to be kept awake.
    (b) She will have anything on offer that would keep her awake.
(7) She will have some coffee.

However, there is no reason in principle why an account of implicature in which deduction is a central element should not be

---

13 Grice, 'Logic and conversation', p. 58.

adequate to deal with the interpretation of (2b) and other examples of implicature-carrying utterances.

Some of the authors cited above seem to be making not just the definitional point that implicatures cannot be deduced from the content of the utterance alone, but the stronger claim that deduction plays no significant role in their derivation, and in particular that an account like the one just suggested cannot be correct.[14] To be able to evaluate this claim we would have to have not only a clearer idea of the deduction-based account, but also some idea of possible alternatives to it. By what non-deductive inference processes might the hearer of (2b) arrive at the conclusion in (3), and how would the alternative conclusion in (7) be ruled out?

It is now fairly widely recognized that there can be no non-demonstrative inference *rules* (in the sense that there are deductive inference rules) which, given a set of premises, simply enumerate a set of valid conclusions. Instead, the process of reaching valid non-demonstrative conclusions is standardly broken down into two distinct stages: hypothesis formation and hypothesis confirmation. For example, the hearer of (2b) would have first to form the hypothesis in (3), or the hypothesis that the speaker was trying to communicate (3), and second to confirm or disconfirm this hypothesis.

As Fodor points out,[15] we are very far from having an adequate account of the psychology of hypothesis formation and confirmation. It is well known that from the purely logical point of view any empirical proposition confirms or disconfirms an infinity of others. For example, (8) is logically equivalent to (9), and any proposition that confirms the latter confirms the former:

(8) All snow is white.

(9) Anything that is not white is not snow.

Proposition (9) is confirmed by anything that is not white and not snow: for example, a green apple. Hence, (10) confirms the claim that all snow is white:

14 See, for example, Levinson, *Pragmatics*, p. 116; and Brown and Yule, *Discourse Analysis*, pp. 33–5.
15 J. Fodor, *The Modularity of Mind* (MIT Press, Cambridge, Mass., 1983).

(10) This is a green apple.

Someone who says (10) would not normally, of course, be construed as encouraging the hearer to derive either (8) or (9) as a conclusion. The problem is that there is as yet no principled account capable of explaining which of the infinite set of possible conclusions that the hearer of a given utterance *could* draw will actually be drawn.

Hypothesis formation, according to Fodor, is a creative process involving analogical reasoning, about which virtually nothing is known. Once formed, a given hypothesis will be accepted or rejected on a basis which is again very little understood. As Fodor sees it, the difficulties with hypothesis formation and confirmation arise from the fact that they are *global* as opposed to *local* processes. The distinction beween global and local processes corresponds roughly to a distinction between processes which have free access to contextual information and those which do not. A global process is one in which any item of information, however remote and unrelated to the information being processed, may legitimately be used. So, for example, in creating a scientific hypothesis to account for a certain range of data it is legitimate to rely on analogies with other domains of knowledge, seemingly random association of ideas, and any other source of inspiration that comes to hand. Once a hypothesis has been formed, the extent to which it is regarded as confirmed will depend on how well it fits not only with neighbouring domains of knowledge but with one's whole overall conception of the world. A local process, by contrast, is one which needs to take nothing into account apart from the information actually being processed. For example, deductive reasoning from fixed premises is a purely local process in which no attention need be paid to information not contained in the premises themselves. Fodor's argument is that although we have a fair understanding of a variety of local processes, the working of global processes remains a mystery.

Given the haziness of our understanding both of the psychology of hypothesis formation and confirmation and of the effects of context on information processing, it is perhaps not surprising that pragmatists who express scepticism about the role of deductive reasoning in comprehension have said little about the processes by which implicatures are recovered. Bach and Harnish, after establishing that the working out schema is not deductive, add:

> Our empirical thinking in general is rife with generalizations and inference principles that we are not conscious of when we use them, if we are conscious of them at all. It would take us well beyond present-day cognitive psychology to speculate on the details of any of this. . . . Whatever these processes are, whatever activates them, whatever principles or strategies are involved, they work, and work well.[16]

But the fact that these processes work well enough in everyday utterance comprehension does not absolve us from saying what they are. If anything, the lack of any existing framework for describing them should make us more, not less, interested in their nature. Given the 'probabilistic' nature of implicatures as illustrated in (2b) above, an adequate theory of how implicatures are recovered might shed light not just on utterance comprehension but on the more general psychological problem of hypothesis formation and confirmation which, for the reasons Fodor has given, has proved to be so intractable.

The claim that pragmatics must be based on *either* deductive *or* non-demonstrative inferential systems, or that the adoption of one type of system must inevitably lead to the rejection of the other, seems to us to be unfounded. For the last few years we have been working on a theory of spontaneous non-demonstrative inference in utterance comprehension and other cognitive domains, in which deductive reasoning plays a central role. In previously published work[17] we have concentrated on the central, deductive element of the theory, which will be outlined briefly in the next section. In the remainder of this paper we will sketch in some of the broader

---

16 Bach and Harnish, *Linguistic Communication*, p. 83.
17 See, for example, D. Sperber and D. Wilson, 'Mutual knowledge and relevance in theories of comprehension', in *Mutual Knowledge*, ed. N. V. Smith (Academic Press, London, 1982), pp. 61–87; and D. Wilson and D. Sperber, 'On defining relevance', in *Festschrift for Paul Grice*, ed. R. Grandy (OUP, Oxford, forthcoming).

background against which this central deductive element is set, and show how 'probabilistic' implicatures would be handled in this framework.

RELEVANCE THEORY

Grice's work on the maxims of conversation[18] can be seen as providing the elements of a pragmatic hypothesis confirmation system. Given (a) a source of hypotheses about the speaker's communicative intentions and (b) an adequate account of what it is for a speaker to observe the conversational maxims, it seems reasonable to claim that the most favoured hypothesis, the one the hearer should choose, would be the one which best satisfies the maxims. In at least a few cases, it is easy to see how this proposal might work. Consider disambiguation, for example. Here the source of hypotheses is the grammar, which assigns a range of possible senses to an utterance. On the approach now being considered, the sense the hearer should assume that the speaker wanted to communicate is the one which best accords with the assumption that Grice's maxims have been observed.

Or consider how a hearer might decide which of the deductive consequences of an utterance the speaker wanted to communicate. Here the source of hypotheses is the deductive inference rules. On the approach now being considered, the hearer should assume that the speaker wanted to communicate any subset of consequences needed to satisfy him that the maxims have been observed. Consider, for example, the exchange in (11):

(11) (a) *He*: Is Jacques a good cook?
    (b) *She*: He's French, and all the French are good cooks.

Here, in order to satisfy himself that the speaker of (11b) is observing the maxims of relevance and informativeness, the hearer must assume that she wanted him to deduce from her utterance the conclusion in (12):

18 Grice, 'Logic and conversation'.

(12) Jacques is a good cook.

In these two types of case, Grice's maxims can thus be used, if not to generate a set of hypotheses about the speaker's communicative intentions, at least to choose among them.

To provide an adequate account of implicature along these lines, two questions would have to be answered. First, what is the source of hypotheses about the possible implicatures of an utterance? Second, is it possible to show more precisely what it is for a speaker to observe Grice's maxims? In previously published work[19] we have offered, in outline, an answer to the second of these questions. We have proposed a definition of relevance and suggested what factors might be involved in assessments of degrees of relevance. We have also argued that all Grice's maxims can be replaced by a single principle of relevance – that the speaker tries to be as relevant as possible in the circumstances – which, when suitably elaborated, can handle the full range of data that Grice's maxims were designed to explain.

We treat relevance as a relation between a proposition P and a set of contextual assumptions $\{C\}$. In previously published work we have made the simplifying assumption that the only propositions used in the comprehension process are those believed to be true. On the basis of this assumption we defined relevance as follows:

(13) A proposition P is relevant in a context $\{C\}$ if and only if P has at least one contextual implication in $\{C\}$.

A contextual implication is a special type of logical implication, derived by the use of a restricted set of deductive rules which derive at most a finite set of conclusions from any finite set of premises.[20]

---

19 For example, D. Wilson and D. Sperber, 'On Grice's theory of conversation', in *Conversation and Discourse*, ed. P. Werth (Croom Helm, London, 1981), pp. 152–77; and Wilson and Sperber, 'On defining relevance'.
20 The details of this system will not concern us here. See, for discussion, D. Sperber and D. Wilson, 'Reply to Gazdar and Good', in Smith, ed., pp. 101–10; Wilson and Sperber, 'On defining relevance'; Sperber and Wilson, *Relevance*.

Inference and implicature

The contextual implications of a proposition P in a context $\{C\}$ are all those conclusions deducible from the union of P with $\{C\}$, but from neither P alone nor $\{C\}$ alone. For example, (2b) above contextually implies (3) in a context containing (5), and contextually implies (7) in a context containing (6); it would thus, by our definitions, be relevant in a context containing either (5) or (6).

The intuitive idea behind these definitions is that relevance is achieved when the addition of a proposition to a context modifies the context in a way that goes beyond the mere incrementation of that context with the proposition itself and all its logical implications. As we will show, the production of contextual implications is a special case of a more general notion of contextual modification which emerges once we drop the assumption that the only propositions used in comprehension are those believed to be true. For the moment we will continue to assume that a hearer who wants to establish the relevance of an utterance should be looking for a context with which it will interact to yield contextual implications.

Consider, in this framework, how a hearer might set about processing the information in (14):

(14) *She*: Susan doesn't drink alcohol.

One possible line of interpretation would be to think of the names of some alcoholic drinks, as in (15), and conclude that Susan doesn't drink them, as in (16):

(15) (a) Sherry is alcoholic.
    (b) Gin is alcoholic.
    (c) Whisky is alcoholic.
    . . .

(16) (a) Susan doesn't drink sherry.
    (b) Susan doesn't drink gin.
    (c) Susan doesn't drink whisky.
    . . .

One of the conclusions in (16) might in turn combine with further contextual assumptions to yield a range of further contextual implications, which could in turn combine with further contextual assumptions, and so on indefinitely.

Another line of interpretation would be to think of conditional premises with (14) as antecedent, as in (17), and derive their consequents as conclusions, as in (18):

(17) (a) If Susan doesn't drink alcohol, she may prefer a soft drink.
 (b) If Susan doesn't drink alcohol, she probably disapproves of getting drunk.
 (c) If Susan doesn't drink alcohol, she never has hangovers.
. . .

(18) (a) Susan may prefer a soft drink.
 (b) Susan probably disapproves of getting drunk.
 (c) Susan never has hangovers.
. . .

Again, one of the conclusions in (18) may combine with further contextual assumptions to yield further contextual implications, and so on indefinitely.

We assume that in processing a proposition the hearer begins by systematically searching for contextual implications in a small, immediately accessible context consisting of the propositions that have most recently been processed. To these, further assumptions may be added subject to the following constraint. We assume that information is stored in memory in encyclopaedic entries attached to concepts, and that the information in a given encyclopaedic entry can only be accessed via the presence in the set of propositions currently being processed of the concept to which it is attached. For example, an utterance mentioning alcohol makes accessible (to varying degrees) the set of propositions in the encyclopaedic entry attached to the concept *alcohol*; these in turn give access to the encyclopaedic entries attached to the concepts they contain, and so on indefinitely.

It can be seen that in this framework not all the contextual implications of a given proposition will be equally easy to obtain. Those derived from small, easily accessible contexts will be relatively cheap in processing terms. Those derived from larger, less easily accessible contexts will be relatively expensive in processing terms, because of the additional effort required to access the contexts needed to derive them and to search these contexts systematically for contextual implications. We assume that the universal aim in processing is to obtain the maximum of contextual implications in return for any processing effort expended. However, at a certain point in processing – which will vary from person to person and situation to situation – the cost of obtaining any further contextual implications will become too high, and processing will stop.

Let us say that, other things being equal, the relevance of a proposition increases with the number of contextual implications it yields and decreases as the amount of processing needed to obtain them increases. Maximizing the relevance of a proposition is thus a matter of accessing, as quickly as possible, a context in which it will yield the maximum of contextual implications in return for the available processing effort. The most relevant propositions will be those which yield a wide range of contextual implications in a small, immediately accessible context.

We assume that the universal goal in cognition is to acquire relevant information, and the more relevant the better. We also assume that a speaker who thinks it worth speaking at all will try to make his utterance as relevant as possible. A hearer should therefore bring to the processing of every utterance the standing assumption that the speaker has tried to be as relevant as possible in the circumstances. It is this assumption that we call the principle of relevance.

A speaker cannot observe the principle of relevance without believing that his utterance will convey some relevant information to the hearer. Sometimes, he may have only the most general grounds for thinking so. For example, if I know you follow the pop music charts, I can reasonably assume that it will be relevant to you to know the name of the new number one hit, even though

I may have no idea what specific implications this information will have for you. At other times, however, a speaker may have a much more specific idea of the sort of context that will be brought to bear and the sort of conclusions derived. It is in situations like this that we believe implicatures arise.

Consider, for example, the exchange in (19):

(19) (a) *He*: Does Susan drink whisky?
(b) *She*: She doesn't drink alcohol.

On what grounds might the speaker of (19b) have thought her utterance would be relevant to the hearer? What sort of context might she have expected him to supply that would be both accessible enough and rich enough in contextual implications for it to be worth his while to process her utterance? The answer is clear. He has just asked her whether Susan drinks whisky. In our framework, he would not have asked this question if he had not had immediately accessible a context in which the information that she did (or did not) drink whisky would be relevant – and indeed more relevant than any other information he thinks she will be able to provide. By providing this information directly, she would therefore be sure of satisfying the principle of relevance.

In fact, her utterance does not provide the information directly: the hearer has first to supply the contextual assumption in (15c) and then to derive the conclusion in (16c):

(15) (c) Whisky is alcoholic.
(16) (c) Susan doesn't drink whisky.

However, the speaker can reasonably expect him to do this. On the one hand, her utterance gives him immediate access to his encyclopaedic entry for *alcohol*, which should in turn provide access to propositions of the form (15a–c). On the other hand, on normal assumptions about the organization of memory, the immediately preceding mention of whisky should act as a prompt, making (15c) more accessible than other propositions of this form. It would therefore be reasonable to assume that one of the grounds on which the speaker of (19b) thought her utterance would be relevant was that she expected it to be processed in a context which contained (15c) as an assumption and yielded (16c) as a contextual implication.

We want to say that the speaker of (19b) implicates both (15c) and (16c). On this approach, the implicatures of an utterance are those contextual asssumptions and implications which the hearer has to recover in order to satisfy himself that the speaker has observed the principle of relevance. Here, (15c) is a necessary precondition on the recovery of (16c), and (16c) is a necessary precondition on the recovery of the whole range of contextual implications on which the main relevance of (19b) depends. We will call (15c) an *implicated assumption* and (16c) an *implicated conclusion* of (19b).

In fact, as we have described it, the interpretation of (19b) does not conform to the principle of relevance. The speaker could have conveyed the whole of this interpretation more economically by producing the direct answer (16c). Instead, she has forced the hearer to process the proposition expressed by (19b), to access (15c) and to deduce (16c) as a contextual implication, each step requiring some processing effort which would not have been required by the direct answer (16c). Suppose the hearer asks himself why she might have thought that the indirect answer (19b) would be more relevant to him than a direct answer. The only possible explanation is that she must have expected it to yield some additional contextual implications, not derivable from the direct answer (16c), which would more than compensate for the extra processing cost. In other words, the only possible explanation is that she believed that the surplus of information she was providing had some relevance in its own right.

As always, the speaker must have some reason for thinking that this surplus of information will be relevant, and more relevant than any alternative information she could provide. She may know, for example, that the hearer is wondering what drink to offer Susan. In these circumstances, her response in (19b) would encourage him to derive conclusions along the lines of (16) and (18c) above: that she doesn't drink sherry, gin, etc., and that she may prefer a soft drink. Or he may be wondering whether to invite Susan to his party. In these circumstances, the response in (19b) would encourage him to derive conclusions along the lines of (18b) above: that Susan may disapprove of getting drunk, that he should maybe not bother inviting her to his party, and so on.

Grice suggests that many implicatures are indeterminate:

> Since to calculate a conversational implicature is to calculate what has to be supposed in order to preserve the supposition that the Co-Operative Principle is being observed, and since there may be various possible specific explanations, a list of which may be open, the conversational implicatum in such cases will be a disjunction of such specific explanations; and if the list of these is open, the implicatum will have just the kind of indeterminacy that many actual implicata do in fact seem to possess.[21]

His commentators have been divided in their reaction to this suggestion. Some, realizing the difficulty of providing an explicit treatment of indeterminacy, have largely ignored it. Gazdar, for example, notes the existence of indeterminacy, but adds: 'Because indeterminacy is hard to handle formally, I shall mostly ignore it in the discussion that follows. A fuller treatment of implicatures would not be guilty of this omission, which is really only defensible on formal grounds.'[22] Others, less interested in explicit treatment of the processes by which implicatures arise, tend to use the indeterminacy of implicatures as an argument against deductive models of the recovery process and in favour of 'informal', 'loose' or 'probabilistic' models.[23] In our framework, the indeterminacy of implicatures can be dealt with without losing the explicitness of the deductive approach.

Sometimes, as we have shown, a speaker can observe the principle of relevance without having any idea of the sort of context the utterance will be processed in, or the sort of conclusions that will be derived. In these cases, the utterance will have no implicatures at all. In other cases, as with (19b) and its implicatures

---

21 Grice, 'Logic and conversation', p. 58.
22 G. Gazdar, *Pragmatics: Implicature, Presupposition and Logical Form* (Academic Press, New York, 1979).
23 See, for example, Leech, *Principles of Pragmatics*, chapters 2 and 7.

(15c) and (16c), it is impossible to see how the speaker could have observed the principle of relevance without expecting a specific contextual assumption to be supplied and a specific conclusion derived. In these cases the utterance will have fully determinate implicatures. Between these two extremes lie a whole range of intermediate cases. We have discussed a situation where the indirect answer (19b) would encourage the hearer to think of assumptions along the lines of (15) or (17) and conclusions along the lines of (16) or (18). Here, the speaker has a general idea of the type of assumption to be supplied and the type of conclusion to be derived, but may not know or care which specific assumptions and conclusions of this type will be supplied. The clearer an idea the speaker must have had of the specific assumptions and conclusions to be supplied, the more determinate the implicatures will be; the vaguer an idea he could have had and still have been observing the principle of relevance, the less determinate the implicatures will be, up to the point where they vanish altogether and the choice of contexts and conclusions is left solely up to the hearer.

In every case, the method of processing is the same. The hearer supplies specific contextual assumptions and derives specific contextual implications. What varies is not the specificity of the assumptions and conclusions derived, or the formality of the reasoning processes involved, but simply the amount of foreknowledge the speaker must be taken to have had of the way the utterance would be processed, and with it the degree of responsibility he must take for the particular conclusions derived. Suppose, for instance, that I could not have observed the principle of relevance without expecting you to supply a certain assumption and derive a certain conclusion in processing my utterance. Then by encouraging you to supply them, I take as much responsibility for their truth as for the truth of the proposition I have explicitly expressed.

To take an example, suppose that after the exchange in (19) has taken place it turns out that Susan does drink whisky. Although (19b) does not *entail* that Susan does not drink whisky (the additional assumption that whisky is alcoholic is needed), the speaker could be quite rightly accused of having misled the hearer by allowing him to suppose that she did. Similarly, a speaker who secretly believed that whisky was not alcoholic could be accused at least of having *tried* to mislead the hearer by uttering (19b) and thus encouraging him to suppose that whisky was alcoholic. In other words, the speaker is committed to the truth of all determinate implicatures conveyed by her utterance, just as much as if she had expressed them directly.

With less determinate implicatures, the speaker cannot be held solely responsible for their truth. Suppose, for example, that the exchange in (19) takes place in the circumstances described above, where the speaker of (19a) is wondering whether to invite Susan to his party. Here, (19b) would clearly carry implicatures to the effect that Susan may disapprove of getting drunk, is unlikely to enjoy rowdy behaviour, may inhibit the proceedings, and is thus not a suitable person to invite to a party. However, it would be a little strong to say that the speaker of (19b) had specifically indicated that the hearer should not invite Susan to his party: this is only one among a range of roughly equivalent conclusions that the hearer could have drawn, any of which would have satisfied him that the speaker had observed the principle of relevance by providing some information with a bearing on his deliberations. The weaker the implicature – that is, the wider the range of roughly equivalent alternative assumptions and conclusions that would have satisfied the hearer that the speaker had observed the principle of relevance – the weaker the speaker's responsibility for its truth, up to the point where the implicature disappears altogether and the responsibility for the assumptions used and the conclusions drawn from them lies solely on the side of the hearer.

Talk of degrees of responsibility for the truth of implicated assumptions and conclusions takes us outside the simplified framework we have been assuming so far – a framework which abstracts away from the fact that a proposition can be expressed by the speaker with a stronger or weaker guarantee of truth, and that this guarantee may be more or less trusted by the hearer.[24] In the next section we will outline only as much as is needed to account for the 'probabilistic' nature of implicatures.

---

[24] The full framework is developed in detail elsewhere. See Sperber and Wilson, *Relevance*.

AN EXTENSION TO THE THEORY

What would happen, in our simplified framework, if the hearer of (20) tried to process it in a context such as (21a–d), which directly contradicts it?

(20) *She*: Peter is not coming to the party.

(21)(a) Peter is coming to the party.
    (b) If Peter is coming to the party, Jane will come.
    (c) Jane will come to the party.
    (d) If Peter is not coming to the party, Harry will not come.

We assume that no contextual implications at all are derivable from a contradictory set of assumptions.[25] The hearer of (20) must therefore either reject the utterance as irrelevant, or modify his assumptions in (21). By eliminating (21a) he could, in the simplified system outlined above, establish the relevance of (20) in a context consisting of the remaining assumptions (21b–d), deriving (22) as a contextual implication:

(22) Harry will not come to the party.

However, this is a rather unsatisfactory account, for two reasons. First, it implies that if (21d) had not been present in the context to enable (22) to be derived, (20) could not have been relevant at all. Yet intuitively it is always relevant to discover that one has been mistaken. In such cases, our original intuition that a proposition achieves relevance by interacting with, or modifying, the context in which it is processed, is not matched by our formal definition. Second, it is clear that a hearer in real life might neither reject (20) and retain (21a) nor accept (20) and reject (21a). He might decide that on the whole (20) is more likely to be true than (21a), or that (21a) is more likely to be true than (20), or that he has no idea which of (20) and (21a) is true. To account for these facts we must abandon the assumption that the only way a proposition can

---

25 See ibid. for discussion.

modify a context is by yielding contextual implications, and that the only propositions which play a role in processing are those regarded as certainly true.

A proposition may be put forward, and accepted, with varying degrees of confidence. Some account of how this can happen must be provided by any adequate theory of cognition. We argue elsewhere that a logical theory of confirmation, involving the assignment of numerical confirmation values, is not the best starting point for such an account.[26] For the purposes of this paper, however, let us say that when a proposition is processed it is assigned some form of gross absolute confirmation value representing its estimated likelihood of being true. Positive values represent the estimate that it is more likely to be true than false; the highest positive value, *true*, represents it as certainly true. Negative values represent the estimate that it is more likely to be false than true; the lowest negative value, *false*, represents it as certainly false. The absence of a value represents the absence of an opinion either way. When (20) is added to the context in (21), some complementary assignment of values to (20) and (21a) must be achieved: for example, by giving (20) the value *true* and (21a) the value *false*, or by giving (20) some positive value less than *true* and (21a) some negative value greater than *false*. The greatest possible effect that (20) could have would be to make the hearer entirely abandon his former assumption (21a), assigning (20) the value *true* and (21a) the value *false*. Let us assume that this readjustment takes place.

The deductive rules must now be applied to a context in which one premise, (21a), is *false*. Moreover, (21a) combines with (21b) to yield (21c) as a conclusion. What happens to this conclusion now that one of the premises used to derive it is *false*? Let us say that only conclusions based on premises with positive confirmation values can have confirmation values of their own, so that once (21a) is assigned the value *false*, (21c) automatically loses its own value. Any further conclusions involving (21c) will in turn be affected. Let us also assume that (21d) has some positive value less than *true*. How does this affect the value of (22), a contextual

---

26 Ibid.

implication based on (20) and (21d) as premises? Let us say (simplifying slightly) that a conclusion based on a mixture of premises with positive values will inherit at most the lowest value of any premise used in deriving it. Thus (22) will inherit at most the value of (21d).

The total effect of a proposition on a context can now be assessed by answering the following questions. First, did it directly affect the value of any proposition already present in the context, as (20) affected the value of (21a)? If so, how large was the change? Second, did it indirectly affect the value of any proposition already present in the context, as the modification of (21a) indirectly affected the value of (21c)? If so, how many propositions were affected, and how large was the change? Third, did its addition to the context yield any new contextual implications, as (20) yielded (22)? If so, how many were there, and how high were their values? We assume that the higher the value of any new contextual implication, the greater the modification to the context, and that a new contextual implication which lacks a confirmation value does not modify the context at all. With this extension to the framework, the recovery of contextual implications becomes just a special case of a more general notion of contextual modification in terms of which relevance can be redefined.

Let us say, then, that the proposition P is relevant in a context $\{C\}$ if and only if it modifies $\{C\}$ in one of the ways described above. Let us say that other things being equal, the more P modifies the context the more relevant it is, but that other things being equal, the greater the amount of processing required to bring about this modification, the *less* relevant it is. As before, the aim of the hearer in processing P will be to access a context which makes the best possible use of the available processing resources – that is, a context that maximizes the relevance of P.

From this very brief account, one or two general principles emerge. In particular, the only new contextual implications worth deriving will be those based on assumptions with positive values, the higher the better. The use of other assumptions will incur processing costs, but without leading to any reward in terms of contextual modification, since no new contextual implication based on them will be assigned a confirmation value at all. The use of such assumptions will thus detract from the relevance of any proposition being processed. Retrieval strategies geared to the maximization of relevance should therefore be aimed at retrieving, as quickly as possible, assumptions with positive confirmation values, the higher the better, and this fact should be known to any speaker. The hearer should also be able to infer, from the fact that the speaker is observing the principle of relevance, that he must have believed that all implicated conclusions, and all assumptions needed to derive them, had positive confirmation values, even if the hearer, of his own knowledge, would have been inclined to treat them as *false*.

Let us return, in the light of this discussion, to (2b) and its implicature (3):

(2) (a) *He*: Will you have some coffee?
    (b) *She*: Coffee would keep me awake.
(3) She won't have any coffee.

We can now answer the two questions raised earlier: how is (3) derived, and how is the alternative derivation of (7) ruled out?

(7) She will have some coffee.

The answer to the first question is that (3) is a contextual implication of (2b) in a context containing (5):

(5) (a) She doesn't want to be kept awake.
    (b) She won't have anything that would keep her awake.

Moreover, (5a–b) are implicated assumptions, and (3) is an implicated conclusion. By parallel arguments to those used in the discussion of relevance theory, the hearer knows that a speaker observing the principle of relevance must have expected him to supply the assumptions in (5) and derive the conclusion in (3). A question we have not yet considered is what confirmation value the speaker expects the hearer to assign to the implicated assumptions and conclusion.

If the exchange was taking place in the evening, the hearer could no doubt, of his own knowledge, assign some positive confirmation value less than *true* to (3) and (5). Under normal assumptions, it would be no more than a probability that the speaker does not want to be kept awake, and will not have anything that would keep her awake, and hence no more than a probability that she won't have any coffee. In the circumstances, however, the information that the speaker probably won't have any coffee would not be relevant enough. In the first place, she ought to know whether she will or will not have any coffee, and if she knows, she should have told him, since he has indicated that this information would be relevant to him. In the second place, she must realize that the hearer would have been aware that she *might* not want any coffee when he asked his question. What he indicated by asking it was that a categorical answer would be relevant to him. Therefore, if she has this information and is observing the principle of relevance, she ought to have given it. Is there any way of construing (2b) as giving a categorical answer to the question in (2a)? Certainly: all the hearer has to do is upgrade the values of (3) and (5) to *true*. To preserve the assumption that the speaker has observed the principle of relevance, this is what he must do. By the arguments of relevance theory, the speaker, who has encouraged him to do this, will be held just as responsible for the truth of (3) and (5) as if she had expressed these propositions directly.

To complete the interpretation, some justification has to be found for the fact that the speaker has chosen an indirect rather than a direct form of answer. Failure to find such a justification would be *prima facie* evidence that this line of interpretation was not correct. Here, at least on an informal level, the reason is easy to see. A direct refusal, with no explanation, would be likely to raise all sorts of questions in the hearer's mind about why his offer has been refused. The indirect answer (2b) simultaneously refuses the offer of coffee and explains the refusal, thus saving the hearer the time he might have spent speculating on the reasons behind it. This line of interpretation is thus confirmed as satisfying the principle of relevance.

By contrast, an interpretation based on the contextual assumptions in (6) and the conclusion in (7) is unlikely to be considered at all. If considered, it should be rejected as not conforming to the principle of relevance:

(6) (a) She wants to be kept awake.
   (b) She will have anything on offer that would keep her awake.
(7) She will have some coffee.

In the first place, if the exchange was taking place in the evening, the hearer of (2b) would no doubt, of his own knowledge, assign a lower confirmation value to (6) than to (5). On the assumption that retrieval strategies give preferential access to higher-valued assumptions, (5) should be retrieved before (6); and since it gives rise to a satisfactory interpretation, there is no reason why (6) should not be considered at all. However, suppose it is. The interpretation it gives rise to should still be rejected as not conforming to the principle of relevance. There is no reason why a speaker observing the principle of relevance should have preferred the indirect answer (2b), construed in this way, to the direct answer that she wants some more coffee. An acceptance, unlike a refusal, normally needs no justification; it normally raises no questions in a hearer's mind about the reasons behind it. Moreover, a speaker who attempted to justify her acceptance on the grounds that she wanted to stay awake and would accept anything on offer that would keep her awake *would* raise a number of questions in her hearer's mind, and cost him valuable processing time if she did not go on immediately to answer them. Hence, the line of interpretation based on (6) and (7) is ruled out at a number of points as failing to conform to the principle of relevance.

Many standard examples of implicature fit quite straightforwardly into this framework. For example, Clark discusses a class of 'bridging' implicatures needed to establish the reference of the referring expressions in (23b)–(25b):[27]

(23) *She*: (a) I went into the room. (b) The window was open.
(24) *She*: (a) I went into the room. (b) Both windows were open.
(25) *She*: (a) I went into the room. (b) All three windows were open.

[27] H. H. Clark, 'Bridging', in *Thinking: Readings in Cognitive Science*, eds P. N. Johnson-Laird and P. C. Wason (CUP, Cambridge, 1977), pp. 411–20.

Inference and implicature

As Clark points out, in normal circumstances the hearer of these utterances would supply assumptions (26)–(28) respectively, even if there had been no previous mention of the number of windows in the room:

(26) The room had a window.
(27) The room had two windows.
(28) The room had three windows.

Consider how this might happen in the case of (24b). Given the immediately preceding mention of a room, the hearer of (24b) would no doubt, of his own knowledge, have relatively easy access to each of the assumptions in (26)–(28), and be able to assign each of them some confirmation value less than *true*. On the assumption that the speaker has observed the principle of relevance, he will take it that he must upgrade the value of (27) to *true* and use it to establish the reference of the referring expression *both windows* in (24b). As long as this assignment leads to a satisfactory range of contextual implications, he will accept it as correct. The role of the implicated assumption here is not to yield any particular contextual implication, but to establish the referential content of the utterance, which is a necessary precondition to recovering any contextual implications at all.

There may, of course, be many other logically possible assumptions that the hearer of (24b) could have used: for example, the windows might have been in the house opposite, or mentioned in a letter the speaker found in the room. However, in normal circumstances, unless the existence of these windows had already been established, these assumptions would be much less accessible than those in (26)–(28) above, and a speaker observing the principle of relevance could not normally have expected the hearer to supply them. The general principle, for bridging implicatures as for all other implicated assumptions, is that they should – at least in the estimation of the speaker – be virtually instantaneously accessible, and more accessible than any alternative assumption likely to lead to an acceptable interpretation. If not, a speaker observing the principle of relevance should have done something to increase their accessibility – for example by directly mentioning them in the utterance – and thus save the hearer some unnecessary processing costs.

Grice is unsure whether the implicatures carried by (29b) would be categorical or merely probable:

(29)(a) *A*: I am out of petrol.
    (b) *B*: There is a garage round the corner.

He claims that 'B would be infringing the maxim 'Be relevant' unless he thinks, or thinks it possible, that the garage is open and has petrol to sell; so he implicates that the garage is, or at least may be open, etc.'[28]

We can shed some light on his uncertainty. A speaker observing the principle of relevance should expect the hearer, among other things, to supply the contextual assumption in (30) and derive the conclusion in (31):

(30) If there's a garage round the corner, I can get some petrol there.
(31) I can get some petrol round the corner.

However, if it occurs to the hearer that garages may be closed or out of petrol, he will be unable of his own knowledge to assign more than a fairly high degree of probability to (30) or (31). In other words, he will only be able to derive the conclusion that he *may* be able to get some petrol round the corner. So far, the case is exactly like the two previous ones discussed in this section. The difference is that in this case, even the information that he *may* be able to get petrol round the corner might be relevant enough for a speaker who could not make a more categorical claim to think this information worth offering.

More precisely, what the speaker of (29b) indicates is that *as far as he knows* (30) and (31) are true, and therefore that *as far as he knows* the garage is open and selling petrol, etc. In some circumstances – for example if the speaker is coming from the direction of the garage with a full petrol can in his hand – the hearer would be

28 Grice, 'Logic and conversation', p. 51.

justified in assuming that he knew with certainty; in this case the implicatures (30) and (31), and their necessary conditions that the garage is open and selling petrol, would be regarded as categorical. In different circumstances only a weaker attribution of confirmation value would be justified. The general principle is thus that when a less than categorical implicature would conform to the principle of relevance, the hearer is not entitled to assume that the speaker expected a categorical implicature to be supplied.

All the implicatures considered so far have arisen in processing the explicit content of the utterance, or in Grice's terms 'what was strictly speaking said'. As Grice points out, many implicatures arise not so much from the content of what was said as from the saying of it, in those circumstances, to that audience, and so on. Consider (32), for example:

(32) (a) *A*: Where does *C* live?
    (b) *B*: Somewhere in the South of France.

In normal circumstances, *B* would implicate that he does not know more precisely where *C* lives. We would analyse this implicature as resulting not from the explicit content of (32b) but from the fact, which the hearer is expected to notice and process, that the speaker has failed to give more precise information when, in the circumstances, more precise information would have been more relevant. To reconcile this fact with the assumption that the speaker has observed the principle of relevance, the hearer would have to access something like the contextual assumption in (33) and derive something like the conclusion in (34):

(33) If *B* has failed to give more precise information on *C*'s whereabouts, he has no more precise information to give.
(34) *B* has no more precise information to give.

Here, (34) is a contextual implication, not of the content of (32b), but of (35):

(35) *B* has failed to give more precise information on *C*'s whereabouts.

This is a proposition which may, and in this case clearly does, have some relevance in its own right. It would therefore be a mistake to think of a speaker as providing relevant information only through the explicit content of his utterance. An act of utterance may draw the hearer's attention to a number of propositions other than explicitly expressed, and these may contribute to the overall relevance of the utterance.

Grice analyses (32b) as involving a clash between the maxims of informativeness and truthfulness; the desire to give precise information about C's whereabouts is sacrificed to the demands of truthfulness. He says little to explain why the supposed clash is not resolved in the opposite direction, which is a weakness of his system. Any system with more than one pragmatic principle must provide some account of their interaction – an account which is rarely provided. In our framework, with its single principle, there is no possibility of clashes. Notice, too, that there is no appeal to a violation of the principle of relevance, real or apparent, in our account of (32b). The speaker has been as relevant as he can in the circumstances – more relevant, for example, than if he had merely said 'I don't know.' His failure to provide more detailed information is explained not by appeal to deliberate violation of the principle of relevance, but by the assumption that he did not have more detailed information to provide.

We would like to make the more general claim that the recovery of implicatures *never* involves an appeal to deliberate violation of the principle of relevance. Grice himself remarks that it is hard to find cases in which his maxim of relevance is deliberately violated, but offers the following as a candidate example:

> At a genteel tea party, A says 'Mrs X is an old bag.' There is a moment of appalled silence, and then B says 'The weather has been quite delightful this summer, hasn't it?' B has blatantly refused to make what *he* says relevant to A's preceding remark. He therefore implicates that A's remark should not be discussed and, perhaps more specifically, that A has committed a social gaffe.[29]

However, the fact that B's utterance is not relevant to the immediately preceding remark does not mean that it is not relevant

---

29 Ibid., p. 54.

at all. Most of its relevance would be achieved, not through its content, but by drawing the hearers' attention to the fact that *B* is deliberately ignoring *A*'s remark. To reconcile this with the assumption that the principle of relevance has been observed, they would have to access assumptions along the lines of (36a–b) and derive conclusions along the lines of (37a–b):

(36) (a) If *B* is deliberately ignoring *A*'s remark, he believes it should not be discussed.
    (b) If *B* believes *A*'s remark should not be discussed, he believes it was a social gaffe.
(37) (a) *B* believes *A*'s remark should not be discussed.
    (b) *B* believes *A*'s remark was a social gaffe.

In our framework these would be implicatures, since they are needed to reconcile the fact that *B* is deliberately ignoring *A*'s remark with the assumption that he is being as relevant as he can. They would, however, be relatively weak implicatures, since a variety of roughly equivalent assumptions could be made, all of which would reconcile *B*'s behaviour with the assumption that he is observing the principle of relevance. By the arguments outlined above, the speaker could therefore not be held solely responsible for their truth.

Relevance theory thus makes a number of specific claims about the role of implicatures in comprehension and the processes by which they are recovered. First, they are either contextual assumptions or contextual implications which the hearer is expected to supply in satisfying himself that the speaker has observed the principle of relevance. Implicated assumptions are recovered by the same processes used to retrieve other contextual assumptions, with ease of accessibility playing a decisive role; implicated conclusions are recovered by deduction.

Second, the hearer may be expected to upgrade the confirmation value of an implicated assumption to the point where the conclusions it yields conform to the principle of relevance. The speaker is held responsible for the truth (or degree of confirmation) of any assumptions and conclusions upgraded in this way. The hearer may thus acquire new information, not only from the explicit content of an utterance and its implicated conclusions, but also from its implicated assumptions.

Third, implicatures may be recovered either in the course of processing the explicit content of an utterance, or in the course of processing some higher-level description of it which the hearer is expected to construct. It is important, therefore, that relevance is defined not as a relation between utterances, but as a relation between propositions or sets of propositions.

Fourth, there is no essential connection between the recovery of an implicature and the assumption that the speaker has deliberately violated the principle of relevance. On the contrary: in this aspect of comprehension as in every other, it is the assumption that the speaker has *not* violated the principle of relevance that makes all the difference between processing an item of information that has been deliberately communicated and one that has not.

Within this framework, utterance comprehension is ultimately a matter of hypothesis formation and confirmation: the best hypothesis about the speaker's communicative intentions is the one that best satisfies the principle of relevance. However, it does not follow that deductive inference plays no role in the formation and confirmation of pragmatic hypotheses. On the contrary, because relevance is itself defined in partly deductive terms, the description of pragmatic hypothesis formation and confirmation makes essential reference to deductive processing. In particular, the class of possible implicated assumptions must be of a form capable of combining with information derived from the utterance to undergo deductive inference rules, and the class of possible implicated conclusions is itself deductively determined. The assumption that the overall framework in which comprehension takes place is ultimately non-demonstrative is not incompatible with the assumption that deductive processing plays a central role in comprehension.

CONCLUDING REMARK

As we have described them, the processes of pragmatic hypothesis formation and confirmation are clearly context dependent. But to what extent are they global processes in Fodor's sense? They are global in principle because, as we have shown, the interpretation of a given utterance can proceed, in ever expanding contexts, just as long as the hearer thinks that the rewards are likely to outweigh the processing costs. With certain types of utterance, for example a sacred text or a fortune-teller's prophecy, a hearer might be willing to devote a lifetime's effort to the interpretation process. In practice, however, expectations of relevance are generally much lower; there are other demands on the hearer's processing time; and he generally satisfies himself with establishing relevance in the most immediately accessible context, and leaves it at that.

The same point applies to the formation and confirmation of scientific hypotheses. At one extreme are major theories, which may take a lifetime to develop and confirm. At the other extreme are such minor hypotheses as that there is a bird on the grass, or that spring is on the way, which are formulated in passing, processed in the most immediately accessible context and either abandoned or stored for future use.

We see little reason to think that there are differences of principle between relatively local and relatively global processes of pragmatic or scientific hypothesis formation and confirmation. In particular, the role of context and the goal of maximizing relevance are the same for both types of process, although the principle of relevance, of course, applies only to deliberately communicated information. What distinguishes the two types of process is simply a relative difference, in practice not in principle, in their freedom of access to contextual information. We therefore suggest that the most useful way of gaining insight into fully global processes in Fodor's sense is to look at the relatively more local processes of everyday utterance interpretation and the interpretation of everyday sights and sounds, and work on the assumption that other, more global processes of hypothesis formation and confirmation involve the same cognitive principles and goals.

3

Ambiguity and the semantics–pragmatics distinction

Ruth Kempson

Over the past few years, work in formal semantics has increasingly demonstrated that the linguistic meaning of expressions has to interact with contextual parameters of a rich and complex sort to determine the truth-theoretic content of the propositions that a sentence expresses.[1] One conclusion this forced on linguists is that being part of the truth conditions of some proposition expressible by a sentence is not a sufficient condition for some aspect of utterance interpretation to be characterized as part of the meaning of that sentence by a rule of grammar. Moreover it is a familiar, if unexplained, problem that there are so-called conventional implicature phenomena associated with lexical items and constructions[2] which contribute to the interpretation of sentences in a purely linguistic, rule-governed way and yet do not contribute to the

---

1 See D. Kaplan, 'Demonstratives', unpublished manuscript, UCLA; A. Kratzer, 'The notional category of modality', in *Words, Worlds and Contexts*, eds H. Eikmeyer and H. Rieser (de Gruyter, 1981); H. Kamp, 'Semantics versus pragmatics', in *Formal Semantics and Pragmatics for Natural Language*, eds F. Guenther and S. Schmidt (Reidel, 1979), pp. 255–88; G. Stump, 'The formal semantics and pragmatics of free adjuncts and absolutes in English', PhD thesis, Ohio State University; B. H. Partee, 'Compositionality', in *Varieties of Formal Semantics*, eds F. Landman and F. Veltman (Foris, 1984).
2 See P. Grice, 'Logic and conversation', in *Syntax and Semantics 3: Speech Acts*, eds P. Cole and J. Morgan (Academic Press, 1975).

truth-conditional content expressible by the construction in question. These are the cases which demonstrate, in addition, that being part of the truth conditions of the proposition expressed by some sentence is not a necessary condition for an aspect of sentence meaning.

In this chapter I wish first to emphasize this problem by demonstrating that, using two standard truth-conditional tests of ambiguity, we find a problem similar to that posed by context-dependent phenomena: we are faced with far more ambiguity than any linguist would wish to incorporate in a theory of grammar. Indeed, by these standard tests for ambiguity, all cases of scalar implicature are cases of truth-conditional ambiguity.[3] If we wish to retain the pragmatic explanation of the relation between the interpretations in question, we are forced to the conclusions (a) that the linguistic meaning of sentences considerably underdetermines the truth conditions of the propositions they can express, and (b) that pragmatic principles, in particular the principle of relevance, in part determine such truth conditions.[4] Second, I shall give a new analysis of contrary-to-expectation *but* in terms of a lexical constraint on (a) the pragmatic context to be constructed, and (b) the contextual implications (roughly equivalent to implicatures) to be deduced. I am not however going to argue that the semantics-pragmatics distinction be abandoned. On the contrary, I shall suggest that the scalar implicature phenomena, the context-dependent phenomena, and the conventional implicature phenomena all become straightforwardly explicable if we make certain assumptions. These are that utterance interpretation involves a process of context construction by the hearer in addition to recovering some proposition expressed, and that specifying the linguistic meaning of a sentence does not involve the full articula-

---

3 The arguments in this section are adapted from A. Cormack, 'Negation, ambiguity and logical form', unpublished manuscript. I am grateful to her for allowing me to use this material, and also for her comments on a previous version of this chapter. An early version was delivered to the winter 1982 LSA meeting. Work for this chapter was supported in part by ESRC grant HR8602, HR8635.
4 This general conclusion was anticipated in C. Travis, *The True and the False: The Domain of the Pragmatic* (John Benjamin, 1981), but without any detailed indication of how linguistic meaning and pragmatic principles interact.

tion of truth conditions of the propositions expressed by the sentence in question, but rather involves the partial articulation of both these aspects of utterance interpretation.

Take first the problem of ambiguity and scalar implicatures. How do we decide whether a multiplicity of interpretations displayed by different uses of a sentence should be characterized as linguistic ambiguity specified as part of the grammar of that language? On the assumption that the characterization of semantics for a natural language as specified in its grammar is a specification of truth conditions (equivalently, propositional content) associated with sentences of the language, there are two tests for determining whether a sentence should be analysed as linguistically ambiguous. First, a sentence is ambiguous if with respect to a single set of circumstances it can be both true and false: this is the defining property of ambiguity. Second, if a sentence is ambiguous, then an assertion that the proposition expressed by that sentence is false (by the use of the corresponding negative sentence)[5] should be ambiguous in at least the same way as the sentence itself. So we find that (2) is just as ambiguous as (1):

(1) John went to the bank.
(2) John didn't go to the bank.

By contrast, if a sentence has a single specifiable propositional content, then we expect positive and negative forms of the sentence to have equally only one interpretation (scope variation apart), as indeed is displayed by (3) and (4):

(3) Edith is my sister-in-law.
(4) Edith isn't my sister-in-law.

'Sister-in-law' is a property attributable to an individual under apparently two quite different conditions (being one's brother's wife or being one's husband's sister). Nevertheless, its unitary meaning as a linguistic entity is displayed by the fact that the assertion that 'it is false that Edith is my sister-in-law' is an

---

[5] Nothing in these arguments turns on the question of whether failure of so-called presuppositions gives rise to truth-value gaps.

assertion that the referent of Edith meets neither of these two conditions, demonstrating that these apparently distinct conditions have no status as defining properties of the concept 'sister-in-law'.

We can now apply these two criteria for ambiguity to one of the core cases of scalar implicatures – the numerals. Numerals have two interpretations, 'at least n' and 'exactly n', and the question is whether this is a phenomenon of linguistic ambiguity or a case of a unitary core meaning plus implicature imposed by pragmatic principles.

(5) Mark didn't eat three biscuits.
(6) John hasn't got two girlfriends.

It may superficially seem from (5) and (6) that numerals behave as though they merely have the 'at least' understanding as part of their linguistically specifiable core meaning,[6] for on the relevant reading of (5) and (6) in which the numerical expression is interpreted within the scope of the falsity operator, the immediately available understanding in both cases is exclusively the 'at least' one. However, (7) provides contrary evidence:

(7) Mark didn't eat three biscuits: he ate four.

Any speaker of (7) asserts that 'it's false that Mark ate three biscuits' and goes on to provide as a reason for asserting that proposition that he ate four biscuits. But to have eaten either at least or exactly four biscuits entails that one has eaten at least three biscuits. Hence if (7) is taken, as it is, to be non-contradictory, the proposition that Mark ate three biscuits has simultaneously to be false and yet true. By our first criterion of ambiguity, we conclude that the sentence 'Mark ate three biscuits' is ambiguous. Moreover, unlike (5), which appeared only to have 'at least' understanding of the numeral, the use of (5) in (7) has only the 'exactly' understanding of the numeral. Thus (5) displays a range of interpretations

---

6 As argued in L. Horn, 'On the semantic properties of logical operators in English', PhD thesis, University of California, Los Angeles.

Semantics–pragmatics distinction

which parallel the positive form of the sentence. By our second criterion of ambiguity also, numerals are ambiguous.

What is going on here? We have a sentence having two understandings P and Q, where Q entails P, and the negative form of that sentence is being used to deny the truth of the proposition that the positive sentence expresses solely on the basis that Q is false. Indeed, P's truth follows from what is asserted. This phenomenon, if the criteria of linguistic ambiguity are to be relied on, leads to the conclusion that the sentence displays a linguistic ambiguity between its understandings P and Q. But the extra strength of interpretations that distinguishes Q from P is, with some good justification, claimed to be a pragmatically induced property of utterances of the sentence.[7] This problem extends to the whole set of scalar implicatures, as is demonstrated by (8)–(15):

(8) Mark didn't eat some of the biscuits: he ate all of them.
(9) She isn't competent at linguistics: she's masterly at the subject.
(10) He didn't sleep until noon: he slept until one.
(11) He isn't patriotic or chauvinistic: he's patriotic and chauvinistic.
(12) I didn't invite John to supper: I invited John, Mary and Susanna.
(13) The house is in a terrible mess. We didn't have Lily in to play today – we had the whole street in (as well as Lily).
(14) She didn't lose a finger: she lost an arm.
(15) It's no longer a crime to hold left-wing views in Colombia: it's a crime to hold any views whatsoever. (*The Times*)

Each of these is a denial of the truth of the proposition expressed by a positive form of sentence on the basis of a further assertion

---

7 See ibid.
8 Sentence (10) is from G. Miller and P. Johnson–Laird, *Language and Perception* (Cambridge University Press, 1976). Sentence (11) is an example of the type whose existence is disputed by G. Gazdar, *Pragmatics* (Academic Press, 1979), discussed in L. Horn, 'Metalinguistic negation and pragmatic ambiguity', *Language*, 6, pp. 121–74. Sentence (15) occurred in *The Times* during 1980.

which entails the truth of that proposition, the only evidence for the denial involving just that aspect which has been argued to be a pragmatic property. If we take the tests for ambiguity as demonstrating that the ambiguity in question should be characterized within the grammar of that language, we seem forced to the conclusion that there is much more ambiguity in natural languages than anyone has previously envisaged as part of the linguistic specification of natural languages, despite the fact that the variation in interpretation has a pragmatic basis.

Notice that this phenomenon cannot be dismissed as mere lexical ambiguity, predictable by lexical stipulation. For on the basis of (14) we would have to postulate that 'finger' was lexically ambiguous between 'just finger' and 'finger and possibly something else', that 'John' was lexically ambiguous between 'John and no one else' and 'John and possibly someone else', and so on. And in some cases, as in (15), there is no plausible lexical basis whatever. Moreover, this is not a phenomenon which is reducible to questions of focus, even (as in (12)) where this might seem appropriate. The problem of focus and its interpretation is independent of and in addition to this.

There are two ways of avoiding this conclusion of massive ambiguity. The first is to argue that in all such cases the items in question have the stronger of the two interpretations as their meaning, and that a pragmatic device weakens this in those (the 'at least' cases) where the meaning is not so narrowly determined. This proposal can swiftly be rejected. This is no better than claiming lexical ambiguity in all cases. There are some cases for which no plausible basis can be given (see (15) in particular). Second, any such account would have to invoke a quite exceptional pragmatic weakening principle, which would have to be allowed to apply as many times as there are conjuncts. Thus it would have to apply to each of the conjuncts separately in (16), i.e. twice over:

(16) I've invited John and Mary.

and to each conjunct separately in (17), i.e. three times over:

(17) John, Mary or Susanna can come.

and so on. Moreover the principle would have to be sensitive to whether the words in the conjuncts are correlated in some way to be explained as in (19) or not as in (18):

(18) You have to be seventeen to drive a motor bike and you have to be eighteen to drive a car.
(19) You have to be eighteen to drive a car and I'm nineteen so I'm certainly eligible.

No such principle exists. Third, any such account would falsely predict that the sentences (20)–(25) are synonymous, differing only pragmatically:

(20) John hit Bill.
(21) Only John hit Bill.
(22) John hit only Bill.
(23) John only hit Bill.

Finally, by the same line of argument, the analysis would predict that (20) would entail (24)–(26):

(24) No one else hit Bill.
(25) John did nothing else to Bill.
(26) No one else did anything to Bill.

Since these claims are false, this solution is a non-starter.

The second solution to these paradoxical negation cases is to argue that the negation involved in (8)–(15) is a pragmatic negation operator, equivalent, say, to 'I refuse to say p.' Such a pragmatic operator might be sensitive to various factors and not those relating to truth value. One recent proponent of this view is Horn,[9] who argues that (8)–(15) are all examples of what he calls 'metalinguistic negation'; a speaker is not asserting that some proposition is false, but is rather 'indicating his unwillingness to assert something in a given way or to accept another's assertion of it in that way'. Metalinguistic negation, he says, is a non-truth-

9 Horn, 'Metalinguistic negation'.

functional operator which is used to object to any aspect of a previous utterance. He points out that negation can be used to object to pronunciation or stylistic overtone and not just or not even to the propositional content:[10]

(27) I didn't [miʸənĭdʒ] to solve the problem: I [mænĭdʒd] to solve the problem.
(29) I'm not his daughter: he's my father.
(29) He doesn't ever assault any of his customers: he just dusts them down.

What Horn argues is that (8)–(15) parallel (28)–(29) in being not descriptive uses of negation but rather a denial of the assertibility of the positive form of sentence on the grounds of not wanting to convey the associated conversational implicature. Thus, (28) is a refusal to assert 'I'm his daughter' despite believing it to be true, on the grounds that this might convey, say, 'I am moody and difficult'. In the same way, he contends, (8) is a refusal to assert 'Mark ate three biscuits' despite believing the proposition expressed by the sentence 'Mark ate three biscuits' to be true, because of not wanting to convey what an utterance of that sentence conversationally implicates – that Mark ate exactly three biscuits.

That there is a metalinguistic use of negation is incontrovertible. Any negative sentence can be used in the way Horn terms 'metalinguistic', as witness (30) and (31):

(30) He didn't clean the 'parrots': he cleaned the carrots.
(31) He isn't to eat 'four mats': he's to eat more fats.

These contain negative sentences used metalinguistically despite their potential for straightforward descriptive use. So it does not follow that, because a metalinguistic analysis is available for (8)–(15), there should be no other analysis. The question is rather whether (8)–(15), like (27)–(29), have only a metalinguistic use.

I offer four reasons for doubting this. First, Horn specifically claims that these metalinguistic uses are only used as an objection

10 Sentences (27) and (28) are Horn's examples.

to some previous utterance. This is not true of genuine uses of negation, and it is not true of (8)–(15). As evidence of this, consider (32):

(32) A: How did your tour go?
    B: We had to work very hard.
      (a) We didn't give three concerts: we gave eight concerts.
      (b)? We didn't give 'three' concerts: we gave free concerts.

There is no denial of any immediately previous utterance in the use of the negative sentence, but (a) is entirely acceptable. By contrast, (b), containing a metalinguistic use of 'three', objecting to 'three' and rectifying it by 'free', is not.

Second, in genuine descriptive uses of negation, one may be able to reconstruct the speaker's reasons for uttering the negative sentence. A characteristic use of negative sentences is one in which people assert a proposition by using a negative sentence and go on to provide evidence for holding such a belief. Sentences (33)–(35) are examples of this:

(33) John didn't hit the target: he hit the wall.
(34) Sue didn't help Mary: it was only Joan who did.
(35) Sue didn't help Mary: she hindered her.

In each of these cases, the second sentence of the example is an assertion of the evidence on which the speaker has formed his belief in the negative proposition. In metalinguistic uses, this is not possible. Having more students cannot provide evidence for or against having four students:

(36) He's got more students, not 'four' students.

Giving free concerts doesn't provide evidence for or against giving three concerts (cf. (32)). And so on. By contrast, however, (8)–(15) are in this respect exactly like (33)–(35): the addition of the second conjunct in (8), for example, does provide evidence for holding the belief that Mark didn't eat three biscuits if 'three' is understood to mean 'exactly three'. Thus the relationship between the second conjunct and the negative assertion parallels ordinary uses of negation and not metalinguistic uses.

Third, if the negation in (8)–(15) is a pragmatic refusal-to-assert operator, it should parallel the 'not that' construction exemplified by (37):

(37) It's not that Mark ate three biscuits
$\begin{Bmatrix} \text{– though he did –} \\ \text{– in fact he didn't –} \end{Bmatrix}$
it's that I'm too tired to cook breakfast.

'Not that' is a pragmatic operator which is sensitive to pragmatic factors such as relevance and is not a falsity operator. In virtue of this property, it allows non-contradictory co-ordination with an assertion of the positive sentence *tout court*, as in (37). Indeed it is indifferent to the truth value of its complement sentence. Negation itself does not parallel this behaviour: co-ordination of a negative sentence with any form of its positive congener is invariably contradictory:

(38) Mark didn't eat three biscuits, though he did.

Therefore the negation in the problematic cases (8)–(15) is not a pragmatic operator, varying over factors other than truth relevant ones.

Finally, as Horn himself points out, (8)–(15) can be replaced by 'it is not true that' paraphrases, whereas (27)–(29), the definitive examples of metalinguistic negation, cannot. Sentences (39) and (40) stand in contrast to (41)–(43), for (39) and (40) are perfectly natural ways of conveying the same information as (8) and (10) whereas (41) and (42) are odd, and (43) is only not odd if 'assault' is taken to be truth-conditionally distinct from 'dust down':

(39) It's not true that Mark ate some of the biscuits: he ate all of them.
(40) It's not true that he slept until noon: he slept until one.
(41)?It's not true that he [miʸənīdʒ] to open the door: he [mænīdʒd] to open the door.

(42) ?It's not true that I'm his daughter: he's my father.
(43) It's not true that he ever assaults any of his customers, he merely dusts them down.

Horn suggests that this merely shows that 'it is not true' should not be taken literally in examples such as (39) and (40), but his single argument to this effect is quite unconvincing. It is that (i) is acceptable:

(i) It is not true that they had a baby and got married: they got married and had a baby.

He argues, on the assumption that the temporal sequence and causal implications are implicated rather than being part of the content of what is said, that 'it is not true' is used non-literally both in (i) and in (39) and (40). However, there is good reason to think that temporal sequence (and causality) may be part of the propositional content asserted, thus affecting truth value judgements, despite this aspect being contributed by pragmatic principles.[11] Thus the existence of (i) provides no evidence at all that 'it is not true' is being metalinguistically used in (39) and (40), or in consequence that (8)–(15) can only be interpreted metalinguistically.

Horn provides two diagnostics of exclusively descriptive use of negation which, if reliable, confirm the view adopted here. They are (a) that the use of negative polarity items precludes a metalinguistic use of negation, and (b) that lexically incorporated negation precludes a metalinguistic construal. If these diagnostics were taken to be reliable, they confirm the view adopted here that (8)–(15) are not necessarily metalinguistic for we not only have

(ii) He didn't [miʸənīdʒ] to open $\left\{\begin{array}{l}\text{??any}\\ \text{some}\end{array}\right\}$ doors, he [mænīdʒd] to open some doors.

(iii) It's $\left\{\begin{array}{l}\text{??impossible}\\ \text{not possible}\end{array}\right\}$ to see him – it's essential.

---

11 See R. Carston and D. Wilson, 'Pragmatic analyses of *and*', unpublished manuscript, where this is explicitly argued.

but also (29) and

(iv) It's most unlikely that he'll have two pints – it's more likely to be three or even four.
(v) If he buys any sweets, he's quite unable to buy two Mars Bars – he always buys five or six.

However, these diagnostics are not entirely convincing, as witness the acceptability of

(vi) The hero didn't ever bump anyone off – he just used to help people to their final resting place.
(vii) It would be impossible for Jo to [mi^{y}ənîdʒ] anyone, though he might admit to [mænədʒ1ŋ] people.

On the strength of my arguments, I conclude that though a metalinguistic analysis is available for these paradoxical negation cases, the problems they present cannot be pushed aside by only providing a metalinguistic analysis; they can and naturally are interpreted as straightforward cases of descriptive negation. The conclusion that there is a lot more truth-conditional ambiguity than is contributed by the language in question itself is unavoidable. Another way of putting the same conclusion is that the truth-functional falsity operator is not restricted to ranging over aspects of sentence meaning: it also ranges over those aspects of propositional content determined by pragmatic principles. In consequence, the negation test of ambiguity does not provide a sufficient condition for some element to be part of the linguistic specification of meaning.

There is also the converse, familiar problem, posed by the conventional implicatures mentioned initially, that being part of the truth-conditional content of propositions expressed by a sentence is not a necessary condition for some element of interpretation to be part of the semantics of a natural language either. In other words, the concept of truth conditions does not provide a basis for determining what is part of semantics and what part of pragmatics if we take semantics to be that aspect of content specified within the grammar of the language. Many would argue that the distinction between semantics and pragmatics should be abandoned.[12] I would urge to the contrary that this is an impossible stance for a linguist to take, for semantics, as a component part of grammar, is the specification of the rule-governed contribution that sentences of the language make to utterance interpretation, and pragmatics is the set of general language-independent principles which complete the picture, to determine how utterances are understood. What alternative account of linguistic meaning could we propose which would enable us to absorb the insights achieved by assuming that natural language semantics was exclusively concerned with truth-conditional content? A straightforward answer is available from a consideration of pragmatics.

The pragmatic theory I propose to make use of is that of Sperber and Wilson.[13] The pragmatic theory of Sperber and Wilson is a complete theory of utterance interpretation. It turns on four principal claims. One is that the only principle or maxim governing utterance interpretation is that of *relevance*, a concept which is defined as follows:

> An utterance *P* is relevant in a context *C* if and only if the union of *P* and *C* allows the deduction of conclusions which are not derivable from either *P* or *C* alone (subject to the third claim below).

For example, take (44):

(44) *P*: We are going down the Baja.
    C: If we go down the Baja, we shall go down the East Coast and go snorkelling.
    Contextual implication: We shall go down the East Coast and go snorkelling.

The proposition expressed by utterance *P* against context *C* automatically leads to the deduction of the specified pragmatic implication; and according to the definition of relevance the

---

12 See Kamp, 'Semantics versus pragmatics'.
13 Chapter 2 in this volume; and D. Sperber and D. Wilson, *Relevance: Communication and Cognition* (Basil Blackwell, Oxford, 1986).

proposition is relevant against this context. Associated with the deductive concept of relevance is the *principle of relevance*:

> The speaker has tried to express the proposition which is of optimal relevance to the hearer.

where to be optimally relevant means that the maximum number of contextual implications can be deduced in the shortest possible time. In other words, what is required in applying the principle of optimal relevance is not merely applying the definition of relevance itself in computing numbers of contextual implications, but is rather selecting a context which balances the factors of processing time and information content derivable – to put it informally, balancing the effort involved against the information extracted. We shall see a detailed application of this shortly with numerals.

The second main claim concerns the concept of context. The interpretation of an utterance by a hearer is said to involve three aspects: (a), as is uncontroversial, the recovery of the proposition expressed; (b) the construction, by the hearer, of some context set of propositions (possibly as small as a single proposition); (c) the consequent deduction of contextual implications from the combination of context and proposition. In other words, there is no presumed context or body of mutual knowledge in some sense prior to the utterance itself. There is minimal use of the concept of speaker's propositional intentions, and there is no unanalysed concept of appropriacy. The hearer does all the work of utterance understanding, including creating a context. The way the speaker is involved is in making it as easy as possible for the hearer. This works in the following way. The principle of relevance, which governs utterance interpretation, is one which both speaker and hearer know. The speaker produces an utterance, trying to make sure that the proposition recovered from it by this principle will be the one she intended to convey. The hearer using the principle simply recovers a proposition from the utterance. He does not *have* to recover the speaker's intentions, the speaker's beliefs, or the presumed knowledge which the speaker believes he believes she believes he has. He simply interprets the utterance according to the principle of relevance, which acts as a guarantee that the speaker believes that the form that he has selected makes

Semantics–pragmatics distinction

immediately accessible to the hearer a proposition and a context set from which he can derive contextual implications. Successful communication is where the hearer recovers at least what the speaker intended him to, and normally a whole lot more. In particular the speaker does not have to intend each one of the contextual implications that the hearer may derive from her utterance; she merely has to intend that the hearer will find the appropriate number of contextual implications to achieve a satisfactory level of relevance. (We shall come to an example of this with *but*.)

The third main claim of the theory concerns the logic. The deduction process is assumed to be syntactically driven as in systems of natural deduction,[14] and the logic is non-standard in that it is a concept logic. Deductive inferences are allowable only in so far as they are definable on particular concepts expressed by the utterance. There are no introduction inference rules (which can apply recursively), with an initial proposition variable on the left-hand side, and connectives introduced on the right-hand side, of the inference rule. In other words there are no such rules as vel-introduction. Thus the problem of every proposition having an infinite number of inferences is resolved by claiming that the logic underlying communication does not contain introduction rules of inference which would lead to such infinite sets of inferences.

The fourth main claim is implicit in what I have said already, namely that the principle of relevance is applied in determining all three aspects of utterance interpretation (and not merely in the deduction of contextual implications, as proposed within Gricean theory). The principle of relevance is claimed in particular to determine reference assignment, disambiguation and domain selection, all three of these pertaining to the proposition expressed. Consider (45):[15]

(45) Place of utterance:
Playground full of kids with adults, displaying the whole range from misery to ecstasy.

---

14 In such systems, the inference rules apply in virtue of some well-formed formula meeting the structural condition imposed by that rule.
15 The informality of the notation is for exegetical purposes only.

Conversation between two adults:
A: Can I talk about our mutually miserable circumstances?
B: Everyone seems to be happy.

Context:
B is in charge of six kids.
For all set of six kids (if k is happy then k does not need attention from B).
For all set of six kids (if k does not need attention, then B can take part in an adult-oriented conversation).
Talking about our mutually miserable circumstances is an adult-oriented conversation.

Contextual implication:
A can talk to B about A and B's mutually miserable circumstances.

In interpreting B's reply as an affirmative reply to her question, A is expected to construct a context along the lines specified. The significance of this example is that in order for A to understand B's answer as an answer to her question, A has to construct a fixed domain for the quantification and to set up a series of inferential links from which a direct answer to A's question can be deduced. And it is only if B's quantification is understood in this way that B's answer can be seen as an answer to A. Furthermore, the domain is not that of the total context of utterance; in particular it does not contain either the speaker or the hearer, who – given the suggested topic of conversation – are presumably not happy. This example demonstrates that domain selection cannot be stated in terms of indexical co-ordinates of any straightforward sort other than stipulation of some arbitrary fixed set. However, it is naturally explained in terms of relevance: given that the domain of individuals is totally undetermined by the sentence itself, the constraint of relevance guarantees that the domain of individuals has to be narrowed to a point at which it is compatible with the requirements of optimal relevance. Here, that principle predicts that the domain is the six individuals that B is in charge of, because it is only if the domain is this restricted that B's reply constitutes any answer to A's question. Indeed, on all broader domains, B's assertion is transparently false. Moreover, A is only able to interpret *B*'s reply as providing this (indirect) answer via the construction of the requisite context set of propositions. Thus this example demonstrates (a) how the principle of relevance determines aspects of the proposition expressed (here the selection of the domain of individuals in question), and (b) how context construction is an essential part of utterance interpretation.

What I have given is of course only a sketch of the theory. Even from this minimal account, however, the phenomena of conventional implicatures can be predicted without any stipulation as an exception mechanism. What I propose is that conventional implicatures are by definition phenomena which involve lexical restrictions on aspects of utterance information other than (merely) the proposition expressed.[16] I shall take here only the contrary-to-expectation sense of *but*. This is an aspect of *but*, distinguishing it from *and*, which has been regularly noticed in the literature. Consider the discourse (46):

(46) *A*: John's coming tonight.
    B: But Sue's coming too.

    Context for interpreting *A*'s utterance: If John comes, we won't play music.
    (*A* plays violin, *B* plays piano, John plays viola.)
    Contextual implication: We will not play music.

    Context for interpreting *B*'s utterance: If John and Sue come, we'll play music.
    (Sue plays cello.)
    Contextual implication: We will play music.

Suppose (46) occurs in circumstances where *A* and *B* like to play music with their friends whenever possible. However, John plays viola, and they don't have any music for the combination of violin, viola and piano. Thus *A* knows that *B* will interpret his utterance

---

16 This was originally suggested in D. Brockway, 'Semantic constraints on relevance', in *Possibilities and Limitations of Pragmatics*, ed. H. Parret *et al.* (John Benjamin, 1981) as the analysis of connectives, such as 'anyway', 'after all', etc.

against a context such as 'If John comes, we won't play music.' B's reply however causes A to access a different context: namely, 'If John and Sue come, we will play music', with the contrasting contextual implication. What is going on? We have an utterance of a first sentence which has a contextual implication which is implicitly denied by the utterance of the second, joined to the first by *but*. I suggest that the contrastive element in *but* is a lexically specified instruction to the hearer to consider only particular kinds of context, namely those in which some contextual implication drawn off the proposition expressed by the first sentence conflicts with some implication to be drawn off the two sentences taken together. Thus part of the linguistic meaning of *but* contains the following restrictions:[17]

In interpreting 'P but Q' where P and Q are propositional variables, construct a context C_m for P such that:

$C_m \;\&\; P \rightarrow R$

and also construct a context C_n for (P &) Q such that:

$C_n \;\&\; (P \;\&) \; Q \rightarrow - R_m$

For a second example, consider (47):

(47) My father's coming to stay in our house but he's going to be out of the house all day.

> Context for interpreting for the first conjunct:
> If the speaker's father stays in her house, she will have to keep the kids quiet.
>
> Context for interpreting the second conjunct:
> If the speaker's father is going to be out of the house all day, she won't have to keep the kids quiet.

In processing (47) one might construct contexts as specified. In the case of the first conjunct, this yields the contextual implication

---

[17] This analysis is similar to that of J. Anscombre and O. Ducrot, 'Deux *mais* en francais?', *Lingua*, 43 (1977), pp. 23–40, recently brought to my attention, though their account is not couched within the framework of relevance theory.

'She will have to keep the kids quiet', and in the case of the second conjunct, the conflicting implication 'She won't have to keep the kids quiet.' Notice that there is no specification in the characterization of *but* as to what the context or the contextual implications ought to be. So in reconstructing what the speaker has said, the hearer is not directed towards any particular pair of conflicting propositions. This matches the indeterminacy as to what the precise point of conflict is that the speaker has intended. As long as we are not reconstructing utterance meaning in terms of a full set of propositions that the speaker is intending to convey, we can reconstruct the phenomenon exactly. If this account of *but* is correct in outline, we have a case where articulating the meaning of the expression involves not only constraining the proposition expressed but also placing constraints on the construction of contexts in which utterances containing *but* are interpreted, and, further, on the range of contextual implications which should be deduced from the combination of context and proposition. This phenomenon is puzzling and exceptional only if we insist on retaining the assumption that linguistic semantics is directed solely towards the propositions expressed by sentences of the language. If, on the contrary, we consider the goal of semantics to characterize what it is that sentences of natural language contribute to utterance interpretation in general, restricting the range of propositions the sentence can express and in part restricting the context with which utterances of the sentence combine, then the linguistic content of *but* reduces to an unproblematic lexical restriction on one aspect of utterance interpretation.

This account of course leaves virtually everything unsaid. I have given no formalism: all I have done is to indicate a direction. Even within the confines of this programmatic chapter, however, there are two further problems I should like to discuss to round out the picture. One is how the principle of relevance determines that, given the linguistic meaning of a scalar predicate expression, the proposition expressed may be the predicate plus the so-called scalar implicature. The second is how the principle of relevance would explain why in negative sentences it is only in the paradoxical negation cases such as (8)–(15) that scalar predicates are understood to have the strengthened interpretation. I shall take the case of numbers as paradigmatic,[18] but the explanation should generalize in a straightforward way. The claim by Sperber and Wilson is that selection of interpretation of the scalar implicature phenomena is like that of selection of domain of individuals, and that of selection of interval of time for tense interpretation. In all cases the principle is as follows. Given that the semantics of the sentence itself does not determine the domain to be selected, the domain is narrowed until it reaches an optimal level of relevance. Thus for example intuitively (48) is relevant given an extremely broad interval of time, but (49) is not relevant unless the domain of time is narrowed to a period of just a few hours:

(48) I've been to Tibet.
(49) I've had breakfast.

In the case of numbers, if the utterance in question is interpreted as involving, say 'at least two', it must be that this satisfies relevance in such a way that narrowing down the interpretation to the more precise 'no more and no less' interpretation would not increase the relevance. This is precisely the case in (50) with context (a):

(50) A: How many children do you have?
  B: I have two children.

Context (a): If you have at least two children, you get a fixed amount of state benefit.

Against context (a), there is no number more relevant than 'two', even if B has a larger number of children. In these circumstances there is no possible increase in relevance as the numbers increase (for in these cases even knowing that a larger number is applicable does not provide any conflict in relevance.) So if A accesses context

---

18 I leave on one side here the precise form of the operation involved in changing a propositional construct representing 'at least n' for any number n into a construct representing 'exactly n', but see R. Kempson and A. Cormack, 'Ambiguity and quantification', *Linguistics and Philosophy*, 4 (1981), pp. 259–310, for a specification of such 'strengthening' rules (albeit against a different set of assumptions).

(a), he will interpret the number as having the weaker of the two interpretations, as predicted by the principle that the requirements of relevance narrow the domain until an optimal level of relevance is attained.

In the more common case of the 'exactly' interpretation, the position is more complicated. Consider the same exchange between A and B, but this time in a scenario in which A and B are both mothers. On this occasion, in interpreting B's reply to her question, A cannot derive a determinate set of pragmatic implications if the number is interpreted only as 'at least two'; for the information accessed by knowing someone has two children is quite different from that accessed by knowing someone has four or five children. Without the interpretation of the number as 'exactly two', the hearer does not have enough information to construct a context from which she can derive contextual implications. Moreover, in using the number, B must have tried to produce an utterance that would be optimally relevant for A. If she knew of any other number which could be substituted for two which would have led to a greater number of contextual implications, then she would have been violating the principle of relevance not to have given that alternative number. On the assumption that she is not, she therefore means exactly that number – to wit, no more and no less than two.

The explanation of why, in negative sentences, the 'at least' understanding is normally predominant follows directly from the principle of relevance. In order to be able to interpret an utterance of 'Mark didn't eat three biscuits' as compatible with 'Mark ate three biscuits' one has to be able to process both the linguistic meaning of the sentence and its narrowed 'exactly 3' interpretation simultaneously and yet separately, as it were, ignoring the lexically stipulated meaning in favour of the relevance-restricted one. Unless to do so leads to a sufficient number of contextual implications to offset the increased processing complication involved in doing this, the 'exactly' interpretation will not be considered. Other things being equal then, this predicts that a negative sentence containing a numeral construed as within the scope of the negative element will be interpreted as 'at least n'. Other things are not equal if either the word 'exactly' is inserted, or the speaker uses a paradoxical negation sentence of the type (8)–(15) which demands an 'exactly' interpretation in order to be non-contradictory. In these cases, the speaker is explicitly drawing her hearer's attention to the interpretation she intends by the form of her utterance, and the interpretation of the utterance as having an 'exactly' interpretation is thus directly in accordance with the principle of relevance; after all, the speaker is doing her best in such circumstances to guarantee that that is the interpretation the hearer should recover.

Let me now give the overall picture I am proposing. We have a pragmatic theory of utterance interpretation in terms of the three aspects: proposition recovery, context construction, and contextual implication deduction, all three governed by the principle of relevance. On the assumption that this theory is correct, a natural requirement on a semantic theory for natural languages is that it should provide an input to the constructs of this pragmatic theory, specifying for each sentence partially articulated propositional forms, a set of constraints on the contexts to be constructed and (for some cases) constraints on the range of contextual implications to be selected.

There are immediate consequences for linguistic theory if this outline of a program is correct. One prediction is that natural languages may display diversity of propositional context for a linguistically unitary phenomenon. The numerals have provided an example of this. Any numeral is a linguistically unitary expression, yet all numerals can be used with more than one interpretation, and the variety in their interpretation is subject to a pragmatic explanation. A second prediction is that the linguistic content of an expression may require specification in representational (and in this sense syntactic) terms which may be opaque with respect to the truth-theoretic properties of the expression in question. A third is that general information retrieved from memory and not from specification by a rule of grammar may play a part in determining these truth-theoretic properties of propositional content. Processes of anaphora exemplify all three of these predictions. First, pronouns and definite NPs have extremely divergent semantic properties: they are sometimes referential, sometimes not; sometimes bound to a quantifier, sometimes not. They can be referring expressions even though their antecedent is not. And any one pronoun or definite noun phrase (NP) can display a range of these properties. Pronouns have been analysed as at least three or four ways ambiguous: as indexical, bound-variable, discourse-anaphoric, co-referential, or E-type; and much energy has been spent on arguing for different ways of reducing this list.[19] This variation in semantic properties is shared also by definite NPs, as witness (51)–(54):

(51) John got into his car. The car needed servicing and wouldn't start.
(52) John got into his car, hoping that the car would start easily.
(53) Everyone who bought a car found out later that the car wouldn't start easily.
(54) John sold many cars last year. The cars were all Volvos.

Thus it appears that we cannot give a unitary account of anaphor-antecedent relations unless this explanation is in terms which ignore this semantic divergence, i.e. in syntactic terms (in the sense specified above). Finally, the third prediction. It has largely gone unnoticed that the truth-theoretic properties of propositions expressed by sentences containing such anaphoric expressions are not determined exclusively from information specified linguistically as part of grammar. In each of (55)–(58) the specification of the propositional content expressed by the sentence, in particular the anaphor-antecedent dependency, requires a specification of the interaction between principles of grammar and pragmatic principles which explain how general encylopaedic knowledge is accessed:

---

19 See H. Lasnik, 'Remarks on co-reference', *Linguistic Analysis*, 2 (1976), pp. 1–22; R. Cooper, 'The interpretation of pronouns', in *Syntax and Semantics 10*, eds F. Heny and H. Schnelle (Academic Press, 1979); R. Hausser, 'How do pronouns denote' in Heny and Schnelle (eds), *Syntax and Semantics 10*, pp. 93–107; G. Evans, 'Pronouns', *Linguistic Inquiry*, 11 (1980), pp. 337–62; J. Higginbotham, 'Pronouns and bound variables', *Linguistic Inquiry* 11 (1980), pp. 679–708; T. Reinhart, 'Co-reference and bound anaphora: a restatement of the anaphora questions', *Linguistics and Philosophy*, 6 (1983), pp. 47–88.

(55) John opened up his car. The battery needed recharging.
(56) John opened up his car to recharge the battery.
(57) Jo sold many cars last year. The registration numbers are listed in this book.
(58) Every car needed the battery recharging.

In (55) and (56) the interpretation of 'the battery' as anaphorically linked to the expression 'his car' is made possible by making use of the knowledge that cars have batteries. In (57), an example of E-type dependency,[20] the information required is that cars have registration numbers. And in (58) the information that cars have batteries has to interact with the binding principles which determine quantifier-variable dependencies, a phenomenon whose explanation is normally argued to be the exclusive provenance of grammar.[21]

If we assume that part of the task of grammar is to provide a set of rules which recursively fully define the mapping from each string of the language on to its propositional content, then every one of this list of properties is problematic.[22] On the view proposed here, however, these phenomena are immediately predicted, without any *ad hoc* parasitic stipulation or exception mechanism. Anaphoric expressions are paradigm cases of expressions whose linguistic meaning involves a specification in syntactic terms which underdetermines the form they take in a fully specified propositional form, and which by definition therefore underdetermines their truth-theoretic content. An NP anaphor, for example, is not assigned a translation into a syntactic expression of the selected logic directly as part of grammar, but rather is analysed as a metavariable whose value at the level of the fully

---

20 See Evans, 'Pronouns'.
21 See Reinhart, 'Co-reference'.
22 On this view, it needs to be argued in particular that the bridging cross-reference phenomenon is merely parasitic on anaphoric dependencies reconstructed solely on the basis of intra-sentential configuration, and, that as a phenomenon based on some process of analogy, it can be put on one side as an exception of little theoretical consequence (see Higginbotham, 'Pronouns and bound variables', where a comparable dismissal is given of the interaction between contexual effects and quantifier binding.)

specified propositional form ranges over syntactic expressions of the required type (individual constants or individual variables). This analysis thus assigns a single pronoun or definite NP a single linguistic meaning despite its diversity of content. The diversity is predicted by the interaction of this linguistically specified information with the principle of relevance, which determines the form the anaphoric expression takes at the level of the fully specified propositional form. More precisely, the value the anaphoric expression should have is selected by the hearer from a set of representations immediately accessible to him as he interprets the utterance (in line with the principle of relevance). On this view the cases where linguistic information provides the antecedent are not the paradigm cases on which others are parasitic, but merely a consequence of the rather trivial observation that information immediately accessible to a hearer includes the immediately previous linguistic expressions (whether in the same sentence or in immediately previous sentences of the discourse). Other information retrieved from memory, or constructed from visual information available to him at the time, may equally be accessible to him in ways which enable him to construct the appropriate representation for the anaphoric expression.[23] Thus relevance theory leads directly to the prediction that expressions of natural language may have a unitary linguistic characteristic while having diverse truth-theoretic properties – properties which furthermore may involve computations over general background information and not merely linguistically specified information. In other words, relevance theory predicts the existence of phenomena generally considered to be problematic, and in combination with a particular linguistic account of anaphora makes the correct predictions of detail without any *ad hoc* stipulation.

The consequence for linguistic theory are not however merely data specific. There are general theoretical consequences as well. Within this framework, grammars do not generate sentence-

---

23 See R. Kempson, 'Anaphora, the compositionality requirement, and the semantics-pragmatics distinction', *Proceedings of the North-Eastern Linguistics Society XIV*, University of Massachusetts, Amherst, for a precise articulation of the interaction between rules of grammar and pragmatically provided information to determine the full range of anaphor-antecedent dependencies.

proposition pairs as part of the semantic characterization of a sentence. Those entities which all truth-based theories of meaning assume as the basis of semantics under one conception or another – the truth-bearing entities, propositions – will not be generated by the grammar at all. What the grammar does specify is for each sentence a set of constraints on constructing propositions, a set which may contain restrictions on the form of the context that can be constructed as well as on the proposition that an utterance of that sentence may be taken directly to express. This set interacts with the principle of relevance on any given occasion to determine the full content of the utterance. Linguistic semantics is then a partial translation algorithm defined in solely syntactic terms for mapping linguistic strings which are not transparent with respect to their inferential properties on to fully specified strings of some selected language of inference which are. In consequence, there is no reconstruction of truth-theoretic content defined directly over strings of natural languages as part of the grammar: truth-theoretic content is defined solely with respect to propositional forms of the language of inference, and model theoretic constructs thus have no part to play in the articulation of formal properties of grammars.

Finally, I return to the problem posed in the early part of this chapter: that of ambiguity and its relevance to the semantics–pragmatics distinction. With the proposed modification in the conception of linguistic semantics, the truth-conditional principles that have been widely assumed as the basis for semantic description of a language can no longer be used as a criterion for determining the limits of a semantic theory for a language if we choose to define this to mean the semantic component of a grammar of that language. The semantic component of a grammar neither completely specifies the propositions to be paired with any given sentence, nor is restricted to specifying such propositions. The semantic component of a grammar indeed does not provide a semantic theory for a language at all in the philosophical sense. In the light of this, the demarcation between semantics and pragmatics that linguists need to draw has to be realigned. Pragmatics is not what is left over after the specification of truth-conditional content paired with each sentence of a language:²⁴ and the specification of linguistic meaning is not a specification of that content. Rather, linguistic meaning is the rule-governed contribution that expressions of a language bring to the process of utterance interpretation. Whether this specification is distinct from the syntactic account of that language I leave as an open question.

---

24 See Gazdar, *Pragmatics*, for the slogan: 'pragmatics = meaning − truth conditions'.

4

Domains of discourse and common-sense metaphysics

Adam Morton

'There are assumptions that we must make and must take each other to make, in order to say what we want to say. Some of these assumptions cannot be stated explicitly in our everyday vocabulary: they give the language expressive power without being within the range of that power.' This is a familiar sort of claim, and perhaps vague enough to be unobjectionable. I will support a particular form of it: that such hidden and hard to express assumptions are involved in the anaphoric relations which tie individual assertions into coherent stretches of discourse. I shall be looking just at quantifiers, and very pedestrian quantifiers at that: 'all', 'some', 'something', . . . , as used in coherent stretches of discourse. (I will write the universal quantifier (all, every) sometimes with the standard logician's (x) and sometimes with a half-way (for all x). Similarly, the existential quantifier (some) will be Ex and (for some x). I will sometimes write ⌐ for negation and ⇒ for the conditional.) My claim is simply that (a) most quantifiers are implicitly restricted to a domain, (b) there is an intricate and important dovetailing of these domains to make a coherent topic for the discourse, and (c) what domain is assigned to a quantifier depends in part on the domains of the preceding domains in the discourse. It is claim (c) that allows me to say that I am concerned with anaphoric relations. It is my most interesting claim: that there is an anaphora of quantifiers.

I will defend two more specific claims.

1 The specification of the domain may change as a discourse develops, and one way in which it changes depends on taking terms as liable to second-order quantification.
2 *Some* of the phenomena which the relation of presupposition has been invoked to explain can instead be explained in terms of the relation of second-order logical consequence.

In 1 and 2 I am using the term *discourse* as a common noun: a discourse is a coherent sequence of communicative speech, typically involving more than one speaker. Defined in this way, the term is vague but not objectionable. What is more problematic is the use I make of the identity of discourses. I will speak for example of a discourse ending at a certain point in a conversation, and another one beginning. I must apologize in advance for this, for I am not going to give anything like necessary and sufficient conditions for two stretches of speech to be parts of the same discourse. I hope to make a case for the usefulness of speaking in this way, though, and intend what I say as the beginnings of an explanation of what could be involved in such claims.

DOMAINS

The theme that hold these theses together is that of a domain of discourse. The term is familiar to most of us from our school-days when we were taught to make Venn diagrams. It is also familiar from the model theory of elementary logic. In that theory a model is defined as a pair (D,F) of a non-empty domain D and a function F which assigns a subset of D to each predicate symbol in the formal language (and a set of ordered n-tuples of D to each n-place relation symbol). Then satisfaction and hence truth under an interpretation are defined for sentences of the language in familiar ways.[1] It is the role of the domain D that I am interested in now.

---

1 See B. Mates, *Elementary Logic* (Oxford University Press, New York, 1965) and J.L. Bell and A.B. Slomson, *Models and Ultraproducts* (North Holland, 1969). For second-order logic, see G. Boolos and R.C. Jeffrey, *Computability and Logic* (Cambridge University Press, Cambridge, 1974).

Domains of discourse

Suppose that we did not explicitly mention any domain, and simply defined an interpretation, as might at first sight seem most natural, as any function which assigns extensions to predicates. Then ignoring difficulties in defining the notion of a sequence of arbitrary elements (rather than of elements from a D) – which would require accepting the limitations of some standard set theory – one would proceed exactly as usual, ignoring the allusions to D, and saying for example that a sequence s satisfies $\text{Ex}nA$ under the interpretation iff there is an object o such that replacing the nth member of s with o results in a sequence which satisfies A. If A is an atomic predicate, this boils down to saying that $\text{Ex}A(x)$ is true under F if the set $F'A'$ has a member. And this is just like the standard definition except that on the standard definition the set and thus its members are constrained to be taken from D. Similarly for the universal quantifier. Then one could define logical validity and logical consequence in the usual way. And in a sense the result would be more intuitive than the usual definitions, since it would be a direct rendition of the idea that, for example, a sentence is logically valid whatever its non-logical terms are taken to mean. Since 'all' and 'there is' are logical terms, they should be left to mean what they do mean, namely 'all things (whatever)' and 'something (or other)'. Or do they?

I have put a little effort into thinking out what the result might be of rewriting standard first-order model theory along these lines. As far as I can see quite a lot of the model theory of first-order logic without identity remains fundamentally unchanged, though everything, particularly statements and proofs of completeness results, is a bit more cumbersome (cumbersome enough to make the suggestion that quantifiers be relativized to a domain an appealing one, without appeal to any deeper considerations). The reason most things work out all right is the simple fact that anything that is true in the universe as a whole is true in some subdomain of it. So a domain can always be cobbled together by taking the union of the extensions (under F) of the predicates in whatever sentences one is considering and then adding a few elements as quantifiers may require. (Consider Ex ($]Ax$ & $]Bx$). Clearly the domain will have to contain more than just the extensions of A and B, but just one thing more.) It is evident, via the Lowenheim-Skolem theorem, that, if a sentence without identity has a model when its quantifiers are taken to range over the universe, then it has a model in a domain got by adding to the union of the extensions of its predicates at most denumerably many elements.) Going the other way, from satisfiability in a domain to satisfiability in the universe can usually be handled by assigning blanket falsehood outside the domain.

Real differences emerge, though, when identity is added to the logic. Consider the sentence $Ex(y)(y=x)$. It says that there is only one thing. It clearly isn't valid, but on the usual model theory it is satisfiable (consistent), since there are domains with only one element. But on the proposed domain-free semantics it would be unsatisfiable, just because there is no such x.

EVERYTHING

The connection between the idea of a domain of discourse and that of a conversational context (a location of an utterance in a discourse) can be seen by considering sentences involving the concept of identity. There are limiting case examples such as 'there is only one thing', discussed above. But there are also much more natural examples. Consider the following. Someone reports that:

(1) When I arrived at the house the burglars must have just left. Everything was gone: the furniture, the curtains, even the ashtrays.

'Everything' here does not mean 'everything in the world'; it is restricted at least to everything in the house. And surely it is restricted even more: the burglars are not taken to have taken the wallpaper or the molecules of air. Evidently we do often intend restrictions on the range of our quantifiers, though it is not obvious what the best representation of these restrictions is. However it works, the restriction often limits the number of objects in the domain, so that, once the restriction is established, the story can continue.

(2) And in the garage only one thing was left, a rusty lawnmower.

The paraphrase of (part of) this as 'there was one thing such that everything remaining in the garage was identical to it' ((for some x)(for all y)(if Rx then $y=x$)) is accurate as long as we allow the 'everything' and 'there is' to be restricted to things within the ambition of burglars.

Let us accept that quantifiers in ordinary usage are usually hedged in by contextually imposed restrictions. Standard model theory is to this extent correct in requiring a domain of discourse. It is also very plausible in requiring that the domain not be empty. This requirement may seem rather arbitrary if taken as a working out of the idea that a valid sentence is one which is true however the non-logical symbols are interpreted. But it is more natural if taken as a consequence of the fact that people usually presume that their discourse is about something. That is, if a domain is assigned to the quantifiers of a segment of actual speech, this domain will be what – under some description – the speakers take themselves to be discussing. They are thus almost certain to make the presumption that the domain has members.

This is certainly a pretty loose argument, and there are likely to be exceptions. I will return to the presumption that the domain is non-empty. Before that, I want to say something about a related idea, which is well known both from the controversies earlier in the century about the relation between symbolic and traditional logic, and from Strawson's work over the past 25 years on the subject/predicate contrast. The basic situation is that the now-standard logician's representation of 'all As are Bs' (or 'As are Bs' or 'each A is a B') is $(x)(Ax \Rightarrow Bx)$, i.e. (for all x) (if Ax then Bx), which is true when there are no As. And, as every beginning logic student is told, this means that 'all As are Bs' does not, despite many people's intuitions, entail 'some As are Bs', and that some sentences are satisfiable which seem not to be permissible members of a discourse, for example Strawson's familiar 'all John's children are asleep, but John has no children.'

Strawson called the relation between 'all As are Bs' and 'there are As' that of *presupposition*. There has been a lot of discussion about the correct analysis of presupposition.[2] Crudely, *s* presupposes *t* when *t*'s denial will prevent either *s* or its idiomatic negation from being admitted into the discourse.

The subsequent literature has brought out very clearly that there is *not* an automatic connection between the assertion of an 'all' sentence and the satisfaction of its subject term. For there are very many examples along the lines of:

(3) If you've picked up all your papers you can go.
    John has no papers.
    Therefore: John can go.

John can go because he has picked up all his papers – that is, no papers. The result seems to be that a simple isolated 'all' sentence does present the appearance of presupposing that its subject term is satisfied, while an 'all' sentence embedded in a more complex context may well not. With just a little setting up of the context one can plausibly say:

(4) All John's children are asleep: *because* he has none.

There is a natural explanation of this situation. An isolated sentence can only be understood as a miniature discourse or as the beginning of a longer one. In either case it must determine (or at any rate must play a large part in determining) what the domain of quantifiction of that discourse is. Let us assume that when an initial 'all As are Bs' is uttered (or for that matter an initial 'some As are Bs', or any of a number of other forms) a presumption is set up – to use a fairly neutral word – that there is a non-empty domain D which bears some systematic relation to A and to B, and which is the domain of quantification of the ensuing discourse. If that relation were simply that D is the extension of A (which I think it

---

2 See P.F. Strawson, *Logico-linguistic Papers* (Methuen, London, 1972); G. Gazdar, *Pragmatics* (Academic Press, New York, 1979); L. Kartunnen, 'Presupposition and linguistic context', *Theoretical Linguistics*, 1 (1974), pp. 181–94; R. Stalnaker, 'Presupposition', *Journal of Philosophical Logic*, 2 (1973), pp. 447–57.

Domains of discourse

sometimes is), then the presumption that the domain is not empty would ensure that the 'all' sentence presumed that its subject term was satisfied. But note that even on this assumption, which is surely in fact too strong, a sentence occurring in the body, rather than at the head, of a discourse need establish no such presumption, even when it occurs as an assertion and not embedded in another sentence.

CHANGE OF DOMAIN

We need now to look at two things: the relation between a sentence and the domain it may be taken as implicitly specifying for its quantifiers, and the way in which this specification may change in the course of a discourse.

Begin with the second of these. I hypothesized that 'all' sentences which do not begin a discourse do not introduce a domain for quantification. This certainly seems to be the case in examples such as the burglary story above. There the 'only one thing' in (2) is clearly to be understood in terms of the domain introduced at the beginning of the story, that of burglarable objects. It is equally clear, though, that sometimes the domain of a quantifier in the body of a discourse is not determined just by the predicates occurring in sentences nearer the head. Consider this conversation, with its three possible continuations.

(5) *A*: The silver spoons have tarnished.
    B: Everything tarnishes in this house. The stainless steel knives have a trace of rust.
(6) *A*: Perhaps the gold-plated forks will be all right?
    B: Oh yes they are. Something is usable then.
(7) *A*: Even plastic?
    B: Well! Plastic spoons for dinner?
(8) *A*: And our marriage has lost its glimmer, dear.

In (5) the domain of 'everything' in *B* is clearly restricted in some way (which is why the 'continuation' (8) is a joke or an assault). But it is not restricted just to spoons or silver things or any combination of these. The range of 'everything' must be something like 'metal household objects'. It is determined in part by the earlier reference to silver spoons, but also by its own predicates.

The continuation (6) fits easily into the domain set by (5). Continuations (7) and (8) modulate the domain, though. Continuation (7) does so in a perfectly comfortable way: the domain is easily expanded to include non-metal household objects. But for all that it is not trivial: the truth value of *B*'s earlier assertion changes under it. And thus *B* may take it as the beginning of a new conversation rather than as the continuation of the previous one. (In this case there is a definite index of whether the discourse is continuous: whether a single truth value is assigned to each assertion.) Continuation (8) has very little continuity with (5); in order to knit them together the hearer (and the participants) have to rethink their interpretations of the preceding quantifiers.

I draw the following conclusions:

1 The domain of a quantifier depends on the predicates, in particular the sortal nouns, which have appeared earlier in the discourse.
2 The domain of a quantifier in the body of a discourse is not automatically determined by the predicates in previous sentences.
3 There must be a coherence to the domains of quantifiers in a discourse. To a first approximation: a common discourse needs a common domain.[3]

There is a tension between these conclusions. If all the quantifiers in a discourse are to have the same domain, or even if their domains are to be related in systematic ways, then it seems that the initial sentences of the discourse cannot set the domain, for this will set the domains of later quantifiers more than seems to be the case. There seem to be two alternatives: either the initial sentences set a domain which is then stuck to, or the domain can only be set, and the quantifiers only understood, after the whole discourse is

---

3 A next approximation would use a many-sorted model theory with a variety of domains. Clearly different domains tend to be set for, for example, the people and the physical objects under discussion.

Domains of discourse

over. Certainly the first of these sometimes occurs, particularly when there is a domain of discourse clearly set by particular common nouns ('we're talking about cars: ...'). And certainly the second occasionally occurs, for example in (5)+(8). But it seems very implausible that these are the only alternatives.

What we usually have is some kind of anaphora between quantifiers: a discourse begins by postulating a domain, and then later quantifiers continue with 'and in this domain'. But how are we to take this postulation and this 'this'?

The initial postulation clearly does not require that the domain be completely specified. The speakers must understand that there is a domain involved and that it covers certain classes and does not cover others. (For example, within a couple of sentences in a typical discourse the speakers might have adopted a restriction which could be made explicit: as 'We're talking about animals. Not all animals but middle-sized ones – cats, elephants, snakes and the like. Tiny beasts like protozoa or even fleas are not included, nor are long-extinct creatures such as dinosaurs.')

Let us represent this by the introduction of a predicate D into the discourse, to which all quantifiers are relativized. Thus (5) will be represented as

(9) A: (for all x in D)((silver x & spoon x) $\Rightarrow$ tarnished x)
    B: (for all x in D)(in this house x $\Rightarrow$ tarnishes x)

Relativized quantifiers, such as (for all x in D), can be defined in terms of unrelativized ones: for example A could have been written out as (for all x)((Dx & silver x & spoon x) $\Rightarrow$ tarnished x)). D obviously need not be a fully interpreted predicate. But neither is it a mere cypher. A and B agree to a large extent about its extension. So if we write out as well some of what they take themselves to be leaving unsaid bracketed off with [] before their utterances, we get:

(10) A: [(For some D)(A will be talking about Ds. D includes objects relevant to the table setting job)]
    (for all x in D)((silver x & spoon x) $\Rightarrow$ tarnished x)
    B: [Ditto & D certainly includes silver spoons] (for all x in D)(in this house x $\Rightarrow$ tarnishes x)

Thus in the bracketed [] part of this representation – giving the assumptions that speakers take each other to be making and the conclusions that they will assume each other to be drawing – D functions as a quantified variable. And in the unbracketed part – giving the explicit spoken level of discourse – it functions as a partially interpreted predicate.

The situation is roughly parallel to what happens when a new proper name is introduced into a discourse.[4] A says 'James was at the party last night' and B, not knowing more than this about James, registers the belief that 'there is someone whom A believes to have been at the party and who in this discourse we shall call "James".' And then for the rest of the discourse B will intend to refer to whatever it was that A was alluding to, while reserving the right to disagree about some of its characteristics (A: 'James is a very sensible person.' B: 'Not if he went to that party.') Similarly, when a discourse acquires a domain from one person's contribution, others will intend to speak about that same domain, though they may well disagree about what is true or false of its members.

There are disanalogies too. The specification of a domain is a more co-operative and a less retrospective business than the determination of a name's reference. While B in the previous paragraph must acknowledge 'James' to refer to whomever A had in mind, the domain predicate D will usually mean roughly 'those things we will have been talking about'. The 'we' and the 'will have' clearly go together.

What remains when the analogies and the disanalogies are weighed up is that quantifiers in natural discourse seem to involve implicit 'pro-predicates' – indefinite predicates which cross-link the interpretation of one quantifier to that of another. The pro-predicates function much as do free names in a natural deduction system for quantificational logic, but with the great

---

4 See S. Kripke, *Naming and Necessity* (Basil Blackwell, Oxford, 1980); C. Chastain, 'Reference and context', in *Language, Mind, and Knowledge* (Minnesota Studies in the Philosophy of Science 7), ed. K. Gunderson (University of Minnesota Press, Minneapolis, 1975). There are also connections between my account of the common domains of different sentences and the issues of H. Bohnert, 'Communication by Ramsey-sentence clause', *Philosophy of Science*, 34 (1967), pp. 341–7.

Domains of discourse

difference that since they are pro-predicates rather than pro-names the resemblance is to a natural deduction system for *second-order* logic.

PRESUPPOSITIONS

The resemblance to second-order logic connects us with existential presuppositions again. The general pattern is easiest to see with an example.

A and B are discussing animals. It is clear to them that they are not talking about mythical or extinct animals, so that they both tacitly accept a second-order background ('bracketed') assumption which, still using D for the domain predicate, letting Ax be 'x is an animal', and writing $\Rightarrow$ for 'if . . . then', can be written:

(11) (for all P)((for all x)(x is $P \Rightarrow Dx$ & Ax) $\Rightarrow$ (for some y)(Py))
(That is, all animal species in this discussion have members.)

Then A says either of the following:

(12) A: All thrushes sing.
(That is, (for all x in D)($Tx \Rightarrow Sx$).)
or
(13) A: The thrush in the syringa sings.
(That is, S(the x in D such that Tx & Ix).)

To which B replies:

(14) B: No thrushes sing.
(That is, (for all x in D)($Tx \Rightarrow \rceil Sx$).)
or
(15) B: The thrush in the syringa does not sing.
(That is, $\rceil S$(the x in D such that Tx & Ix).)

Now in standard logic (13) but not (12) or (14) entails:

(16) There are thrushes.
(That is, (for some x)(Tx).)

Sentence (15) entails (16) if the x is given a 'wide scope' reading, and otherwise not. But intuitively all of (12)–(15) 'presuppose' ('take for granted','indicate')(16), in the context of the discourse. What this amounts to can easily be explained if we assume that A and B are assuming (11) above, and also

(17) (for all x) $(Tx \Rightarrow Dx)$
   (That is, 'thrushes are in the domain.')

which presumably is introduced by (12), and also the 'analytic' (common-sense, trivial)

(18) (x) $(Tx \Rightarrow Ax)$
   (That is, 'thrushes are animals.')

Then we find that any of the sentences in question will, *when conjoined with (11), (17) and (18)* logically entail (16).

The quarrel between standard logic and our intuitions is thus resolved, in this case, if we allow that often we take one assertion to imply another when what bears the strictly logical relation to the second assertion is not the first assertion alone but the conjunction of it with propositions implicitly assumed in the conversational context. The logic involved is second-order logic, of course. If we were working out the details of the inference, though, we would find that the crucial second-order step was from

$$(\text{for all } x)(Tx \Rightarrow (Ax \,\&\, Dx))$$

which is derived from (11) and (18) to

$$(\text{for some } P)[(\text{for all } x)(Px \Rightarrow (Ax \,\&\, Dx)) \,\&\, (\text{for all } x)(Px \Leftrightarrow Tx)]$$

which when conjoined with (11) yields (16). It is transparently valid. Intuitively, it amounts to the inference from 'all thrushes are animals and are under discussion here' to 'there is a species of animals under discussion which contains all and only thrushes.'

I think that there is a fairly general phenomenon at work here, which can account for *some* of what is discussed under the heading

Domains of discourse

of presupposition. Let me call it *discourse presupposition*. Discourse presupposition certainly will not explain what is usually called lexical presupposition: the relation which holds for example between both 'John spoke to Mary before she died' and 'John did not speak to Mary before she died' and 'Mary died.' This depends on the meaning of particular words, in this case 'before' in various subtle ways. What it will account for are general connections between the introduction of a predicate into a discourse and presumptions about its extension. The pattern will be that, when a sentence s is explicitly asserted in a discourse, a general assumption A, usually about the relation between the predicates occurring in s and the domain of discourse, is also implicitly made. I will only consider such assumptions which are independent of the logical form of A, that is, which are made just by the fact of having made an utterance introducing certain predicates into the discourse. There will usually also be a set of assumptions S made at earlier stages of the discourse. Then the conjunction of s, A, and S will logically entail various propositions p. The relation between s and p is that of discourse presupposition when p is entailed by both 's & A & S' and 'not-s & A & S', that is, when p 'follows from' the introduction of either s or not-s at that point in the discourse.

Discourse presupposition will almost inevitably involve second-order logic. For the simplest logical patterns which go from both a sentence and its negation to a common conclusion involve second-order existential generalization (the inference from a sentence '... P ...' involving a predicate P to the assertion '(for some P) ... P ....'). For both '(... P ...)' and 'not (... P ...)' entail '(for some P)(... P ...)'. But of course this is much too weak a conclusion to be interesting. The propositions we actually think of as being presupposed by an utterance are entailed by the combination of conclusions like this, got by second-order existential generalization, with the particular assumptions of the discourse. This is as it should be, because the same sentence when introduced into different discourses may produce rather different presuppositions. (See the next section for a discourse in which the 'standard' existential presuppositions of a sentence fail.)

A comparison with an analogous feature of first-order logic may help. 'All kings are heartless' and 'Groxzdo is bald' together entail 'if Groxzdo is a king he is heartless.' And so do 'all kings are heartless' and 'Groxzdo is not bald.' And we have as a principle of first-order logic that if '$A \& B$' and '$A \& \text{not } -B$' both entail C then A entails C alone. Thus 'all kings are heartless' alone entails 'if Groxzdo is a king he is heartless.' Or does it? The principle of logic I have just referred to applies to sentences of a formal language, and thus holds only within the vocabulary of some such language. '$(x)(Ax \Rightarrow Bx)$' will entail '$Ag \Rightarrow Bg$' only when the constant g is among those of the formal language in question, and is assigned values by interpretations of that language. It is thus relevant to ask whether if we take a fragment of English containing 'all kings are heartless' it is appropriate to represent it by a formal language containing, besides symbols for the predicates 'king' and 'heartless', a constant representing the name 'Groxzdo'. The answer is clearly discourse relative: if 'Groxzdo' is in the vocabulary of the discourse then the right formal language should include such a constant and the right account of logical consequence should include this inference. And if not, not.

Thus, by asserting 'Groxzdo is bald' in a discourse in which 'Groxzdo' had previously been used, a speaker can enlarge the vocabulary of the discourse, and thus bring it about that sentences such as 'all kings are heartless' have consequences which they would not otherwise have had. Just as with the examples of discourse presupposition above, it is the introduction of the vocabulary in question that does most of the work. And in fact a very similar formal analysis can be applied.

Again take a discourse implicitly to involve a partially defined predicate D representing the domain. Then an utterance of 'all As are Bs' is to be represented as '(for all x in D)(if Ax then Bx)'. This will not in general entail 'if Ag then Bg', without the additional premise Dg'. Then a later assertion of 'g is C' – or for that matter 'g is not C', or just about any utterance involving 'g' – is to be taken as an explicit assertion of 'Cg' and an implicit assertion of 'Dg'. And thus from this implicit assertion and the earlier assertion '(for all x)(if Ax then Bx)', the conclusion 'if Ag then Bg' follows. And here too the conclusion would have followed in exactly parallel fashion if 'g is not C' had been uttered instead.

An example of slightly more complicated presuppositions generated in this way is provided by the following discourse:

(19) *A*: Many of the eleventh-century kings had very strange habits. Travis used to boil Dutchmen for breakfast.
B: And Beo buried the rector of Tilbury in a dung-heap.

A's assertion specifies a domain of eleventh-century kings. When the names 'Travis' and 'Beo' are introduced they are implicitly assimilated to the domain of the discourse. And thus 'Beo was a king' enters as a presupposition, following logically from the implicit assertions '(for all x)(if Dx then Kx)' and 'Db'. The first of these is slightly unstable: *A*'s initial assertion ensures only that D includes eleventh-century kings, and not that everything in D is an eleventh-century king. In practice I think the implicit assertion would be 'D consists of eleventh-century kings and others relevant to their histories.' This is shown by the contrast between two possible continuations of the discourse:

(20) *A*: Beo wasn't a king, of course.
B: I know. But he was the father of three and the murderer of six.

(21) *A*: I'm afraid I've never heard of Beo.
B: He was my great uncle and a famous professor of sociosophy. The incident with the rector was in 1902.

Discourse (20) is a perfectly natural continuation of (19). The domain has been refined; it now definitely contains eleventh-century kings, a king called Travis, and a villain called Beo, and no doubt also family members and contributors to the life and death of kings. But these refinements are consistent with an initial specification of D as containing eleventh-century kings and those relevant to them. The presupposition 'Beo was a king' has now been overturned, but it has been replaced with the weaker one 'Beo was involved in the lives of kings'. If *A* continues (20) with 'Ah yes, and Groxzdo was if anything even more villainous', the presupposition is that Groxzdo is either a king, a king's relative, a king's assassin, or otherwise closely connected with the life of a king. (Notice how in the transition from (19) to (20) the specification of D has tightened as well as loosened. Discourse (19) could have been continued with a reference to eleventh-century people who were not kings – queens or bishops, for example – but after (20) the emphasis has definitely gone from eleventh-century life to eleventh-century kings.)

Discourse (21), on the other hand, is just not a continuation of (19) at all. The domain has shifted so much that it makes more sense just to say that a new discourse has begun. There is no continuity of presupposition.

COMMON-SENSE METAPHYSICS

My discussion of one rather particular class of presuppositional phenomena was meant to illustrate the claim that in everyday discourse we treat some predicates – in particular some common nouns – as quantifiable. That is, we reason from 'a is P' to 'there is some class (or king, or property) Q such that a is Q.' That claim was also central to my treatment of domains of discourse, for there I was arguing that the particular assertions of a discourse are implicitly prefixed by such a second-order quantification: there is a domain (kind, class) D such that . . . . The prefix evolves as the discourse does, in the direction of a greater specification of D – implicit clauses are added requiring D to include the extension of this or that noun entering the discourse – but it need never be completely specifiable, and is thus not in principle eliminable. The controversial element of this is not the claim that (first-order) quantifiers are usually restricted to a domain or, I imagine, even that in a coherent discourse the domains of restriction have to be closely related to one another. What is controversial is the idea that the domain is often indefinitely specified, that often we must take the implicit form of the discourse to be: there is a domain D.

Such second-order quantification is obviously not an unlimited affair. We do not take all noun clauses, let alone all predicates,

Domains of discourse

occurring in a discourse to represent actually existing subclasses of the domain. For example, in the discourse (11) onwards the noun clause 'singing thrush' is not quantifiable: the background assumption that all animal species in the discourse have members does not lead to the conclusion that there are singing thrushes because it is not assumed that *there is* such a kind as 'singing thrush' (though there may or may not be singing thrushes'). But why?

Well, it does depend on the discourse. If the conversation had begun:

(22) *A*: Some kinds of thrushes are easily seen even against a dull background: for example, those with white spots on their throats.
  B: Singing thrushes are pretty easy to spot, too.

Then unless *A* had quickly come in with 'but there are no singing thrushes' the discourse would have picked up the assumption that among the kinds of thrushes being talked about is that of singing thrushes. To put it generally, both this discourse and that of (11) onwards share a fairly common pattern, in which the opening assertions indicate a range of kinds: of animals in the first example, thrushes in the second. A conversational convention then builds into the discourse the assumption that it is these kinds that are being discussed, that is, later quantifiers are to be restricted to a domain D which includes the extensions of these kinds, and that they form a substantial topic for discussion, that is, that these kinds have members.

The conversational rules that inject these assumptions into discourses are not laws of logic. They are simply generalizations, tacitly understood by speakers of the language, determining the assertions that are made by uttering a particular syntactic form in a particular context. Thus *A* says the words 'some kinds of thrushes . . .', and in so doing he asserts that there is a domain of discourse, that it includes kinds of thrushes, that the kinds of thrushes under discussion have members, and no doubt many other things. *Then* laws of second-order logic operate on these in conjunction with particular later assertions (for instance, 'old female thrushes are particularly hard to see') to generate consequences which do not follow from those later assertions alone (for instance, 'there are old female thrushes').

The body of assumptions about the quantifiability of particular words and about the decoding of utterances into implicit assertions is part of what I call common-sense metaphysics. It contributes towards a framework of assumptions about the nature of speech and the nature of the world speech refers to, which makes communication possible.[5]

These assumptions are often very subtle. Consider another example. *A* and *B* are trying to fix a rusty bicycle.

(23) *A*: Do we have anything that could loosen this bolt?
  B: A number five wrench would do the job, but there are none.

The example is interesting in two ways. First: the presupposition that the subject of an 'all' sentence is satisfied fails. For the domain of the discourse, set by *A*'s question, includes tools in their possession, and very little else, as *B*'s reply shows: whether or not number five wrenches exist outside the domain, since there are none in their possession it is intelligible to say simply 'there are none'. Yet for all that the 'all' sentence 'a number five wrench would do the job' ('Any (all) number five wrench(es) would do the job') does not presuppose that its subject is satisfied, that there are number five wrenches.

One might suppose that at least a weaker proposition is presupposed, that there are number five wrenches in existence somewhere, even if not in the domain of discourse. But I do not think this is so. For the conversation could continue

(24) *B*: In fact, no number five wrenches were ever manufactured.

The other thing that is interesting about the example is that *A*'s initial assertion sets up the domain in such a definite way that only tools at that moment within their possession fall within it. (The

---

5 See S. Korner, *Metaphysics, its Nature and Function* (Cambridge University Press, 1984).

domain is not totally definite, though. *B* could have replied: 'That bottle-top, gripped by a pliers, might do it.' The domain has a definite restriction to objects within their possession, and definitely includes tools, but has a rather indeterminate stretch outwards towards things which while not officially tools could be used to manipulate bits of bicycles.) A just slightly different beginning, for example:

(25) *A*: Is there anything which could loosen this bolt?

would not have set up such a definite domain, and this would have made *B*'s reply (24) much less natural. Instead, *B* would have said

(26) *B*: A number five wrench could do the job, but we have none.

This reply is subtly different from (24). It refrains from saying that there are no number five wrenches, since *A*'s opening has not restricted the domain and thus the 'there are' in such a way that this would mean what *B* intends.

The evident conclusion from these two points is that in setting up a very specific domain, of tools, *A* has somehow not built into the discourse the assumption that all kinds of tools to be spoken of have members in it. Various similar asssumptions *are* built in: if for example the conversation continues:

(27) *B*: A spanner from the green box might well work, too.

and then *A* finds that the green box is, as *B* knew, full of nails, he will naturally think that *B* has spoken very misleadingly. He has violated a conversational convention, even if what he said was true, taken literally (as '(for all x in D) (if x is a spanner in the green box then x may loosen the bolt)').

What is the difference between 'number five wrench' and 'spanner from the green box' in the context of this conversation? There are neither number five wrenches nor spanners in the green box, within the domain of discourse. The conversation assumes that there *could have* been either, though: common sense has built into it the Aristotelian idea that the nouns we use represent kinds which are potentially instantiable. This particular conversation makes assumptions which tie the user of 'spanner in the green box' to a claim that there are such things, though, and does not require a similar tie for 'number five wrench'. What is the difference between them?

I do not know the answer to this question. It represents in miniature many of the things that baffle me here: what general assumptions do we make about the quantifiability of our predicates? What is the exact form of the rules which equip discourses with assumptions about the extent of their domains of quantification and their relation to the predicates occurring in them? What is required to block such assumptions? These are large questions, and all I can hope to have done in this chapter is to have made it plausible that they are real questions, and potentially answerable.[6]

---

6 I had help with an early draft from Christopher Williams and Simon Orde, and at the Tilburg conference from Peter Gardenfors, Barbara Partee, and Hilary Putnam.

Part II
Structure in Language and Thought

5

Tacit knowledge, and the structure of thought and language

Martin Davies

This chapter is about not throwing out the stock with the marrow bone. Over many years, the philosophy of language has been nourished by a certain idealized view of natural language. One consequence of that view has been the idea that the semantics of natural language will require mere variations on techniques drawn from systematic semantic theories for formal languages. Recently, a more radical conception of natural language meaning has been emerging, and great stress has been laid upon pragmatic factors in communication.[1] But, while this changed perspective is welcome, and although the idealized view arguably misconstrued the systematicity of meaning in natural language, we shall not do well to discard altogether the idea of the compositionality of meaning.

COMPOSITIONALITY AND TRUTH CONDITIONS

Here then are two very familiar thoughts about natural languages. First, natural languages have semantic structure – meaning is compositional. Second, meaning determines truth conditions – if a sentence s means that p then s is true if and only if it is the case that p. Together, the two thoughts suggest a certain picture of what

---

1 See, for example, chapter 2 by Wilson and Sperber, and chapter 3 by Kempson, in this volume.

sentence meaning is: first, the meaning of a sentence is determined by the meanings of its constituent words and the way they are put together; and second, the meaning of a sentence determines the conditions under which an utterance of the sentence is strictly and literally true or false. According to this picture, truth conditions are determined compositionally by the semantic properties of words and ways of putting words together.

Of course, no one is in the grip of quite such a simple picture as this. For everyone knows that natural languages contain indexical expressions; and the meaning of a sentence containing an indexical expression determines truth conditions only relative to a context of utterance. A more realistic picture will thus have the meaning of a sentence *plus context* determining truth conditions. But this revised picture, although marginally more realistic than the original one, is still potentially misleading.

One way of elaborating the revised picture is to say that contexts can be regarded as formal objects – some kind of ordered n-tuple, perhaps – and that sentence meanings are simply functions from such objects to truth conditions. For example, one element of a context will be the *speaker* in the context. An utterance of a sentence containing the indexical expression 'I' will then have its truth conditions determined in a very simple rule-governed way by the meaning of the sentence uttered, together with the transparent fact that a particular person is the speaker in the context of utterance. According to this elaboration, the phenomenon of indexicality – which necessitated the revision of the original picture – is simply the result of the occurrence in natural languages of half a dozen or so words which function formally rather like 'I'. The compositionality of truth conditions is, in a sense, retained in the elaboration, for the interaction between linguistic meaning and context of utterance takes place at the level of individual words. Truth conditions are determined compositionally from the semantic values of the words relative to the context.

The revised picture of sentence meaning, thus elaborated, can be further adapted to include many more varieties of context dependence than merely the indexical expressions 'I', 'here', 'now', and the rest. But in the adaptation one crucial feature remains. This is that, even if the formal study of context dependence is called pragmatics, it is quite different in character from another branch of pragmatics, namely, the theory of conversational implicature or the *implicit content* of utterances. The latter theory adverts to global principles of, for example, the expectation of *relevance* in the light of mutually accessible background information, and it is only via such expectations and in the light of such background knowledge that implicit content can be communicated. But such principles are entirely absent from the theory of context dependence that goes with the revised picture of sentence meaning. According to that picture, the theory of truth conditions or the *explicit content* of utterances needs to go beyond linguistic meaning only to the extent of acknowledging the systematic dependence of truth conditions upon local, transparently recognizable, features of contexts of utterance.

It is now widely accepted that this picture is mythological; explicit content is, as one might say, 'pragmatically penetrated'.[2] Consequently, it will not do for theorists of language to idealize away from indexicality and other features of context dependence – including dependence upon *linguistic* context. The study of natural language is not facilitated by an obsession with the (non-existent) ideal of isolated, strict and literal utterances of context-independent sentences. Rather, it requires a careful exploration of the joint contributions of narrowly linguistic factors, on the one hand, and more global principles of rational co-operation, on the other, to the determination of the explicit content of utterances. The two kinds of contribution – one relatively insensitive to, and the other highly sensitive to, background information – need to be considered both in generality and as applied to particular cases. And such consideration will – without confusion between *what* is being computed and *how* it is being computed – surely include both *a priori* and empirical elements.[3]

---

2 See again Wilson and Sperber, chapter 2 in this volume; and D. Sperber and D. Wilson, *Relevance: Communication and Cognition* (Basil Blackwell, Oxford, 1986).

3 At this stage, we shall want to leave it open that sometimes narrowly linguistic information may be arrived at by a route that does make use of background information and expectations.

It would however be a serious error if, in this interdisciplinary investigation of semantic and pragmatic factors in utterance comprehension, the familiar thought that natural languages have semantic structure were to be ignored. For it was not that thought itself that led to the mythological picture, but rather a particular way of combining the twin ideas of compositionality and truth conditions. To the extent that sentence meaning is compositional, meaning is not a determinant of, but a constraint upon, explicit content and truth conditions. And because this is so, we need to take care in choosing a scheme for representing sentence meaning – the narrowly linguistic contribution to truth conditions. But none of this is to deny that there is such a thing as semantic structure in natural languages, or to deny that there is such a project as systematic semantic theorizing.

A semantic theory for a particular natural language will – whatever the exact schematic form of its canonical pronouncements – articulate an assignment of meanings to sentences. But an adequate semantic theory will do more than this. It will also display just how the sentences come to have the meanings they do, given their construction out of more basic constituents: it will reveal semantic structure.

Since a semantic theory is a theory, it will have axioms. If the canonical pronouncements about whole sentences are themselves taken as axioms then, of course, precisely nothing about semantic structure will be revealed. But, if the assignments of meanings to whole sentences are derived from more fundamental principles that assign appropriate semantic properties to constituent expressions, and to ways of putting these together, then the semantic structure of a given sentence will be revealed in the derivational path leading from the axioms of the theory to the meaning assignment for that sentence. More generally, the semantic structure of the language will be revealed in the derivational structure of the theory. The *recurrent* contribution that a constituent expression makes to the meanings of the several sentences in which it occurs will be revealed in the use of a *common axiom* – the principle assigning a semantic property to that expression – in the derivations of meaning assignments for all those sentences.

It is thus a reasonable condition of adequacy upon a semantic theory for a particular language that its derivational structure should articulate and display the semantic structure of the language in question. But this basic idea can be given a more aprioristic or a more empirical slant. For the structure to be articulated may be conceived as an abstract (or mathematical) structure or as a psychological structure.

By distinguishing the two kinds of conception of semantic structure we can, I claim, make good empirical sense of the idea that a speaker has *tacit knowledge* of the semantic rules of her language. This distinction, together with further clarification of the notion of tacit knowledge, is the business of part I of this chapter. One question addressed – albeit briefly – is whether mere tacit knowledge can be sharply separated from common-or-garden belief and knowledge; that is, from ordinary propositional attitudes. Any remarks on this topic are inevitably inconclusive. But one apparently promising line of enquiry concerns the essentially structured character of propositional attitudes.

In part II of this chapter I turn to the relationship between the structure of language and the structure of thoughts expressed. There are plausible arguments for a very close connection between the two – for what I call the doctrine of essential linguistic structure. But the fundamentally correct idea behind the doctrine concerns, once again, the essentially structured character of our thoughts. The doctrine itself errs in taking for a requirement upon language what is really a condition upon thought.

I

FOUR CONCEPTIONS OF SEMANTIC STRUCTURE

The structure to be articulated by a semantic theory can be conceived as abstract or as psychological. In fact, there are at least two notions of abstract structure, and at least two notions of psychological structure, that we need to distinguish.

One notion of an abstract structure in a language is that of a systematization – however arbitrary and unnatural – of the facts about the meanings of sentences in the language. This is a purely formal notion, and there is no one preferred structure in this sense.

As far as this mathematical notion of structure goes, a language has countless – indeed, infinitely many – different structures. And the requirement that a theory should articulate semantic structure, conceived in this way, places precisely no constraints upon semantic theories.[4]

There is, however, a different, more interesting, though still abstract, notion of semantic structure. This is the notion of a structure that an ideally rational creature would recognize. It is an abstract, rather than a psychological, construal because there is no assumption that the structure is realized in the actual speakers of the language. If this is how semantic structure in a language is conceived, then an appropriate constraint on a semantic theory for the language would be along the following lines.

> If someone could (by rational inductive means) come to know what sentence s means purely on the basic of her knowledge of what other sentences $s_1, \ldots, s_n$ mean, then a semantic theory should reveal the meaning of s as a product of the same semantic resources as are deployed in $s_1, \ldots, s_n$.

Since systematic dependences of meaning are to be revealed by patterns of derivation in the theory, the resources – principally, axioms assigning semantic properties to primitives – employed in the derivations of meaning specifications for $s_1. \ldots, s_n$ should already suffice for the derivation of the meaning specification for s.[5]

To conceive of semantic structure as psychological, rather than abstract, is to conceive it as the causal-explanatory structure of the semantic ability of actual speakers. It is the kind of cognitive structure that permits speakers to recognize the meanings of previously unencountered sentences. But there are at least two

---

4 This notion is rather like that of a mathematically possible, rather than a humanly possible, grammar.
5 Such a constraint pushes a theorist in the direction of exposing the maximum amount of semantic structure in the language, irrespective of any details about the linguistic behaviour of actual speakers. For more on this constraint, see my 'Meaning and structure', *Philosophia*, 13 (1983); 'Meaning, structure and understanding', *Synthese*, 48 (1981); and *Meaning, Quantification, Necessity: themes in philosophical logic* (Routledge and Kegan Paul, 1981), chapter 3, 'Structure'.

such notions of structure. On the one hand, we can consider normal or optimally functioning actual speakers.[6] On the other hand, we can consider an individual actual speaker, who may be abnormal and less than optimally functioning.

If we make use of the first notion of psychological structure, then an appropriate constraint on a semantic theory would require that the derivational structure of the theory should mirror the causal-explanatory structure to be found in normal speakers. The crucial question this time is not whether an ideally rational speaker/theorist could work out the meaning of s given the meanings of $s_1, \ldots, s_n$. It is, rather, whether the cognitive resources which in fact underlie the ability of a normal speaker to recognize the meaning of s are among those which underlie her ability to recognize the meanings of $s_1, \ldots, s_n$. It is not guaranteed *a priori* that the answers to these two questions will be the same.[7]

In contrast, if we make use of the second notion of psychological structure, than an appropriate constraint on a semantic theory, relative to a particular speaker, would require that the derivational structure of the theory should mirror the causal-explanatory structure to be found in that speaker.

Suppose, for a moment, that this notion of a causal-explanatory structure to be found in speakers is both tolerably clear and empirically respectable. Then we can distinguish an empirically substantial sense in which a speaker might be said to have internalized a set of semantic rules. For a particular speaker can be said to have internalized the rules that figure as axioms in a theory whose derivational structure mirrors the causal-explanatory structure to be found in that very speaker. This is in contrast to the empirically feeble, and indeed philosophically misleading, idea that a speaker can be credited with having internalized a set of rules simply in virtue of facts that have nothing to do with the psychological states of that speaker. For example, a speaker might be described as having internalized the rules that figure as axioms in a theory which articulates semantic structure conceived either as

---

6 We may need to distinguish normality from optimality of function.
7 One way of putting a familiar point about syntax would be to say that the answers to the two corresponding questions for syntax are not the same.

normal – rather than individual – psychological structure, or as one or other kind of abstract structure.

It has sometimes been claimed that doctrines about internalization, or tacit knowledge, of linguistic rules trade upon a grotesque confusion between causal generation (of psychological states) and derivational generation (of theorems in a theory).[8] According to that claim, friends of tacit knowledge mistakenly take for an empirically substantial doctrine something which really amounts to no more than this: that a speaker somehow assigns meanings to sentences, and that those assignments can be mathematically systematized by a particular set of axioms. The distinction between the abstract notions of structure and the second – individualist – psychological notion reveals clearly that the claim of confusion is unjustified. That, indeed, is my main purpose in labouring the distinction. Friends of tacit knowledge do not *need* to trade on any such confusion.

It would be reasonable to ask whether, apart from this defensive purpose, any significance attaches to the abstract notions of semantic structure – particularly to the second abstract notion, and its associated constraint on semantic theories. Crispin Wright has argued that there is, indeed, a philosophical project to which a theory governed by that constraint would make a contribution. It is the project of 'explaining how a complete knowledge of a particular natural language could be a rational achievement';[9] a project of *rational reconstruction*. For such a theory would reveal how an ideally rational speaker/theorist could infer the meaning of a sentence s from the meanings of other sentences $s_1, \ldots, s_n$, using a mixture of inductive and deductive methods.

We have introduced four different notions of semantic structure. The distinction between the second abstract notion of structure –

---

8 M. Levin, 'Explanation and prediction in grammar (and semantics)', in *Contemporary Perspectives in the Philosophy of Language*, eds P.A. French *et al.* (University of Minnesota Press, 1979), p. 183. Cf. G.P. Baker and P.M.S. Hacker, *Language, Sense and Nonsense* (Basil Blackwell, Oxford, 1984), pp. 243–368 *passim*.

9 C. Wright, 'Theories of meaning: compositionality and speakers' knowledge', in *Philosophy in the United Kingdom*, ed. S. Shanker (Croom Helm, 1986). There is much else in this paper that deserves careful attention, for Wright conducts a close examination of the notions of implicit and tacit knowledge.

call it *a priori semantic structure* – and the second psychological notion – call it *individual cognitive structure* – gives a sense to the theoretical possibility of there being structure in a language, although some, or even all, of the actual speakers of the language are quite insensitive to it. That distinction, and also the distinction between *normal* or *optimal cognitive structure* and individual cognitive structure, requires the theoretical possibility of a difference in causal-explanatory structure between two speakers, even though the speakers assign the same meanings to the same sentences. The distinctions require, that is to say, that there be theoretical slack between *meaning* and *structure*, and it is this that is denied by the doctrine of essential linguistic structure.

CAUSAL-EXPLANATORY STRUCTURE AND NEUROPHYSIOLOGY

In the previous section I assumed that the idea of a causal-explanatory structure is an empirically respectable one, and then drew some distinctions with a view to legitimizing the Chomskyan notion of tacit knowledge. In this section I want to say more about this idea of a cognitive psychological structure in speakers. In particular, I shall aim to make it clear that acceptance of the idea does not involve any commitment to neurophysiological localization of function. The strategy will be to contrast my preferred notion of internalization with a different notion that has been described – though not espoused – by Simon Blackburn. The difference turns out to be analogous to a difference between two notions of a *syndrome*.

The basic idea was of a psychological structure that allows language users to recognize the meanings of new sentences built from familiar constituents; of common cognitive resources at work in the comprehension of different sentences with common constituents. This was then to legitimize the notion of tacit knowledge as follows: a speaker can be credited with tacit knowledge of the axioms of a semantic theory whose derivational structure mirrors the causal-explanatory structure underlying her ability to comprehend sentences.

A quotation from Gareth Evans will serve to make the basic idea clearer.

> I suggest that we construe the claim that someone tacitly knows a theory of meaning as ascribing to that person a set of dispositions – one corresponding to each of the expressions for which the theory provides a distinct axiom. . . . It is essential that the notion of a disposition used in these formulations be understood in a full-blooded sense. . . . The ascription of tacit knowledge . . . involves the claim that there is a single state of the subject which figures in a causal explanation of why he reacts in this regular way to all the sentences containing the expression.[10]

In a semantic theory, an axiom for a primitive expression makes a common contribution to the derivations of meaning specifications for sentences containing that expression. The contribution is only partial, because, of course, the sentences will also contain other expressions. So, the axiom for an expression makes a *common partial* derivational contribution to the meanings of sentences containing the expression. On Evans's account, tacit knowledge of that axiom involves there being a *state* of the subject which makes a common, though of course partial, contribution to the causal explanation of the subject's comprehension of sentences containing the expression. The crucial notion is that of a *common partial* causal explanation.

Evans went on to give examples of the sorts of empirical evidence one might have for the thesis that there is one, rather than another, causal-explanatory structure underlying a subject's comprehension of sentences. These were: evidence from patterns of acquisition; evidence from patterns of loss or decay in understanding, resulting perhaps from brain damage; and evidence relating to perceptual strategies. We might add to these: evidence from patterns of revision.[11] By appeal to evidence of these kinds, the

---

10 G. Evans, 'Semantic theory and tacit knowledge', in *Wittgenstein: To Follow a Rule*, eds S.H. Holtzman and C.M. Leich (Routledge and Kegan Paul, 1981), pp. 124–5. This was a response to C. Wright, 'Rule-following, objectivity and the theory of meaning', in the same volume.
11 Evans, 'Semantic theory', pp. 127–9. I focused on revision of semantic beliefs in 'Meaning, structure and understanding', and *Meaning, Quantification, Necessity*, chapter 4, 'Understanding'.

notion of tacit knowledge was to be defended against the hard-line Quinean charge of empirical vacuity.

Now, Evans said that the explanation of comprehension is 'presumably neurophysiologically based', and in explaining the 'full-blooded' sense of 'disposition' he appealed to the idea of a 'state of the subject'. But, on my reading, he did not advance any more committed view about the relation between states of tacit knowledge (cognitive psychological states) and neurophysiological states. There is, for example, no claim of type–type identity, functionalist type–type identity relative to a subject at a time, or even token–token identity. And it was no part of Evans's position that states of tacit knowledge would be underpinned by strictly localized brain states. The implication of the same brain area in the comprehension of two sentences would in no way be *sufficient* for the presence of the relevant kind of structure. It is also worth noting that Evans distinguished clearly between *evidence* for structure, and what is *constitutive* of structure. Facts about language acquisition, and particularly facts about loss resulting from brain damage, are evidence for the relevant kind of structure; they do not themselves constitute that structure.

In his influential book *Spreading the Word*, Simon Blackburn has distinguished a number of different positions one might take on the relationship between ordinary language users and syntactic and semantic rules.[12] One, according to which 'psychological reality' is allowed to the rules, is of course *Chomsky's realism*. This position is characterized by Blackburn in terms of its commitment to computations and the Fodorian analogy between language comprehension and visual perception.[13] The position that I am defending – what I take to be Evans's position – is intended to be some version of Chomsky's realism.

Opposed to Chomsky's realism, in Blackburn's taxonomy, are two positions on which 'psychological reality' is denied to the rules. One of these, unsurprisingly, is the hard-line Quinean position. The other is a position which 'finds the missing link

---

12 S. Blackburn, *Spreading the Word* (Oxford University Press, 1984), pp. 26–37. Here, I do not in fact discuss Blackburn's own preferred position.
13 Ibid., pp. 27–8. Commitments to meaning preserving transformations and to nativism are also included in Blackburn's sketch. But these are surely separable from Chomsky's view about what constitutes tacit knowledge in adults.

between us and the rules in neurophysiology' (rather than in psychology). It is this position that serves as a useful contrast to mine. It can best be understood by looking both at Blackburn's positive account and at his objections to it.

On the positive side we have this: 'The idea is that our brains have a causal structure. Some "bits" are responsible for some aspects of our competence, and other "bits" are not.'[14] Also, it might be that a particular kind of brain damage is found to produce a loss of linguistic ability structurally analogous to the derivational loss consequent upon the removal of a particular rule or axiom from a semantic theory: 'This would be empirical evidence that the rule or axiom is actually embodied in the user's neural processes.'[15] And, on the side of objections, we have this: 'But it *might* be that our brains . . . do not encode information bit by bit. It is simply not true of them that if you destroy a particular area you lose one particular piece of information.'[16]

Now, suppose that it were nomologically impossible to produce localized brain damage in a subject in such a way as to delete precisely her ability with a particular word W, or a particular construction C. Then, according to the position under consideration, no semantic theory that had an axiom assigning a semantic property to the word W or to the construction C could be structurally adequate. But, says Blackburn, 'that seems incredible.'[17] And he is surely right. For we do not intuitively reckon the imagined fact about the subject's brain – even if it were a fact about *all* subjects' brains – to be sufficient by itself to show that the word W, or the construction C, is not a significant element of semantic structure.

This position, described by Blackburn, has a number of notable features which differentiate it from my preferred account of tacit knowledge. First, and most important, although the position makes use of the notion of a structure in subjects that mirrors the derivational structure of a theory, the structure in question is *not*

14 Ibid., p. 32.
15 Ibid.
16 Ibid., pp. 33–4.
17 Ibid., p. 34.

psychological. This is not merely the point that tacit knowledge is somehow unlike common-or-garden conscious knowledge and belief. It is the claim, rather, that the structure is not even psychological in the sense in which the early stages of visual processing are psychological. The remarks about bits and areas of the brain reveal that, on this view, the structure is *neurogeographical*.

Second, there is not, on the position as described, a sharp distinction between what is constitutive of structure, and what is evidence for structure. It appears at first that, on the neurogeographical view, what would be constitutive of a structure corresponding to the presence of an axiom for the word W would be the presence of a brain area, location, or bit, precisely responsible for mastery of W. In that case, facts about neurophysiologically possible damage would only be *evidence* for structure. For there could be an alternative explanation of those facts. It might be, for example, that although one area *is* specifically responsible for word W, and a nearby area for word X, still the paths of blood vessels in the region are such that damage to the W-area will inevitably impair the nutrition of the X-area, and so result in damage to it too. However, by the end of Blackburn's description of the position, facts about the possibilities or impossibilities of patterns of damage are taken as actually *sufficient* for facts about structure.

This neurogeographical notion of structure is an empirically respectable one, but it cannot be used to legitimize Chomskyan tacit knowledge, for that was supposed to be a cognitive psychological notion.

The contrast between the neurogeographical notion and the notion that I am attempting to characterize is rather like the contrast between two notions of a *syndrome*. The two notions that I have in mind are both distinct from the 'minimal' notion that a syndrome is nothing more than a constellation of symptoms. Both agree that only some constellations of symptoms constitute syndromes. According to the first notion, these are the constellations that have some common neurophysiological explanation, while according to the second notion, what is required is a common cognitive psychological explanation. Someone who uses the term 'syndrome' in this second way – who uses it as it is used in *cognitive* neuropsychology[18] – will not, of course, claim that *all* explanations of the co-occurrence of psychological symptoms are themselves psychological. On the contrary, he will acknowledge that an explanation may be merely physiological, and will draw the consequence that co-occurrence of psychological symptoms – even non-accidental co-occurrence of symptoms – does not by itself provide decisive evidence in favour of one, rather than another, map of *psychological* structure (one, rather than another, 'functional boxology').

A speaker's mastery of a particular sentence containing a word W or a construction C is a psychological 'symptom', and mastery of a host of sentences containing W, or containing C, constitutes a constellation of symptoms. According to the account of tacit knowledge that I am defending, a speaker has tacit knowledge of a semantic rule for W, or for C, only if that constellation of symptoms constitutes a syndrome in this second sense.

BELIEFS AND SUBDOXASTIC STATES

Two hard questions about tacit knowledge are these. First, is there a theoretically important distinction between common-or-garden states of knowledge and belief and states of (mere) tacit knowledge? Second, if there is such a distinction, on which side of it does a speaker's internalization of the syntactic and semantic rules of her language fall? In this section, I shall briefly address the first of these questions.

Whether or not Chomsky is correct that, for the purposes of cognitive psychology, the legimate domain is that of his neologism 'cognize',[19] still we ought to explore the differences between propositional attitudes and other information-containing cognitive states. Examples of the latter, which fall outside the folk psychological, would be states of the optic nerve and the striate cortex,

---

18 See, for example, M. Coltheart, 'Cognitive neuropsychology and the study of reading', in *Attention and Performance XI*, eds M.I. Posner and O.S.M. Marin (Erlbaum, 1985).
19 N. Chomsky, *Reflections on Language* (Fontana/Collins, 1975), p. 165; *Rules and Representations* (Basil Blackwell, Oxford, 1982), pp. 97–8.

investigated in the psychology of visual perception. Some of the states and processes implicated in utterance comprehension – those responsible for phonological analysis of the acoustic signal, for example – would also be clear cases. But we should not begin by begging questions about just how much falls within or without folk psychology; the status of semantic rules is itself not uncontroversial.

The examples just given involve creatures, namely us, who are *inter alia* bearers of propositional attitudes. Some of the cognitive states of such creatures are not propositional attitude states. But there is another aspect to the present topic. For there are information-processing systems *none* of whose states we reckon to be propositional attitudes. There is a clear enough analogy between what a room thermostat does, and what a believer and desirer does. But, for all that, a room thermostat is not a bearer of propositional attitudes.

Thus there are two aspects to the distinction between, as we might pretentiously say, the genuinely mental and the merely cognitive. In Stephen Stich's terminology, this is the distinction between beliefs and *subdoxastic states*.[20] An ultimately satisfying account of the distinction would clarify both aspects. But sadly, an ultimately satisfying account is what we do not have.

Psychological states certainly differ in respect of *accessibility to consciousness*. Ordinary beliefs are conscious states, and beliefs are typically articulable. In contrast, at least some of what is merely cognized is 'forever hidden from consciousness'.[21] A language user may have a conscious belief that, and be able to report that, she is being told that she has missed the bus. But much of the registered information is not accessible. She is quite unaware of acoustic features such as voice onset times. And although she tacitly knows various rules relating, say, phonological and syntactic representations of the utterance that she heard, these rules are quite inaccessible; and if formulations of the rules are explicitly presented she is virtually certain not to recognize them.

A second difference concerns *inferential integration*, as against *insulation*. The belief that a certain food is poisonous, and the

20 S. Stich, 'Beliefs and subdoxastic states', *Philosophy of Science*, 45 (1978).
21 Chomsky, *Reflections on Language*, p. 165.

belief that consumption of small doses of a poison renders one immune to its effects, can lead inferentially to the belief that consumption of small doses of *this food* will render one immune to *its* poisonous effects. And this belief may, with an appropriate desire, lead to action. Furthermore, new beliefs can lead inferentially to the adjustment of previously held beliefs with which they are incompatible.[22]

These are familiar facts. A person's beliefs form a holistic inferential and evidential web. But states of mere cognizing are not integrated with ordinary beliefs. In contrast, they are inferentially insulated from the subject's ordinary beliefs and other attitudes. Stich gave an example involving linguistic rules:

> Suppose that for some rule, you have come to believe that if r then Chomsky is seriously mistaken. Suppose further that, as it happens, r is in fact among the rules stored by your language processing mechanism. The belief along with the subdoxastic state will not lead to the belief that Chomsky is seriously mistaken.[23]

A third difference concerns *mastery of concepts*. A subject cannot believe that p while lacking the concepts involved in the proposition that p. But a subject can certainly cognize that p while lacking those concepts. Highly sophisticated propositions are reckoned to be cognized by quite unsophisticated thinkers.

Very serious unclarities surround each of these putative differences between beliefs and subdoxastic states, and it would be a particularly bold theorist who would rest a distinction upon accessibility *versus* inaccessibility to consciousness. What is more, although Stich's example of inferential insulation seems initially to be quite clear, the distinction between rules (computations) and representations can be used to blur its significance.[24]

---

22 See Evans, 'Semantic theory', pp. 131–2; and for further discussion of this point, see J. Campbell, 'Knowledge and understanding', *Philosophical Quarterly*, 32 (1982), and Wright, 'Rule–following'.
23 Stich, 'Beliefs', p. 509.
24 Stich's example involves *modus ponens*. A subject is supposed to have an ordinary belief of the form 'if P then Q', where what is in the 'P' place is a linguistic rule of which the subject has tacit knowledge. The subject typically

Nevertheless, the difference between inferential insulation and inferential integration is very reminiscent of the difference between what Fodor calls *informationally encapsulated* and *unencapsulated* systems.²⁵ This might suggest to some that Fodor's distinction is the psychological *real essence* of a distinction between beliefs and subdoxastic states – a distinction whose *nominal essence* is partially given by the three differences mentioned.

That is one line well worth pursuing. And there is another. For we can at least catch a glimpse of a theoretical connection between the second and the third differences.

The inferential integration of beliefs is very closely related to the fact that a belief can be 'at the service of many distinct projects', in Evans's phrase. 'To have a belief requires one to appreciate its location in a network of beliefs.'²⁶ But then, he goes on, the inferential properties or potential of various beliefs are related. There are inferential similarities between the belief that a is F and the belief that b is F, and a subject's 'appreciation' of the inferential potential of these two beliefs is, in part, the product of a common capacity, namely mastery of the concept *being F*: 'Behind the idea of a system of beliefs lies that of a system of concepts, the structure of which determines the referential properties which thoughts . . . are treated as possessing.'²⁷ An inferential web thus requires a network of concepts; and the nodes in the web are themselves to be regarded as structured items having concepts as constituents. Conversely, concepts do not come in ones and twos, but in networks – we have local holism – and to possess a network of concepts is to be able to appreciate the inferential properties of states involving those concepts.

Immediately after establishing the connection between inference and concepts, Evans went on: 'We shall not be prepared to

---

does not draw the conclusion Q. The rule of *modus ponens* is more like a computation than a representation, and it needs representations to apply to. But what is in the '*P*' place – an internalized linguistic rule – is itself more like a computation than a representation.

25 J.A. Fodor, *The Modularity of Mind* (MIT Press, 1983); see especially pp. 64–86.
26 Evans, 'Semantic theory', p. 132.
27 Ibid.

attribute to a subject the belief that a is F unless we can suppose the subject to be capable of entertaining the supposition (having the thought) that b is F, for every object b of which he has a conception.'[28] This doctrine is developed much more fully in *The Varieties of Reference* where it becomes the *generality constraint* – a constraint on the contents of propositional attitudes:

> If a subject can be credited with the thought that a is F, then he must have the conceptual resources for entertaining the thought that a is G, for every property of being G of which he has a conception. We thus see the thought that a is F as lying at the intersection of two series of thoughts: on the one hand, the series of thoughts that a is F, that b is F, that c is F, . . ., and, on the other hand, the series of thoughts that a is F, that a is G, that a is H, ...[29]

Both beliefs and other propositional attitudes, on the one hand, and subdoxastic states, on the other, have propositional contents. Evans's claim was that the generality constraint applies to the former but not to the latter.[30]

For example, a theory of visual processing might involve the attribution, to a state of the visual system, of the informational content that a certain visually presented surface is 'smooth', in a technical sense which is beyond the ordinary conceptual sophistication of the subject. (Say, the surface is twice differentiable, with continuous second derivative.) Suppose now that the subject has a belief with the content that the backs of his eyeballs are hairy. If the total domain of propositional attitudes and other cognitive states were subject to the generality constraint, as the domain of attitudes by itself is, then there would have to be some actual or potential state of the subject with the content that the backs of his eyeballs are smooth (in that forbiddingly technical sense). But no ordinary propositional attitude will have that content, for the

---

28 Ibid., p. 133.
29 G. Evans, *The Varieties of Reference* (Oxford University Press, 1982), p. 104. On the generality constraint, see also J. Campbell, 'Possession of concepts', *Proceedings of the Aristotelian Society*, 85 (1984/5); and chapter 6 by Campbell in this volume.
30 Evans, *The Varieties of Reference*, p. 104, footnote 22.

subject cannot think about smoothness, and no state of the visual system will have that content, for the visual system does not contain information about the rear surfaces of the eyeballs.

Illustrations of this kind can be easily multiplied. They do not, by themselves, rule out a model on which there are two domains – the domain of propositional attitudes and the domain of subdoxastic states – each of which, considered alone, is subject to the generality constraint. But an example that Evans gave was surely intended to rule out that idea:

> When we attribute to the brain computations whereby it localizes the sounds we hear, we *ipso facto* ascribe to it representations of the speed of sound and of the distance between the ears, without any commitment to the idea that it should be able to represent the speed of light or the distance between anything else.[31]

The point of this example is that the generality constraint will be infringed by the contents of what are intuitively subdoxastic states, as long as we consider several systems together.

It would thus far be left open, however, that if the mind has a modular structure then the informational states of one module considered by itself – a perceptual system, for example – might meet the generality constraint. To the extent that the generality constraint is a characteristic mark of the mental, what is left open is that informational states of a module are propositional attitudes. They would not be attitudes of the subject but of the individual module; alongside the subject's mental life there would be several homuncular mental lives. If what is left open is indeed the best description of the situation, then the distinction that matters is the distinction between personal and subpersonal propositional attitudes.

Actually, though, it seems to me that this is not the best description of the situation. The idea that states of modules are genuine propositional attitudes faces a dilemma. On the one hand, one can cut modules relatively coarsely. But then examples can be constructed that seem to constitute breaches of the generality

---

31 Ibid.

constraint within a single module, say the auditory processing system. On the other hand, one can cut modules more finely so that there are fewer contents and so fewer building blocks whose recombination the constraint can demand. But this does not really help. For together with the constraint we should have in mind the point that concepts come, not in ones and twos, but in families or networks. The more finely we discriminate modules, the more hopelessly impoverished are the sets of concepts that would be attributed.

It remains plausible, then, that there is a genuine distinction between beliefs and subdoxastic states. And the last few paragraphs support Evans's idea that while the applicability of the generality constraint is a necessary feature of propositional attitudes, states that are intuitively subdoxastic – particularly states of input systems – are not subject to that constraint.

Let us pause to review the discussion so far. For essentially defensive reasons, a notion of *a priori* semantic structure was distinguished from two psychological notions of structure – one individual, the other normal. The cognitive psychological notion of a causal-explanatory structure needed to legitimize the idea of tacit knowledge was then distinguished from a merely neurogeographical notion. And in comparing tacit knowledge with ordinary propositional attitudes, we have appealed to the generality constraint, which captures the essentially structured character of thoughts.

Typically, speaking a language is a matter of deploying a cognitively structured ability to use semantically structured sentences to express intrinsically structured thoughts or meanings. What exactly are the relationships between these three kinds of structure?

II

MEANING AND STRUCTURE

In the section entitled 'Four conceptions of semantic structure' I distinguished more aprioristic and more empirical ways of developing the idea that a semantic theory should articulate and display semantic structure. I noted that the conceptual distinction between *a priori* semantic structure and individual cognitive structure gives a sense to the theoretical possibility (however empirically far fetched) of there being mathematical structure in a language without the corresponding psychological structure in actual speakers of the language. More generally, the distinctions drawn require the theoretical possibility of differences of causal-explanatory structure between speakers who assign the same meanings to the same sentences. Consequently, they require the possibility that an individual speaker may lack the structured ability that normal speakers of her language possess, even though she assigns the same meanings to sentences as do other speakers.

Consider a particular language. In the abstract, it is partly constituted by an assignment of meanings to sentences. Suppose that there is a systematic dependence of meaning upon the syntactic form of the sentences, and that this dependence is recognizable and can be rationally mastered. Suppose too that speakers normally attain tacit knowledge of this systematic dependence. Then, the theoretical possibility in question is that of there being individual users of the language who are, to a greater or lesser extent, psychologically insensitive to this systematic dependence. Such language users would attach the right *meanings* to the sentences, yet be blind to the semantic *structure* of the sentences. They would use syntactically complex sentences to express correspondingly complex thoughts, but would treat each sentence as if it were semantically unstructured.

Someone who maintains that this is *not* a theoretical possibility will say that any use of sentences with complex meanings must involve a psychologically structured linguistic ability. *A fortiori*, the sentences themselves must be complex. According to such a theorist, where there is an *apparent* absence of the expected structure in the ability, it is inevitably the case that the language user is attaching less complex meanings to her sentences. Let us call this the doctrine of *essential linguistic structure*. Evidently, the doctrine could be refined into various more precise versions.

The doctrine of essential linguistic structure rests on some fundamentally correct insights – insights that are too easily forgotten if one is primarily concerned with the defensive project of

'Four conceptions'. Nevertheless, the doctrine itself is – in my view – incorrect.

Here is an uncompromising statement by Elizabeth Fricker: 'The initially plausible thought that there could be structure in a language, though its speakers were blind to it, is wrong.'[32] This claim is rather stronger than some others for which Fricker argues explicitly, such as: 'Facts about sentence-meanings are not independent of facts about their structure.'[33] The latter claim need not be in dispute. If it means only that there are some *a priori* connections between the structure of a speaker's ability and what her sentences can be taken to mean, then it is both true and important. It is one of those fundamentally correct insights. But it does not have the very strong consequence that Fricker draws.

There is no mystery about the initial plausibility of the thought that there could be structure in a language – whether conceived as *a priori* semantic structure or as *normal* cognitive structure – although some individual speakers of that language were blind to it. Consider the following sort of example. Many common nouns take an '-s' plural. There is system here; plural common nouns are semantically structured. The regularity is recognizable and can be rationally mastered. When it is mastered – explicitly or tacitly – it typically results in overextension, since there are irregular plurals in the language. Imagine, now, a child learning the language. She has a fair repertoire of common nouns, and uses them appropriately for objects of various salient kinds. She is also sensitive to the difference between one brick and more than one, between one mouse and more than one, and starts to learn a few plurals. Perhaps, early on, she overextends the '-s' rule and is then brought up short by the occurrence of irregular plurals. Perhaps, on the other hand, she begins with a range of irregulars. It is not impossible that this circumspect language learner could behave as if she thought every common noun to be irregular, and treat the occurrences of '-s' plurals as mere coincidence. She could be cognitively quite insensitive to the systematic relation between

---

32 E. Fricker, 'Semantic structure and speakers' understanding', *Proceedings of the Aristotelian Society*, 82 (1982/3), p. 65.
33 Ibid., p. 60.

form and meaning, treating each plural common noun as a one-off case – as something to be mastered *ab initio*.

It is not really very plausible to say that there can be no such child who still means the right things by plural nouns. Yet, according to the strongest version of the doctrine of essential linguistic structure, this is what we would have to say. For, if she means the right things by '-s' plurals, then clearly she is speaking a fragment of a language in which there is semantic structure; yet she herself is blind to any such structure.

Fricker invites us to think more generally about cases of this kind:

> Consider what it would be to find a speaker of English with less than the canonical amount of structure to his ability: it would be to find someone who failed to understand new sentences which he ought to be able to understand, given the sentences he is already familiar with. If this happened to only a trivial extent, we should no doubt brush it aside; but if it happened on a massive scale we surely could no longer regard an utterance by him of a sentence of English as expressing the same thought that it would in the mouth of a normal speaker.[34]

Whether the case of the child learning plurals is a counter example to this claim depends upon whether it is deemed to be a case of trivial, or of massive, absence of structure in linguistic ability. But even if the case is deemed trivial, that does not constitute a wholly satisfactory resolution, for we do not yet understand the crucial difference between the trivial and the massive cases.

Furthermore, it is crucial to see how it can be true *both* that there are *a priori* connections between the structure of linguistic ability and sentence meaning, *and* that – in a slightly pedantic way – the initially plausible thought is indeed correct.

STRUCTURE AND RADICAL INTERPRETATION

One way in which facts about structure are crucial to facts about sentence meaning concerns the project of radical interpretation:

---

34 Ibid., p. 64.

> In so far as interpretation is determinate the primary feature ensuring this is the fact that the assignment of a meaning to one sentence constrains and is constrained by the assignments made to other sentences. . . . Some principle for discerning semantic structure in sentences is essential to interpreting a language.[35]

This fact about radical interpretation is reckoned by Fricker to provide a decisive argument in favour of her position, so let us look at an example.

Suppose that a speaker comes out with a sentence that seems, syntactically, to have an articulation into subject and predicate. Suppose that she seems to be saying something about – to be expressing a belief about – a particular nearby mountain. But what is she saying about it? Her behaviour surrounding the utterance of just this sentence is likely – indeed, virtually certain – to leave the interpretation massively indeterminate. Suppose that she utters, and then sets off in the direction of the mountain, carrying what seems to be climbing equipment. Was she saying that the mountain is good for climbing, or that the mountain is icy (imagine she believes icy mountains are fun to climb), or that the moutain is a source of food, or of a good view? This is the problem that confronts the radical interpreter.

What would help the interpreter would be another fix on the contribution made to the meaning of the uttered sentence by the presumed predicate. This help could be furnished by an utterance of another sentence in which the same syntactically distinguished predicate is coupled with a different subject, provided, of course, that it could be assumed that the predicate was making the same contribution to sentence meaning in the two cases.

Suppose that our speaker, on returning from the mountain, uses the same predicate in what seems to be a remark about an ice cube placed in a much needed drink. Unless she has some very peculiar beliefs about climbing up very small objects, it is more likely that she is expressing the belief that the cube is icy than that she is saying that it is good for climbing. And, subject to the assumption just mentioned, the interpretation of the later remark constrains the interpretation of the earlier one.

35 Ibid., p. 59.

This little example demonstrates well enough how semantic structure in a language – recognizably regular connections between form and meaning – crucially facilitates radical interpretation. But it does not quite demonstrate that radical interpretation depends upon there being structure in the speaker's ability.

However, there is a little more to be said. For systematic connections between form and meaning do not occur and persist by magic. Expressions which are treated as idioms tend to take on idiomatic meanings. So, in a real-life case, a preponderance of speakers with more or less fully structured abilities seems to be needed, in order to ensure the persistence of systematicity through time.

This is not, perhaps, all that the defender of the doctrine of essential linguistic structure might have hoped for. But what we have is that structure in the ability of speakers is a practical requirement for the systematicity that facilitates radical interpretation.

The significance of this is, however, rather greater than it may initially appear. For we should take into account that the members of a speech community are involved in interpreting each other; radical interpretation begins at home. I need to know, for example, that sentences mean the same in the mouth of another speaker as they mean in my mouth. Members of a speech community need the clues provided by structure, as does the novice who is becoming a member of the community. And, once again, causal-explanatory structure in the linguistic ability of speakers is what enables the clues to persist. So, a preponderance of structured linguistic ability is, at least, a practical requirement for the existence in use of a shared natural language.

These conclusions about *prima facie* practical requirements are, of course, quite consistent with the theoretical possibility of individual speakers of a structured language who themselves have a less than fully structured ability. It is also consistent with the theoretical possibility of a language that is partially or wholly lacking in semantic structure.

One wholly imaginary case would have speakers innately endowed with a correlation between form and meaning. If that were so, and universally believed to be so (perhaps innately), then interpretation would, it seems, be facilitated. But the correlation might be wired in sentence by sentence, rather than word by word. In that case the speakers would have, at least initially, an unstructured linguistic ability.

This far-fetched case is borrowed from Blackburn.[36] Early in *Spreading the Word*, he too appears to defend a version of the doctrine of essential linguistic structure. But as one might expect – given the example – he does not rest his conclusion on the argument from radical interpretation.

ATTRIBUTING COMPLEX MEANINGS

Blackburn's argument adverts to a second, more radical, way in which facts about structure are crucial to facts about sentence meaning.

It is not merely the case that, unless we can discover a syntactically distinguished predicate in other sentences, it will be massively indeterminate exactly *what* property is being ascribed to a certain object. There is a further intuition that, unless the putative predicate is discovered in other sentences, there is a reason to doubt that any property is being ascribed to any object at all. There is reason to doubt, that is, that the belief being expressed is the belief that an object (a particular) exemplifies a property (a universal), and correlatively, reason to doubt that the syntactic articulation within the sentence is an articulation into logical subject and logical predicate.

It is on this potent intuition that Blackburn bases his version of the doctrine.

> What reason could there be for allowing that a person means that Fred is asleep by some noise, unless the noise is structured in a way which permits us to see it as made of a name for Fred, and a predicate for being asleep? . . . You cannot . . . mean by a sentence that Fred sleeps unless you can take an element of it and use it to say

---

36 Blackburn, *Spreading the Word*, p. 122. He uses the example in a quite different connection.
37 Ibid., pp. 35–6.

other things about Fred, and take another element and use it to say that other things than Fred are asleep.[37]

A familiar instance of this same intuition is to be found in the thought that, unless we discover in a linguistic expression of pain a predicate that can be coupled with other subject expressions, we do not readily allow that the expression of pain means that a particular object (this person) exemplifies a property (being in pain).[38]

The intuition is not restricted to the subject-predicate mode of combination. Quite generally, doubt can be cast on the correctness of an attribution of a complex meaning to a sentence by the absence of a range of structurally related sentences.

Strawson once described a language game that he called 'the naming game'.[39] The idea was that one would say 'cat' to respond to the presence of a cat or cats nearby, yet without having the notion of reidentifiable particular cats. Lacking that notion, one would not distinguish between the two cases of 'the same cat again' and 'another cat'. All later cat appearances would be classified simply as 'more cat'. The presence of the one-word sentence 'cat', used appropriately, and the absence of any structurally related sentences used to distinguish the case of the same cat again from that of another cat, would thus have consequences for the ascription of a meaning to 'cat'. It would cast doubt on the idea that 'cat' – as used in the naming game – means that there is *a cat* here. For the concept of a cat is the concept of a continuant – an object for which the question of identity through time arises. And the absence of structurally related sentences to mark the distinction between identity and difference over time suggests that the speakers lack that concept; they have the concept only of the *cat feature*.

What exactly is wrong with interpreting a sentence as meaning that Fred is asleep, when the sentence lacks articulation into

---

38 See P.F. Strawson, *Individuals* (Methuen, 1959), p. 99; and Evans, *The Varieties of Reference*, p. 103.
39 Strawson, *Individuals*, pp. 205–7. For a related, though more complex, example, see G. Evans, 'Identity and predication', *Journal of Philosophy*, 72 (1975); and for more on the attribution of attitudes, see C. Peacocke, *Sense and Content* (Oxford University Press, 1983), pp. 78–86, on the *tightness constraint*.

subject and predicate, or is treated by the speaker as if it lacked such structure? Blackburn's answer is this: 'It pretends they are saying complex things when the absence of any elements corresponding to the complexities *proves* that they are not.'[40] The obvious first move here is to point out that it is possible to set up a special language containing a sentence – structured or unstructured – and to stipulate that this sentence means that Fred is asleep. A sentence can be stipulated to have that, or any other, meaning.

The equally obvious response is that the stipulation will itself have to be performed in a language; and it can then be claimed that in *that* language there will have to be elements corresponding to the complexities of meanings, and there will have to be a range of structurally related sentences.

The doctrine of essential linguistic structure is at its most plausible in respect of first languages, and is so restricted by Blackburn. However, even restricted to first languages, a strong version of the doctrine – requiring that *all* complexity of meaning should be matched by complexity of expression – would not be very plausible.

Is it, for example, absolutely obvious that the word 'bachelor' could not mean 'unmarried male' unless we had words that individually meant 'unmarried' and 'male', in terms of which 'bachelor' was stipulatively introduced? Is it not conceivable that someone might use the word 'bachelor' in such a way that his total linguistic and non-linguistic behaviour provided very good evidence that the word meant 'unmarried male'? And if an unstructured expression could mean that, then why could not 'unmarried male' mean that, and yet be treated as unstructured by speakers?

Once again, we must suspect that the doctrine of essential linguistic structure elevates a *prima facie* requirement into an absolute requirement.

---

40 Blackburn, *Spreading the Word*, p. 36 (my italics). In fact, the claim in this sentence is stronger than the position Blackburn argues for when he returns to the topic at pp. 139–40. So it should not be taken as perfectly representative of Blackburn's view.

MEANING AND THE STRUCTURE OF THOUGHT

There is no incompatibility between rejection of the doctrine and acceptance of the *prima facie* practical requirements on radical interpretation. In the absence of structure, interpretation – including domestic interpretation – is more difficult. But special circumstances surrounding the use of even an unstructured sentence may render interpretation feasible. It might be, for example, that particular objects (say, Fred) and particular properties (say, being asleep) play such a role in the life of the community as to make particular thoughts (say, the thought that Fred is asleep) peculiarly salient.

The view that I wish to defend is thus as follows. Facts about linguistic structure are indeed constitutively connected to facts about sentence meaning. For it is *a priori* the case that facts about structure are *prima facie* evidence for and against particular attributions of sentence meaning. Nevertheless, the *prima facie* evidence can sometimes be overridden, for there may be other relevant evidence that renders very plausible the attribution of a sentence meaning which was *prima facie* implausible given the absence of structurally related sentences. There may be some alternative explanation as to why a speaker fails to make use of structurally related sentences that we would expect her to produce and comprehend.

Indeed, if the *prima facie* evidence is to be overridden then there *must* be some alternative explanation of the lack of the expected linguistic structure. And the need is heightened by the considerations about what would make interpretation possible in the absence of structure.[41] But alternative explanations are not utterly inconceivable; failure to make any use of structurally related sentences could be explained by the speaker's false belief that a particular sentence lacked significant syntactic structure, for example. It is in this sense that the doctrine of essential linguistic

---

41 I am grateful to Simon Blackburn for stressing the point that, in order for the *prima facie* evidence to be overridden, an alternative explanation of it must be available. See Blackburn, *Spreading the Word*, pp. 139–40, where his position is not very different from the one that I am defending.

structure expresses a constitutive *prima facie* requirement rather than an absolute requirement.

What is crucial here is that intuitions about the significance of the absence of certain sentences rest upon a more fundamental – and absolute – principle. If a subject is to mean that Fred is asleep by an utterance of hers – if she is to express that belief – then she must, of course, be capable of the thought that Fred (that particular object) exemplifies the property of being asleep. Now, according to the generality constraint, if she is to have that thought then she must be capable of entertaining the supposition that b is asleep, for every object b of which she has a conception, and of entertaining the supposition that Fred is G, for every property of being G of which she has a conception. She cannot mean that Fred is asleep unless she can think other things about Fred, and think of objects other than Fred that they are asleep. According to the generality constraint, that is not merely a *prima facie* requirement, but an absolute condition. But then, the pattern of a subject's linguistic behaviour is a crucial source of evidence about what thoughts the subject is capable of entertaining – about what concepts she deploys, and what distinctions she makes. So, at one remove, there is a connection between the presence or absence of certain sentences and whether the subject can really mean that Fred is asleep; but the connection is now *prima facie* rather than absolute. It is an absolute condition that there be two series of *thoughts*, with the thought that Fred is asleep at their intersection. It is a *prima facie* requirement that there be a corresponding pair of series of *sentences*, with the sentence that putatively means that Fred is asleep at their intersection.

On this view, the intuitions about structure and sentence meaning rest upon a fundamental principle about thought – the generality constraint – plus a crucial evidential connection between language and thought. So, for example, the reason why the absence of a certain range of sentences can cast doubt on the idea that a particular expression means that I am in pain comes in two stages. First, it cannot be that I am capable of the thought that I am in pain, but incapable of entertaining the supposition concerning any other object that it is in pain. Second, the absence of related sentences is *prima facie* evidence for the absence of related thoughts. For if I mean by an expression that I am in pain, and am able to frame other thoughts – b is in pain, c is in pain, . . . – then one would reasonably expect that I could use related expressions to express those related thoughts. If I do not do so, then that fact requires explanation.

CONCLUSION

In his widely influential paper 'On the frame of reference',[42] John Wallace suggested a kind of structural constraint on semantic theories:

> If we are thinking of translating natural languages, and of applying truth theory to natural languages, it seems reasonable to require that every sentence built from vocabulary that occurs in translations be a translation. The motivation for this requirement is that it is hard to see how one can have good reason to attribute to someone the ability to express, e.g., 'someone loves someone' and 'someone is taller than someone' without having good reason to attribute to him the ability to express, e.g., 'someone loves someone taller than himself.'[43]

This imposes a strict requirement on semantic theories. In effect, Wallace's constraint requires that the complexity of sentences must go in step with the complexity of meanings. In my view, this is not quite the constraint we want.[44]

What *is* correct is that if the thought that p can be constructed from the conceptual resources deployed in the thoughts expressed by various sentences $s_1, \ldots, s_n$, then a speaker who uses those sentences to express those thoughts must have the conceptual resources for entertaining the *thought* that p.

There are then three further conditional truths. First, *if* a speaker can express linguistically every thought that she can

---

42 J. Wallace, 'On the frame of reference', in *Semantics of Natural Language*, eds D. Davidson and G. Harman (Reidel, 1972).
43 Ibid., p. 225.
44 I discussed Wallace's constraint at length in 'Meaning and structure' (see fn. 5).

entertain, then there should indeed be some sentence that she can use to express the thought that p. Second, *if* the syntactic articulation within the sentences $s_1, \ldots, s_n$ matches the conceptual articulation within the expressed thoughts, then there should be a sentence s which is structurally related to the sentences $s_1, \ldots, s_n$, and which, in the language in question, means that p. Third, *if*, in addition, a speaker is sensitive to the systematic connection between form and meaning in the sentences $s_1, \ldots, s_n$, then the structurally related sentence s will be one that she can herself use to express the thought that p.

These three conditionals are true, but in my view their antecedents may conceivably fail to obtain. More may be thinkable than is expressible in any given language. A simple sentence may yet express a complex thought. And a speaker may be blind to some of the systematicity that is present in her language.

There is, then, a fundamental truth lying behind Wallace's constraint – as behind the doctrine of essential linguistic structure. But the constraint itself is strictly incorrect, for it imposes directly upon language a requirement of structure that is properly a condition upon thought. That condition, which finds partial expression in Evans's generality constraint, also promises illumination of the distinction between beliefs and subdoxastic states. But the full significance of the essential structure of thought is something that we are, as yet, far from understanding.[45]

---

[45] For comments on an earlier version of this chapter, I am grateful to Simon Blackburn, Jeremy Butterfield, Max Coltheart, Jerry Fodor, Mark Sainsbury, Charles Travis, and Crispin Wright.

6

Conceptual structure

John Campbell

In *The Interpretation of Frege's Philosophy* Dummett characterizes the 'basic tenet' of analytical philosophy as '(i) an account of language does not presuppose an account of thought, (ii) an account of language yields an account of thought, and (iii) there is no other adequate means by which an account of thought may be given.'[1] I want to consider the account which an analytical philosopher gives of a fundamental problem: namely, to explain why a grasp of the truth condition of a thought requires a grasp of its conceptual structure.

Why do we have such difficulty with the idea of, as it were, a *blank* apprehension of the truth condition of a thought; one which does not involve a grasp of the way its structure fixes its truth value? One may grasp a thought by, for example, knowing which thing is in question and which property it is conceived to have. Why could one not, *without* this grasp of structure, know the condition for it to be true? I want to begin by briefly commenting on the way in which an analytical philosopher might approach this question.

The notions of *truth* and *structure* play key roles in Davidson's communication-theoretic approach to thought; let us consider how they are connected. We may remark first that possession of a concept in general requires one to grasp a range of related ideas

---

1 M.A.E. Dummett, *The Interpretation of Frege's Philosophy* (London, 1981), p. 39.

which 'make the concept available', which provide the context in which one finds the concept intelligible. According to Davidson, the capacity for communication provides the conceptual 'surround' required for a grasp of the notion of objective truth. For communication requires the participants to think of themselves as inhabiting the same world; which suggests that the capacity to communicate suffices for the concept of truth. 'To complete the "argument"', Davidson writes, 'I need to show that the *only* way one could come to have the subjective–objective contrast is through having the concept of intersubjective truth. I confess I do not know how to show this. But neither do I have any idea how else one might arrive at the concept of an objective truth.' He concludes: 'Our sense of objectivity is the consequence of [a] sort of triangulation, one that requires two creatures. Each interacts with an object, but what gives each the concept of how things objectively are is the base line formed between the creatures by language.'[2]

On this approach, a grasp of something with an objective truth condition is a grasp of something communicable. We are to look to an account of communication to explain why this must be a grasp of something *structured*. And the approach to communication offered by the theory of radical interpretation may seem to promise just that. For the radical interpreter, on Davidson's account, must discern structure in the language he seeks to understand.[3]

This does not explain why a grasp of the truth condition of a thought requires a grasp of its conceptual structure, however. The fact that the radical interpreter must discern structure in the language by no means shows that all who grasp it must do so.

Furthermore, even if we waive this point, we have not yet been shown the *connection* between a grasp of truth condition and a grasp of structure; they might simply be independent though complementary aspects of a grasp of a thought. What we want to understand is the connection.

2 D. Davidson, 'Rational animals', *Dialectica*, 36 (1982), pp. 317–27; at p. 327.
3 D. Davidson, *Inquiries into Truth and Interpretation* (Oxford, 1984), pp. 127ff.

It may be that we can in the end provide an analytical or communication-theoretic account of why a grasp of the truth condition of a thought requires a grasp of its conceptual structure. I postpone consideration of this question in order to develop an alternative account of the relation between a grasp of truth condition and a grasp of conceptual structure. I shall then return to the communication-theoretic approach.

OBJECTIVE TRUTH

I want to begin by questioning Davidson's conception of the conceptual 'surround' required to make available the notion of objective truth. An account of communication must surely depend on the idea of different perspectives on the same temporal order; but the dependence appears to be asymmetric. No appeal to communication-theoretic notions seems to be needed in explaining what makes available the conception of the objective temporal order.

The fundamental idea here is rather that the subject takes his perceptions to be *explained* jointly by the way things objectively are, and his own place in the objective order. In filling out what makes this conception available to the subject, we show what provides him with the notion of objective truth.

The subject must have the conception of the objective temporal order being as it is independently of whether he perceives it. He must be able to make sense of the notion of existence unperceived. What makes this notion available is the subject's conception of the *enabling conditions* of perception.

For us, the enabling conditions of perception are *spatial*. Thus in order to see something, for example, one must be appropriately located with respect to it, appropriately oriented, and there must be nothing in the way. To touch something, one must be spatially contiguous to it. And so on. Further, one must meet these spatial conditions at an appropriate *time*. What constitutes an appropriate time? We might naturally suppose that to perceive something, one must be there when it happens – that perception and the perceived are in general simultaneous.

What makes it intelligible that a is F, even though one cannot perceive that a is F, is one's knowledge that a's being F is not sufficient for one to perceive that a is F. There are further, enabling conditions, both spatial and temporal, which must be met.

One's view of the enabling conditions of perception is *corrigible*. This is illustrated by the discovery of time lags in perception. The point should not lead one to conclude that there is a 'state of nature' in which one operates with *no* conception of the enabling conditions of perception; one's view of the enabling conditions is something which can only be developed from within.

To say that one conceives of one's perceptions as explained jointly by the objective temporal order and one's own position in it, is to say that one can make sense of the idea that the objective order of events is not uniquely determined by the order of one's perceptions. Thus one must be able to distinguish between perception of successive states of affairs and successive perceptions of coexistent states of affairs. So for example, suppose that one is observing a fairground. One has to be able to distinguish two cases. In the first, one observes a big wheel which stops rotating just as one ceases to observe it, and then observes another big wheel which starts rotating just as one begins watching it. In the second case, one successively observes two big wheels which are rotating simultaneously. One cannot apply this distinction by reference simply to the order and content of one's perceptions of the events in question; for they may be the same in both cases. What one must appeal to is one's sense of the *causal* order – one's grasp of the processes involved in starting and stopping. One's grasp of the temporal order in which things are happening rests upon one's grasp of causal regularities.

The intuitive physics which we first bring to bear on the objective time order is not true *a priori*. Indeed it is plausible to see medieval 'impetus' mechanics as a formulation of a fragment of our intuitive physics. The commitment of this mechanics to the idea of preservation of circular motion, and to the idea that motion is sustained by impetal force, for example, well match the expectations of untutored common sense. And in these respects, 'impetus' mechanics is not true. The intuitive physics which we use in operating with the notion of the objective time order is not conceived by us to be incorrigible; it can be, and it has been, corrected. What the subject of thought requires in the first instance, however, is just a sufficiency of background theory to enable the process of correction to begin; his conception of the world can be developed only from within.

It would surely be wrong, incidentally, to suppose that the intuitive physics we use is entirely composed of a mechanics of motion. Other factors which we would naturally take into account in operating with the conception of the objective time order include the time it takes for fire to heat and for wounds to heal, and the persistence of enduring objects.

For us, the intuitive physics relates to the behaviour of objects in a three-dimensional space, as opposed, for example, to a world with only one dimension other than time, or a world of purely qualitative features. We can use the idea of the intuitive physics to illuminate a certain widely recognized structural feature of our spatial thinking: that is, the distinction between thought of objects at the level of a cognitive map of one's environment, and demonstrative thoughts of spatial objects.

The contrast is ordinarily drawn in terms of connections with *action*. One uses mental maps in finding one's way around. The utility of one's mental map of, say, the centre of a town with which one is familiar, depends upon the fact that there is no unique viewpoint which one must occupy in order to think of the landmarks in the town centre at the level of the mental map. Wherever one is, the map is available to help one find one's way around. Contrast demonstrative ways of thinking. Such a way of thinking of an object is made available by one's current perception of it; the availability of this way of thinking of the thing does depend upon one's current viewpoint. Such ways of thinking of objects are not used directly at the level of one's mental map; but they are needed if one is to bring the map to bear upon the objects one perceives. One can act with respect to an object only if one can demonstrate it. That is how the contrast between mental maps and demonstratives is ordinarily drawn, in terms of connections with action. From our standpoint, however, the more fundamental contrast has to be drawn in terms of *cognition*. For in operating with the conception of the objective time order, one must use an intuitive physics; and for us, the intuitive physics applies in the first instance to spatial objects thought of at the level of the mental map. One has to be able to think in terms of a network of law-governed processes going on around one whether one perceives them or not – quite independently of whether one is in a position to demonstrate the objects involved or not. That is how one must think of objects in using the conception of the objective time order; it is how one must think of the big wheels at the fairground, for example, in finding whether their rotations were successive or simultaneous. Though the physics applies in the first instance at the level of the cognitive map, however, one must ultimately be able to bring it to bear upon demonstrated objects if its bearing upon the time orders of the things one perceives is to be recognizable. And it must ultimately be brought to bear upon perceptually demonstrated objects if it is to be possible to *correct* the physics in the light of experience.

This account provides, in barest outline, a statement of what is involved in possession of the idea of a shared world about which we can communicate. What the communicator has is a conception of his own perceptions as explained by the objective temporal order, together with a sense of the general enabling conditions of perception and his own route through that order. What provides him with his conception of other points of view on that same objective order is just his grasp of the possibility of the last component being filled out in different ways, yielding different courses of perception of the same world – a world about which communication is therefore possible.

The account I have given surely provides *enough* to make intelligible the idea of objective truth. Yet it has been possible to give the account without any overt appeal to communication-theoretic notions. What role could there be for concepts of communication in explaining what makes available the notion of objective truth?

GRASP OF STRUCTURE

What may be maintained is that only an approach in terms of communication-theoretic notions can explain why it is intrinsic to a grasp of the objective truth condition of a thought that one grasp the conceptual articulation of the thought. I shall begin by setting out the datum, then provide an explanation of it in terms of the account so far, and finally return to the approach in terms of language.

We are concerned here with the idea of conceptual structure which one must grasp in grasping a thought. This idea imposes global constraints on the ascription of thought – constraints which may be summed up by saying that subjects of thought are possessors of concepts.

We have already touched on one of these constraints. To have any concepts at all, one must have a repertoire of concepts, a range of concepts providing the surround within which each is intelligible. To grasp any concept at all, however elementary, one must already grasp a *system* of concepts.

It is to some such constraint as this that Wittgenstein was pointing when he wrote: 'When we first begin to *believe* anything, what we believe is not a single proposition, it is a whole system of propositions. (Light dawns gradually over the whole.)'[4]

This 'intelligibility' constraint is not the only one imposed by the thought that subjects of thought are possessors of concepts. It requires also that a subject ascribed one set of propositional attitudes must be capable of grasping a wider range of thoughts – namely, those obtained by permutating the concepts ascribed to him in the initial ascription (perhaps within categorial limits). So, for example, if we ascribe to a man a grasp of the natural numbers, and the belief that his car is travelling at 50 m.p.h., but then find that there is no state into which he can go which would constitute his having the thought of his car travelling at any other speed, then on the face of it the initial ascription was wrong.

In consequence of this, thought meets what Evans called the *generality constraint*.[5] If someone has the thought that a is F, then he must know what it is for something to be a; so he must be capable of grasping the thoughts that a is G, that a is H, and so on, for each conception of a property he has. Similarly, if someone has the thought that a is F, then he must know what it is for something

---

4 L. Wittgenstein, *On Certainty* (Oxford, 1974), Section 141.
5 G. Evans, *The Varieties of Reference* (Oxford, 1982), p. 100.

to be F; so he must be capable of grasping the thoughts that b is F, that c is F, and so on, for each way of thinking of an object available to him. It is not, of course, that he must be capable of grasping all such thoughts simultaneously; only that for each one, he must be capable of grasping it.

To say that one grasps the truth condition of a thought by grasping its conceptual structure is, then, to say that a grasp of the truth condition of a thought requires that one bring to bear a repertoire of concepts constituting a framework within which the concepts used in the thought are *intelligible*; and it requires that one conform to the 'permutation' constraint just indicated. Yet though we naturally feel very strongly that one grasps the truth condition of a thought by grasping its conceptual structure, there is a question about why this is so.

The alternative view would be that one's grasp of the conceptual structure of a thought is, as it were, *external* to one's grasp of its truth condition; that a grasp of the conceptual structure of a thought is at best *derivative* upon one's grasp of its truth condition. On this view, one's grasp of the truth condition of a thought does not at all *exploit* one's grasp of its conceptual structure.

We can see how this alternative view might be developed by considering first how one might defend the view that it is intrinsic to a grasp of the truth condition of a thought that one grasp its conceptual articulation. When we eschew appeal to the communication-theoretic approach, the natural defence begins with the idea that a grasp of the truth condition of a thought requires that one grasp its inferential relations to other thoughts. And one's grasp of the inferential role of a thought exploits precisely the structure in one's propositional states forced by the 'conceptual' constraints indicated above.

One's capacity to engage in inference to the best explanation may be held to require that one operate with a *range* of concepts which one uses in framing one's background conception of the world. And deductive inference generally exploits the fact that one's thought meets the 'permutation' constraint. For example, it is exploited when one infers that a is F from the thoughts that b is F and that a is identical to b. What the 'permutation' constraint secures is precisely that anyone who grasps the premises must be capable of grasping the conclusion.

Were it not for the availability of some such account as this, the point of the 'conceptual' constraints would be hard to fathom without recourse to the communication-theoretic view. For when we ascribe propositional attitudes to someone, the work of explanation and prediction which this enables us to perform is directed entirely at *propositional* states. Why then in ascribing propositional attitudes should we not ascribe sets of thoughts *en bloc*, without regard to the 'conceptual' constraints? Were the appeal to the notion of *inference* not available, it would be hard to see why those constraints are essential to explanation or prediction. Yet this appeal to the notion of inference does not of itself settle whether one's grasp of the truth condition of a thought exploits one's grasp of its conceptual structure.

We can characterize the position of one who returns a negative answer to this question by first noting a qualification needed in the account proposed so far. Notice to begin with that we ought not to maintain that in grasping a thought one must grasp all the concepts which can be, as it were, *extracted* from it. So, for example, consider the thought 'If Roscoe shot Roscoe, then Roscoe did it with a silencer.' We do not want to have to say that, in grasping what it is for this thought to be true, one must grasp the concept 'if x shot Roscoe, then x did it with a silencer.' At most, we want to say that grasping the truth condition of the thought will involve grasping the way in which the thought is constructed out of simple concepts, which may involve one in grasping such notions as 'x shot y' and 'x did y with z.' There is an element of *conceptual creativity* in recognizing that the thought can be viewed as containing the complex concept 'if x shot Roscoe, then x did it with a silencer.' This conceptual creativity is exploited in one's grasp of the thought 'If anyone shot Roscoe, he did it with a silencer.' Grasping this thought really does require that one grasp it as constructed using the complex concept 'if x shot Roscoe, then x did it with a silencer.' And there is a conceptually creative element, involving one's capacity to spot a new pattern in a familiar thought, in grasping that concept by extracting it from 'If Roscoe shot Roscoe, then Roscoe did it with a silencer.'

We cannot, therefore, maintain that it is *intrinsic* to one's grasp of the truth condition of 'If Roscoe shot Roscoe, then Roscoe did it with a silencer', that one grasp that it can be deduced from 'If anyone shot Roscoe, then he did it with a silencer.' For there is a conceptually creative element involved in discerning the complex concept in the former thought which is used in constructing the latter. It was by appeal to this conceptually creative aspect of inference that Frege in the *Grundlagen* explained the fruitfulness of deduction.[6]

In explaining one's grasp of certain of the inferential relations of a thought, therefore, one will have to appeal to *both* one's grasp of the truth condition of the thought *and* one's capacity for conceptual creativity. It cannot plausibly be maintained that one's grasp of *all* the inferential relations of a thought is internal to one's grasp of its truth condition. We need, therefore, to make more judicious use of the notion of inference if we are to appeal to it in explaining why one's grasp of the truth condition of a thought exploits one's grasp of its conceptual structure.

What I have been pressing here is what Dummett calls the distinction between the *analysis* and the *decomposition* of thoughts.[7] Conceptual creativity enters in grasping the various ways in which the thought may be decomposed, in discerning new patterns within it. It may be pointed out, however, that one's capacity to discern new patterns in a thought depends upon a prior grasp of structure. It depends upon a prior grasp of what we may call its *original* structure – the structure which Dummett describes as revealed by analysis. This shows the stages in which the thought is constructed from constituent concepts. And the thesis now must be that one grasps the truth condition of a thought by grasping its original structure.

So, for example, it may be pointed out that one's discernment of the complex concept 'if x shot Roscoe, then x did it with a silencer' in the thought 'If Roscoe shot Roscoe, then Roscoe did it with a silencer' depends upon one's grasp of the thought as constructed using such concepts as 'x shot y' and 'x did y with z.' And the thesis is that one grasps the truth condition of the thought by grasping the latter structure.

---

6 G. Frege, *The Foundations of Arithmetic* (Oxford, 1978), Section 88.
7 Dummett, *The Interpretation of Frege's Philosophy*, pp. 271ff.

The proponent of the view that one's grasp of the truth condition of a thought does *not* exploit one's grasp of its conceptual structure need not deny the distinction between decomposition and analysis, or the thesis that one's grasp of the structure revealed by decomposition rests upon one's grasp of the structure revealed by analysis. What he maintains is that grasp of the latter structure is extrinsic to one's grasp of the truth condition of the thought. He may acknowledge that the capacity to spot the original structures of the thoughts whose truth conditions we grasp is fundamental to our cognitive lives – something that is even more fundamental than the elementary capacity for conceptual creativity already remarked. His contention is only that this capacity is extrinsic to one's grasp of truth conditions, that grasp of structure is *derivative* upon one's grasp of truth conditions.

This is a view to which, I think, we naturally feel a strong resistance. The task is to explain why. I want to begin by showing that we need not accept the explanation offered by the communication-theoretic approach.

CONCEPTUAL CONTENT

In 'Objective truth' we remarked on certain forms of reasoning which seem constitutive of our possession of the very idea of objective truth. I want now to show that the capacity to engage in these forms of reasoning requires and exploits the fact that one's thought meets the 'conceptual' constraints. The suggestion is that this explains why it is that one's grasp of the truth condition of a thought exploits one's grasp of its conceptual structure; for one's grasp of its truth condition rests upon one's capacity to engage in these core patterns of inference.

As we have seen, we cannot maintain a grasp of all the inferential relations of a thought to be constitutive of a grasp of truth condition; what we have to do, therefore, is appeal to one's grasp of some subset of the inferential relations in which the thought stands as being constitutive of one's grasp of the condition for it to be true. And we have to show that this subset is sufficiently rich to demand that the 'conceptual' constraints be met.

These core patterns of inference concern the application of the idea of the objective temporal order as explaining the succession of one's perceptions. As we remarked, for us the explanatory scheme here is *spatial*. The subject operates with a mental map of his environment, together with some conception of his location and a grasp of the enabling conditions of perception. This requires him to grasp a *range* of ideas of spatial objects.

He has to think of the objective temporal order, conceived of at the level of the mental map, as being what explains the course of his perceptions. We saw that this requires him to be able to think of the states of affairs he successively perceives as having obtained either simultaneously or successively. Notice, however, that if such distinctions are to be intelligible to him at all, he must be capable of varying the temporal indicators while holding constant the remainder of the conceptual content of a thought. He has to be able, for example, to think of each state of affairs he observes as he moves around a village both as obtaining at the time of his perception – the time he then thinks of as *now* – and as having obtained continuously and simultaneously over some past period. And he must be able to think of states of affairs he successively perceives both as obtaining *now* and as having obtained *successively*. He requires, that is, a repertoire of temporal indicators, and the capacity to deploy them in a variety of permutations with his conceptions of particular states of affairs. In this local way, his thought must meet the 'conceptual' constraints.

As we saw, the range of ideas of spatial objects which the subject has must be within the scope of the intuitive physics he uses in finding the objective order of events. If the physics is to be brought appropriately to bear in finding the objective time order, then it must be intelligible that it be *repeatedly* applicable to each of the things he conceives of. The properties mentioned in the regularities constituting the physics must each be intelligibly applicable to the various things he encounters. So again, this minimal pattern of reasoning requires that the 'conceptual' constraints be locally met.

The physics must also be *controlled* by experience; it is not *a priori* true. And this again requires that in developing his physics in response to experience, the subject be able to bring it to bear repeatedly on the objects he perceives. So again, the subject must be able to combine his conceptions of the properties employed by the physics in a variety of permutations with his ideas of the objects perceived.

Evidently, furthermore, to grasp the physics at all requires that one grasp the repertoire of concepts which it employs. For us, basic mechanical concepts, for example, form a system in which each concept is made intelligible by its relations to the rest.

Finally, as we saw, it is not enough that one be able to think of the range of objects around one at the level of the mental map. At the level of the mental map, one must indeed be capable of combining each of one's ideas of a spatial object with each of one's conceptions of the properties invoked by the intuitive physics, and this in combination with any of a variety of temporal indicators. But if the physics is to be appropriately brought to bear upon and controlled by experience, this apparatus must also be related to one's *demonstrative* ideas of spatial objects. So one must be capable of combining one's concepts of the properties invoked by the physics with demonstrative ideas. The 'conceptual' constraints must again be locally met.

This suggests, then, that the *Verstehen*, the sense of how the world seems to the subject, which propositional attitude ascription provides, depends upon the 'conceptual' constraints being met; for they are required and exploited by his capacity for the peculiarly central, peculiarly simple forms of reasoning which constitute his having the conception of himself as in an objective world. That is why we can say that one's grasp of the truth condition of a thought exploits one's grasp of its conceptual structure. For it is constitutive of one's grasp of what it is for this thought to be true that one be able to use it in these forms of reasoning; and that involves a grasp of its structure.

Cognitive science has made us familiar with the ascription of content to input systems, with the view of our perceptual systems as information processors. There is a question whether the ascription of content here is governed by the 'conceptual' constraints. The account I have given so far has been concerned with the thought of a subject, rather than with representational content in general. It leaves it open that input systems are *not* governed by the 'conceptual' constraints, and that in *that* sense their content is non-conceptual.

There are two central differences between this type of content and thought. There is in general, first, no such thing as the world view of an informational subsystem. In ascribing thoughts, we are ascribing a world view and aiming to show the apparent reasonableness, in that context, of the agent's propositional states and doings. In the case of an informational subsystem, what takes the place of this global rationality constraint is, in the simplest cases, some conception of the *point* of the subsystem, of what the subsystem is *for*. This conception of the point of the subsystem will be controlled by our grasp of how it has *evolved*; and in ascribing content, what we are aiming to do is to show *how* the subsystem subserves that point. This global constraint is exactly on a par with the global constraint of rationality; it is not somehow a version of it, as if we were in dealing with an informational subsystem merely dealing with a subject whose world view was severely restricted. There is certainly illumination to be had through the ascription of content to input systems; but that illumination is manifestly not the illumination of *Verstehen*.

The second contrast between this type of content and thought is connected. It is that an informational subsystem need not be capable of the peculiarly central, peculiarly simple forms of reasoning constitutive of possession of the conception of oneself as in an objective world. The computation which input systems perform in general operates by successively bringing to bear stronger and stronger physical assumptions about the environment, to wring stronger and stronger conclusions from the initial data. This computation is often not satisfactorily characterizable as deduction, or as inference to the best explanation of the type in which subjects of thought engage; it is a separate category. Consequently, while there certainly are broadly structural constraints on the ascription of content to informational subsystems, there is no reason to suppose that they are identical to the structural constraints on the ascription of thought. In particular, there is no reason to suppose that input systems are subject to the 'conceptual' constraints we have isolated.

STRUCTURE AND COMMUNICATION

Let us return to the analytical or communication-theoretic approach to a grasp of conceptual structure. We may begin by asking whether such an account can accommodate Dummett's point (made in a passage generally hospitable to the analytic approach) that there cannot be two differently structured sentences which express the very same thought. That is, the structure of language does not merely provide what Dummett calls a 'map-reference' system for the identification of thoughts. There is no room for a third feature of sentences, beyond the thought they express and their truth value, which is the *way* in which they identify thoughts. Rather, we have to say that grasping the structure of the sentence just is grasping the structure of the thought it expresses.[8]

In explaining why a grasp of a thought requires a grasp of structure, the proponent of the communication-theoretic approach has to go by way of an assurance that communication requires a grasp of structure. Yet now, suppose we ask why, on this account, communication requires a grasp of structure. Here a dilemma opens up for the communication theorist. He may, first, maintain that the demand for structure arises because of very general facts about the cognitive powers of human beings. Thus he may with Davidson point to ways in which humans are *finite*.[9] But there is a very general problem for this line of approach. All it provides is an explanation of why the system we use for identifying thoughts is of a certain type; why we require, for example, a finitely structured 'map-reference' system. It provides no explanation at all of how it is that one's grasp of the truth condition of a thought exploits one's grasp of its structure.

Alternatively, it may be maintained that the reason why communication requires a grasp of structure is just that one must grasp the structure of the thought expressed. This actually seems correct, as far as it goes. But it steers us against the analytical approach. For

[8] Ibid., pp. 40ff.
[9] Davidson, *Inquiries into Truth*, pp. 8 – 9.

now we must ask why a grasp of the thought expressed requires a grasp of its structure; and this points us towards an account of the type which I have been outlining, in terms of one's grasp of the conception of oneself as in an objective world.

When we look to Davidson's work for an explanation of why a grasp of the truth condition of a thought requires a grasp of its structure, we may be struck by such comments as: 'A belief is identified by its location in a pattern of belief; it is this pattern that determines the subject-matter of the belief, what the belief is about.'[10] These comments may seem more in sympathy with the account I have outlined. They may, however, be read as ultimately based on appeal to the demand that the radical interpreter must discern structure.

To abandon the analytical approach here would not settle all questions of the relative priorities of language and thought in philosophical explanation. The point would be only that there is *one* axis of explanation, concerning the relation between a grasp of truth condition and a grasp of conceptual structure, along which language is posterior to thought.

This point is however of critical importance if we are interested in the project of finding an account of the various *ways* in which thoughts are structured. *De facto*, a great deal of illumination on this issue has come from work on the way in which language is structured. But if the point I have been pressing is correct, there is another, more fundamental approach.

This approach would take the fundamental structures in our thought to require classification in the light of the way they contribute to our conception of ourselves as in an objective world. And it draws its insights not from the study of language, but from the traditional concerns of metaphysics.

---

10 Ibid., p. 168.

Part III
Content and Truth

7
Meaning and metaphysics
S. D. Guttenplan

Some people believe that there exist objects, events and states, many but not all of which are material, and that the properties and relations of these constitute a world which is independent of human concerns and which can, in many instances, transcend human capacities to know or even form beliefs about it. Such people are realists. However, even though we can recognize the doctrine of realism in the above form of words, this expression of that doctrine is too vague to be of much use in close philosophic examination. Or so it has seemed to a number of writers.

Recently, some have sought to effect a great improvement in the characterization of realism by switching to the 'formal' mode.[1] By their lights, realism is the doctrine that our beliefs and claims are true, when they are, because of the disposition of features of the world, whether or not we are in or can get ourselves into a position from which we can ascertain this. Construed in this way, realism is essentially a doctrine about the truth predicate. The gains which this characterization are meant to effect all flow from the fact that we have a greater philosophic purchase on the concept of truth than we do on any notions in the largely metaphorical description

---

Versions of this chapter were read at Cambridge in 1981 and at St Andrews in 1984. I am grateful for comments on it that were made by Hugh Mellor and Crispin Wright.

1 A very explicit account of this is in D. Wiggins, 'What would be a substantial theory of truth', in *Philosophical Subjects: essays presented to P.F. Strawson*, ed. Z. van Straaten (Oxford University Press, Oxford, 1980).

of realism with which this chapter opened. In particular, since there is a considerable body of opinion which sees the concept of truth as central to meaning, and since the accounts we give of meaning are arguably constrained in many interesting ways, we apparently can expect that, in one way or another, results in the area of meaning theory will have consequences for metaphysics. It is my intention to see whether, and if so how, this expectation can be realized.

This task is, of course, much too ambitious for just one essay, so I shall limit myself here to a more manageable subtask. Dummett and, following him, Wright have argued that constraints which must be respected by any proper account of meaning rule out the possibility of using the realistically construed concept of truth in such an account.[2] They propose that the realistically understood truth predicate must be replaced in the account of meaning by some non- (or anti-) realist predicate such as 'warranted assertability'. Much has been, and continues to be, written about Dummett's arguments *against* realist truth and *for* assertability in accounts of meaning. I shall not add to that corpus here. My interest lies *not* in the so-called anti-realist 'constraints' on meaning but rather in the purported argumentative connection between accounts of meaning so constrained and metaphysics. The central question here is: if we accept Dummett's arguments about meaning, are we thereby committed to a recognizably anti-realist ('non-realist' is a better word here) metaphysics? Dummett seems persuaded of an affirmative answer here. He writes:

> Whether we can attribute to ourselves a grasp of such a conception of [realist truth], or whether our impression that we have it is

---

2 For M. Dummett's views see (among other pieces) 'What is a theory of meaning?', in *Mind and Language*, ed. S.D. Guttenplan (Oxford University Press, Oxford, 1975); 'What is a theory of meaning (II)?', in *Truth and Meaning*, ed. G. Evans and J. McDowell (Oxford University Press, Oxford, 1976); the preface to his collected papers *Truth and Other Enigmas* (Duckworth, London, 1978); and 'The reality of the past' in that volume. For C. Wright's views see: 'Truth conditions and criteria', *Aristotelian Society Supplementary Volume*, XLV, 1976; 'Anti-realist semantics: the role of criteria', in *Idealism: Past and Present*, Royal Institute of Philosophy Lectures (1978).

an illusion caused by an illicit transference from the case of more primitive forms of sentence for whose understanding no such transcendent notions of truth and falsity are required, and in the former case, *when* we are entitled to claim to have such a conception, is the fundamental question underlying the various disputes concerning realism. It is therefore a question having widespread metaphysical repercussions. It is itself, however, a question belonging to the theory of meaning: the whole point of my approach to these problems has been to show that the theory of meaning underlies metaphysics.[3]

Terminology has been a problem in this area; so, before proceeding, I need to make a few remarks about it. One can find four philosophical items in play in the discussion so far. They are: (a) the metaphysical position of realism characterized either materially (and vaguely) or formally by means of features of the truth predicate; (b) the metaphysical position of anti-realism which has yet to be characterized save by its opposition to metaphysical realism; (c) an account of meaning for a language which centrally uses the realist truth predicate; (d) an account of meaning which is not wholly unlike that just mentioned but which uses some assertability predicate in place of the realist truth predicate.

Confusion here can come from two sources. First, even the most careful writers sometimes fail to make clear whether what is being described is metaphysical realism understood in the formal mode by means of properties of truth *or* an account of meaning which employs the realist truth predicate. Similar carelessness occurs in discussions of anti-realism. In each case there will be close links between the semantic and metaphysical views but, since I intend to discuss at least one of those links, I can hardly acquiesce in the misleading habit of using the labels 'realism' and 'anti-realism' indifferently of semantic and metaphysical theses.

The second terminological point is this. Many writers, and especially Dummett, have written as if the truth-conditional account of meaning was one and the same as the account of meaning which has the realist truth predicate as its central concept. This is all right in so far as one has made it clear that the concept of

[3] Dummett, *Truth and Other Enigmas*, p. xi.

truth in the truth-conditional account is stipulated to be the realist one. However, in the preface to *Truth and Other Enigmas* Dummett writes:

> Thus I should now be inclined to say that, under any theory of meaning whatever. . .we can represent the meaning (sense) of a sentence as given by the condition for it to be true, on some appropriate way of construing 'true': the problem is not whether meaning is to be explained in terms of truth conditions but of what notion of truth is admissible.[4]

This way of putting his position is far from happy. That it is explicitly a departure from his previous writings is a possible, though not serious, source of confusion (not made any better by his reversion to the older way of putting the problem later in the preface). What is important is that Dummett has, in this formulation, helped himself to a way of connecting meaning and metaphysics; as this chapter develops I shall show why I think that he has no such entitlement.

To avoid these and other possible confusions, I shall stick to my original classification of realist/anti-realist doctrines even at the cost of some clumsiness. By explicitly indicating whether meaning or metaphysics is at issue, I hope to keep attention more sharply focused on the argumentative connections between anti-realist semantics and metaphysics.

SHARED ASSUMPTIONS IN ACCOUNTS OF MEANING

Despite their disagreement over the central semantic notion, realist and anti-realist accounts of meaning share a number of fundamental presuppositions. Being clear about these (as well as about the disputed notion) will prove important to the later argument of this chapter. In this section I shall briefly outline both the main points of agreement (I have isolated four) and the arguments which separate the positions. The shared assumptions of realist and anti-realist semantics are far from platitudinous, though I shall not

---

4 Ibid., p. xxii.

attempt here to answer criticisms of those who are radically out of sympathy with these assumptions.[5]

The first point of agreement is that philosophical elucidation of the concept of meaning can best be achieved by setting out requirements for a theory of meaning for a specific language. As has been remarked more than once in the literature, this has led to an unhappy ambiguity in the phrase 'theory of meaning'. In this paper it will apply to any specific account of meaning proposed for a given language, and will *not* be used of whatever philosophical illumination we derive from such an account.

The second shared assumption is that the theory of meaning for a given language should proceed by characterizing some one feature of the use of sentences; it should treat some one such notion as central. This requirement is usually reckoned to carry with it a commitment to something like the Fregean distinction between sense and force. This is because the central notion has primary application to one sort of sentence use (usually the assertoric) so that provision for other sorts of sentence use must be made within an ancillary theory of force.

The third common presupposition is that the theory of meaning for a language must show how the meanings of sentences are systematically related – via the central notion – to the meanings of the subsentential components. If we, schematically, call the central notion 'θ', then one can view θ as a predicate of a certain class of sentence whose application is systematically determined by the various contributions which subsentential components make to that application. In a somewhat different idiom, it may be said that a theory of meaning for a language is, in part, a recursive theory of θ. The output of this recursion will consist of sentences of the form:

(A) s is θ if and only if . . .

---

5 I have in mind here those so-called 'convention-intention' views of meaning which seem hard to reconcile with the approach discussed in this chapter, and, of course, views that deny any plausibility to the project of constructing accounts of meaning for given languages.

where s is the name of a sentence of the language under consideration, and '...' can be said to give the meaning (or better, sense) of s. As you will appreciate later, there are reasons for being somewhat coy about the notion of 'giving the sense', but it is clear enough, I think, for present purposes.

There will of course be various constraints imposed on the output schematized in (A) which help to ensure that it appropriately pairs the substitutions for s and sense-giving specifications; spelling these out is not a job for this paper but, perhaps surprisingly, realists and anti-realists do not disagree about them. Where there is disagreement it is over the constraints which deal with possible specifications for θ. I shall insert a brief remark about this disagreement before mentioning the fourth and last point of agreement.

Let us suppose that the predicate θ, in some appropriately constrained recursive theory, is read as the realist truth predicate. That is, let us suppose that the predicate which centrally figures in the theory of sense is a truth predicate whose application to sentences might be such as to escape our ability to tell, in a given type of case, whether it did apply. Remember, for the realist it is perfectly conceivable that a sentence used by a speaker could be true even though that speaker, or indeed any other speaker, could not ascertain whether it is true. Truth, for the realist, is radically non-epistemic, and it is because of this that the anti-realist finds himself compelled to protest.

In barest outline, the protest takes the following form. A theory of sense is at least part of an account of what a speaker of a given language knows. The apparatus of the recursive theory generates, in Dummett's phrase, a theoretical representation of a practical ability to speak and understand a language. Given this, there are reasons for doubting whether the central notion in such a theoretical representation can be the realist's notion of truth. As Dummett has argued in many places, one cannot represent a speaker's knowledge in terms which, by hypothesis, preclude our justifying such a representation. In particular, when a speaker uses a sentence about the past, or a sentence of unrestricted generality – both of these being examples of so-called 'undecidable' or 'verification-transcendent' uses – his grasp of such sentences cannot be represented as a grasp of realist truth conditions. This is because, in as much as these sentences are verification transcendent, nothing the speaker does or could do would manifest, and hence justify, the attribution to him of such a grasp. Of course, the anti-realist in no way wants to be taken as denying the intelligibility of these uses of sentences; his only complaint is against the attempt to explain their intelligibility by means of the realist conception of truth.[6]

As I said at the outset, I shall not question this or related anti-realist arguments. There is a growing literature dealing with these arguments, and it must be apparent, even in my cursory sketch of the 'manifestation' argument, that there is a lot that is questionable.[7] None the less, my interest is in the metaphysical consequences of anti-realist semantics, so I shall concede to the anti-realist the cogency of the arguments that he uses to motivate his semantic programme. In particular, in what follows, I shall allow that these arguments establish the need to do semantics in terms of some epistemic notion such as warranted assertability.

The fourth, and final, point of agreement between the realist and anti-realist that I shall discuss is their acceptance of what Dummett calls the *equivalence thesis*: 'the thesis, namely, that, for any sentence, A, A is equivalent to "It is true that A"'.[8] Quite clearly more needs to be said about the notion of equivalence used in this gloss; that will be taken up shortly. Here it will suffice for me to indicate what I take to be the role of the thesis and to distinguish it, as Dummett also does, from the so-called 'redundancy' theory with which it is often confused.

Dummett's characterization of the thesis is not as general as it could be, so here is a revision of it which is more perspicuous – though it is in no way a distortion of Dummett's treatment. For any concept θ, a necessary condition for θ to be recognized as a truth predicate for a language L is that, for any sentence of L, if s is

---

6 For the mistake that is avoided here, see G. Hunter, 'Dummett's arguments about natural numbers', *Aristotelian Society Proceedings*, LXXX, 1979/80.
7 For a discussion of this see J. McDowell, 'Anti-realism and the epistemology of understanding', in *Meaning and Understanding*, ed. J. Bouveresse and H. Parret (de Gruyter, 1981).
8 Dummett, *Truth and Other Enigmas*, p. xx.

a name of that sentence, then it must be the case that θs is equivalent to either the original sentence of L or a translation of it into the appropriate metalanguage. Spelled out this way, and with a suitable notion of equivalence, the thesis captures a crucially important feature of the predicate 'true', and it guarantees that any predicate of which it holds is necessarily coextensive with the truth predicate.

What it does not do, however, is to provide us with all we need to know, or can know, about the concept of truth. The view that it does is usually called the *redundancy theory* of truth, and no appeal will be made here to this view. In any case, I think that this view is incorrect.

DUMMETT'S ARGUMENT

Running throughout all of Dummett's writings on realism, sometimes above and sometimes below the surface, is the following argument connecting anti-realist semantics with metaphysical anti-realism. I shall state it in the idiom so far established in this paper:

(1) Meaning must be given by θ conditions, where the interpretation of 'θ' is constrained by the anti-realist qualms, mentioned above, about the manifestation of our grasp of verification-transcendent truth. So constrained 'θ' must be seen as some form of assertability predicate.
(2) In an assertability conditions account of the meaning of 'or' and 'not' we cannot derive either the laws of excluded middle or double negation; nor are we justified in asserting the principle of bivalence.
(3) Metaphysical realism entails the justified assertion of bivalence and the laws of classical logic.

Therefore, the acceptance of anti-realist semantics entails the unacceptability of metaphysical realism.

This argument is quite clearly valid, but there are sufficiently serious doubts about two of its premises to render it unacceptable.

Before describing these doubts, let me interpolate a remark about a matter that I left somewhat blurred in the above outline.

In premise 2 I did not commit myself to any specific account of the relationship between the failure of the logical laws and the failure of bivalence. In places, Dummett seems to view that relationship as follows:

(a) The assertability account of 'or' and 'not' does not enable us to derive 'A or not-A' as a theorem.
(b) The following principles hold:
A if and only if 'A' is true.
'A' is false if and only if 'not-A' is true.
(c) Given (a) and (b):
('A' is true or 'A' is false) if and only if (A or not-A).
So, bivalence and excluded middle stand or fall together.

In other places, notably in 'The reality of the past', Dummett describes a way in which we can keep excluded middle as a logical law while yet being faithful to the anti-realist semantics of 'or' and 'not'. The trick, for that is what it is, is effected by a procedure analogous to the method of supervaluations. Though I shall not discuss the details here, it is important to recognize that, by this procedure, we apparently get classical logic, but we do not get the principle of bivalence. Hence, in *both* anti-realist strategies we fall short of endorsing bivalence, even though in the one we are, and in the other we are not, allowed classical logic. Since the connection between anti-realist semantics and metaphysics is made in the main argument via attitudes to bivalence, there is no need to choose here between the two strategies with respect to classical logic.

Returning to that main argument, I shall briefly review the reasons for rejecting premises 2 and 3. As described earlier, metaphysical realism consists in the view that the truth predicate is, at least in principle, verification-transcendent. There is no obvious reason why someone who accepts realism so characterized must also see himself as committed to accepting the principle of bivalence. McDowell has, in fact, argued that there are good reasons for keeping the commitments separate.[9] I do not want to thrash this issue out here, but there does seem sufficient doubt about the truth of premise 3 to make it a very weak link in the connection that the above argument is intended to forge. Surely, the argument connecting meaning and metaphysics must contain no such obviously weak links.

Additionally it has been argued, I think correctly, that Dummett has no right to assume as he does premise 2, in which it is claimed that any commitment we have to an assertability conditions account of the meaning of the logical constants is a commitment to the intuitionist version of that account.[10] There are, as Dummett sometimes admits difficulties with the generalization of intuitionist semantics to non-mathematical discourse. If, as has been proposed, there can be an assertability account of the meaning of the logical constants which respects the anti-realist's scruples about verification-transcendent sentences, but does so without sacrificing classical logic or bivalence, then premise 2 is just wrong.

As I said above, I do not expect that these remarks can, by themselves, convince anyone that Dummett's argument must be abandoned, but they do indicate that the argument is shaky. In this circumstance, it is reasonable that we look elsewhere for a path from semantic to metaphysical anti-realism.

CONCLUSIVE ASSERTABILITY AND ANTI-REALISM

In this section I shall consider a quite direct route from the anti-realist semantic thesis to the metaphysical one. Taking this route requires us, in the first instance, to treat the central semantic notion, the notion I schematized as 'θ', as that of conclusive assertability. The sense of a sentence is to be understood as fixed by those conditions necessary and sufficient to establishing it as conclusively assertable. The senses of subsentential components

---

9 See J. McDowell, 'Truth conditions, bivalence, and verificationism', in Evans and McDowell (eds), *Truth and Meaning*.
10 See D. Edgington, 'Meaning, bivalence, and realism', *Aristotelian Society Proceedings*, LXXXI, 1980/81.

are given by what is, for the present, the imagined recursion which shows how the conclusive assertability of sentences is built up from appropriate features of sentence components.

Treating 'θ' as 'conclusive assertability' is the most natural way of proceeding, given that the source of anti-realist inspiration is intuitionist logic and mathematics. The notion of conclusive assertability is the closest relative of proof or provability as used in intuitionist mathematics.

If we allow that the language in which the recursive theory of meaning is given is appropriately rich in syntactic and semantic resources, then the recursion will issue in theorems of this form:

(I) s is conclusively assertable if and only if p

where s is the name of a sentence of the language under consideration, and p is the sentence of the theorist's language which corresponds appropriately to s. That is, p is a sentence which, in providing a specification of the conclusive assertability conditions of s, provides us with a specification of the content of utterances which can be made by the use of s. The last remark should, of course, be understood as allowing a place somewhere for an account of the different forces with which s can be used, but nothing germane to our business hangs on the actual provision of this account. The important point is that instances of (I) can be viewed, in the way described earlier, as specifications of the senses of the sentences named in them.

Given this description of the instances of (I), we are faced with two questions. First, are instances of (I) acceptable? Second, what is the relationship between conclusive assertability and truth? The first question seems pressing because, *prima facie*, it is not obvious that a sentence used to make a claim is equivalent to the claim that the sentence is conclusively assertable. The second question arises simply because (I) is, in form, a version of the equivalence thesis. I shall consider the first question first.

The worry about the acceptability of instances of (I) has two related sources. Assuming that U is a verification-transcendent sentence, (I) commits us to:

'U' is conclusively assertable if and only if U

which read from right to left is:

If U then 'U' is conclusively assertable

and this last conditional seems just wrong.

What is pretty much the same problem can be traced to a different source as follows. The conclusive assertability account of meaning must provide us with, at the very least, a method which relates the assertability conditions of complex sentences to some semantic feature of the components of such sentences. When these components are themselves sentences, it would appear that what we need is a systematic way of relating the assertability conditions of complex sentences to the assertability conditions of their contained sentences. To take a highly problematic example, consider the sentence: x fears that p.[11] The assertability conditions of this sentence must in some way involve the assertability condition of p, though it seems just wrong to construe the original sentence as claiming that x's fear is the fear that 'p' is assertable. Similarly, in order to understand the assertability condition of 'if p then q', we surely want to avoid the natural, but mistaken, construal: 'if "p" is assertable, then "q" is assertable'.

Clearly, the way for the anti-realist to avoid such difficulties is by his refusing to sanction the simple-minded (if natural) move of constructing the assertability conditions of complex sentences from the assertability conditions of their constituent sentences. Wright, in fact, has offered an alternative account for conditionals. (Propositional attitude contexts can be left on one side here, since they are problematic for reasons not directly related to the present discussion.) He suggests that we construe the assertability condition of 'if p then q' as: 'A state of information justifies our assertion of "if p then q" just in case we can recognize that its enlargement into a state justifying the assertion of p would *eo ipso* transform it into a state justifying the assertion of q.'[12] Here we are given an

11 This example is from Wright's own 'Truth conditions and criteria', p. 235.
12 Ibid., p. 236.

account of the assertability conditions of conditionals which relates them to the assertability conditions of their constituent sentences in a less direct way than that envisaged earlier. What justifies the assertion of a conditional is *not* directly dependent upon our being in an informational state which does in fact justify either of the constituents; rather, it is a state which *would* justify one of them given what would be a justification for the other.

Using this proposal, the anti-realist can defuse the objections raised earlier. In particular, we can understand

U if and only if 'U' is conclusively assertable

as claiming that a state of information which conclusively justifies our assertion that 'U' is conclusively assertable is equivalent to one which conclusively justifies our assertion of U. The problematic half of the biconditional, namely

If U then 'U' is conclusively assertable

is now interpreted as:

Any state of information which would conclusively justify the assertion of U can be transformed into one which would conclusively justify the claim that 'U' is conclusively assertable

and this is surely acceptable.

There is much more that could be said about this account of conditionals and about the problems that arise in connection with the anti-realist project of spelling out a recursive theory of conclusive assertability. I propose to leave all of this on one side and turn instead to the second question raised earlier – the question about the relation of conclusive assertability to truth.

Given that we have now accepted as plausible a reading for the biconditional schema (I), and given that the equivalence thesis licenses

(E) 's' is true if and only if p

we can derive:

's' is true if and only if 's' is conclusively assertable

and this commits us to regarding the truth predicate as necessarily coextensive with the predicate 'is conclusively assertable'. I say 'necessarily' coextensive because both (I) and (E) are necessary consequences of general considerations about s and about the recursive machinery which generates the biconditionals. Given the anti-realist interpretation of the conditional, it might seem unreasonable to see the above as guaranteeing 'coextensiveness'. I ask you to leave this matter for the present. I shall return to it at the end of the paper, at which point it will be easier to assess its significance.

In the light of this, we have reached a point where we can formulate what seems a very plausible argument connecting semantic with metaphysical anti-realism. In outline, it is as follows:

(1) A theory of meaning for a language is a recursive theory of some predicate 'θ' of sentences of the language.
(2) Considerations of speakers' abilities, and the need of theorists to justify attributions to speakers consistent with those abilities, require θ to be epistemically sensitive. That is, θ must be understood as some sort of assertability or verifiability predicate.
(3) Taking 'θ' to be the predicate 'is conclusively assertable', and reading the biconditional as described above, we can show that conclusive assertability is coextensive with truth.
(4) Realism is the doctrine that a sentence can be true without its being even in principle known to be so. A realist, in other words, holds that a sentence could be true while not being assertable.

Therefore, since premise 3 undermines the realist claim in premise 4, realism must be rejected.

I think that this is a plausible argument, and something like it must have been in Dummett's mind when he made the observation, quoted earlier, that the realist/anti-realist debate turns on which notion of truth we need in a truth-conditions theory of meaning. In fact, given my remarks about the bivalence argument, I think the above is the *only* way in which the anti-realist can vindicate Dummett's deeply held conviction that meaning underlies metaphysics. Moreover, a particularly nice feature of this, in contrast to the bivalence argument, is that it justifies the importance of the debate over the anti-realist manifestation argument which is implicit in premise 2. In the context of the above, one's metaphysical position depends crucially on the acceptance or rejection of that premise.

However, in spite of the initial plausibility of the argument, I do not think that it is ultimately acceptable even if we grant the anti-realist the truth of the contentious second premise. In the remaining sections, I shall indicate why this is so, and why I can see no prospect for any more acceptable substitute.

THE TRUTH-VALUE LINK

An obvious source of trouble has already been touched on. The anti-realist was forced to construe the conditional in an intuitionist way in order to make good his claim that a recursive theory of conclusive assertability could be taken as a theory of meaning. It was this construal which allowed us to accept instances of (I) as even plausible. The trouble is that conditional contexts are only one of many difficult contexts for an assertability theory. I mentioned propositional attitude contexts, but there is a much more pressing worry about tensed contexts.

In 'The reality of the past', Dummett considered at some length what he called the 'truth-value link'. He wrote:

> One reason why philosophers have been so chary of adopting an anti-realist view of statements about the past is precisely that there appears at first sight to be a gross incompatibility between this view and the truth-value link. To revert to our example, if it follows from the truth of the present-tense statement A that the past-tense statement B, if uttered in a year's time, will then be true, it seems

thereby also to follow that the past-tense statement B will not then be true just in virtue of something which can then be recognized as justifying the assertion of B: indeed, it is entirely conceivable that no one, myself included, might remember where I was at that particular time, and no further evidence, direct or indirect, be available to settle the question, even though we could never be sure that no such evidence would ever turn up.[13]

The solution he offered the anti-realist was as follows: the anti-realist should maintain that 'a statement in the past tense is (or was, or will be) true just in case there now is or will be a situation whose existence we can now acknowledge as justifying the ascription to that statement of the value true'.[14]

The following relatively concrete example will illustrate both the problem and Dummett's solution. I now have, let us say, conclusive evidence that I am in London. The truth-value link allows me to say *now* of the sentence 'I was in London', when uttered next year, that it will be true. However, it seems possible that conclusively justifying evidence may be lost, so that, whereas 'I am in London' *is* conclusively assertable, the sentence 'I was in London', when uttered next year, will no longer be so. Truth and conclusive assertability would appear to function differently. The way out for the anti-realist is for him to insist that judgements of conclusive assertability must always be tied to evidence now available. He can say *now* that the sentence 'I was in London' will be true, precisely because he *now* has conclusive evidence that 'I am in London' is true. Of course, we are tempted to argue that in a year's time, and supposing all trace of evidence about what is happening here and now is lost, no one will be in a position to claim that 'SG was in London' is true. However, it is precisely this temptation that Dummett thinks the anti-realist ought to resist, since it involves a picture of time and tense – the realist picture – which places us outside time and yet able to distribute truth values to sentences of any tense. Surprising as it may at first seem, the truth-value link

13 Dummett, *Truth and Other Enigmas*, p. 368.
14 Ibid., p. 368.

does not require this; it merely requires us to preserve certain systematic links between sentences made *now* and truth values assigned *now*. So, although the truth-value link seems at first to create trouble for the anti-realist, it would appear that a closer investigation shows this not to be a profound objection.

I propose to accept this view of the truth-value link for the present, but I shall now consider what I think is a much more serious flaw, indeed a fatal flaw, in the anti-realist's use of the conclusive assertability predicate in the theory of meaning. The point about truth-value links will reappear in a slightly altered context.

Confusion over the role of the truth-value link is all too easily created, so let me insert a final remark about it in the present context. It can seem puzzling that Dummett worries himself so much over the truth-value link given that, in the context in which he does so, he is canvassing the anti-realist's position. Why, one is longing to ask, doesn't the anti-realist simply repudiate the link as in any way a constraint on his semantic theorizing? The answer is, I think, that the truth-value link is intended merely as a pre-theoretical intuition that all speakers have about the connection of tense and truth. Moreover, it is an intuition that seems to be central to our use of tense in assertions. Dummett's point is that this intuition can be saved without committing ourselves to a realist version of it. In this sense the form of the truth-value link objection is precisely parallel to that discussed above in connection with conditionals. It is (or seems) that our use of conditionals, in particular biconditionals, rules out the equivalence of a sentence and the claim that it is assertable. The anti-realist recognizes that this pre-theoretical intuition must be honoured, and he does so by offering us a way of understanding what is said in the biconditional which does not offend against this intuition. Given his way of understanding the biconditional, the only residual reason for dissatisfaction would seem to arise if one was abandoning the pre-theoretical stance for the realist's. That is, one is unhappy about the anti-realist understanding of conditionals or tense only in so far as one imports hidden realist assumptions into the debate. Or, at least, that is what the anti-realist would argue.

DEFEASIBLE ASSERTABILITY

Among those sorts of sentence which provided the original motivation for anti-realism are sentences about other minds, the past and about unrestrictedly general domains. In each case the problem, as seen by the anti-realist, is that many uses of these sorts of sentence are such that neither we, nor a linguistic beginner, can gain or demonstrate a competence with them if that competence depends on access to the realistically construed truth conditions of the relevant sentences. This is so, it is claimed, because we can have no such access. I have not challenged the last claim, though I am far from convinced by the epistemological assumptions which support it. What is important for present purposes, however, is that if we take this claim seriously we must, I think, reject the pretensions of conclusive assertability, as well as realist truth, on the strength of it.

Consider, for example, a use of a sentence of unrestricted generality – say, as expressed in a scientific generalization. By the anti-realist's lights, a speaker cannot manifest in his behaviour his grasp of the realist truth conditions, and hence his understanding, of such a sentence since he cannot be credited with epistemic access to the infinite totality which the realist sees as necessary to this understanding. But it is no more plausible to suppose that a speaker can manifest his grasp of the conclusive assertability conditions of such a sentence. In the case of mathematics, it is at least plausible to suppose that a speaker can manifest his understanding of a sentence just in case he knows what would count as a proof of it. This is because the notion of proof in mathematics is codified in such a way as to make possession of a proof a decidable issue. In contrast, in the case of scientific generalizations, we just do not credit ourselves with possessing a notion of what would count as *conclusive* verification, and our understanding cannot, therefore, be based on conclusive assertability conditions. The same point can be made in connection with each of the cases listed above that the anti-realist found problematic for the truth-conditions theorist.

The upshot is that, in order to extend anti-realist semantics to the empirical realm, while remaining faithful to its original motivation, the central notion must be an assertability predicate of less than conclusive warrant.

In many places, Dummett has toyed with the idea of using a less than conclusive assertability predicate, but he has nowhere, to my knowledge, recognized that its use is *required* by the very constraints which inspire semantic anti-realism.[15] Other writers, in particular Wright and Baker, quite explicitly see the assertability predicate as what is called 'defeasible', and they see close connections between this notion and Wittgenstein's use of 'critera'.[16] It is certainly an interesting and difficult question how actually to construct a recursive theory of defeasible assertability, but my present purposes do not require me to pursue it. What this paper seeks an answer to is the question: does the argument (in the previous section) connecting meaning and metaphysics go through when 'conclusive' is dropped in favour of 'defeasible'? I think that the answer to this is negative.

The reason for this answer is that defeasible assertability cannot play the role of conclusive assertability in the framework for meaning described earlier; in short, it cannot serve as an acceptable interpretation of θ. Recall that in the case of conclusive assertability there were *prima facie* worries about whether it could be the central notion in an acceptable recursive theory, and about whether it respected the truth-value link. Of both these charges, with certain adjustments, we acquitted this sort of assertability. It seems to me, however, that nothing can be done to make defeasible assertability immune from the truth-value link objection, and indeed from other objections involving contexts which are sensitive to the truth predicate.

A sentence in the present tense which is *now* true can *now* be said to entail the truth of the same sentence uttered in a year's time and recast in the past tense. But it seems incoherent to say of a sentence which is now *defeasibly* assertable that it entails the

---

15 See Dummett, 'What is a theory of meaning (II)?'
16 G. Baker, 'Criteria: a new foundation for semantics', *Ratio* (1974). Wright's main contributions have been cited in footnote 2.

defeasible assertability of its past-tense version uttered in a year's time. It is important to stress the word 'entails' here. It may seem perfectly plausible that someone who holds that a sentence p is now defeasibly assertable, will also think very likely (indeed, defeasibly) that, when p is uttered in a year's time and in a past-tense version, p will be defeasibly assertable. But he cannot hold that p's present defeasible assertability actually entails this; to think so would be to ignore the very feature of this sort of assertability predicate which made its use seem so attractive in the first place – its essential defeasibility. To think that p is defeasibly assertable must surely commit me to the view that, as time goes on, something could turn up which would force me to withdraw my original thought about p. In thinking that p is now defeasibly assertable, I am certainly betting against this possibility, but it is none the less a possibility. Moreover, it is a possibility *now*. That is, I must surely think now that something could turn up to render the past-tense version of p, when uttered at some time after now, no longer defeasibly assertable. The anti-realist would seem committed to the following two thoughts in his attempt to hang on to the truth-value link while, at the same time, employing a defeasible notion of assertability in his semantic theory:

(1) p now is such that, when uttered in a year's time in its past-tense version, it will definitely be defeasibly assertable.
(2) p now is such that it might not be even defeasibly assertable in a year's time and when recast in the past tense.

Thought 1 comes from the commitment to regard 'defeasible assertability' as a filling for θ and, hence, as a reading for 'true' while, at the same time, respecting the intuition in the truth-value link. Essentially, it is the commitment to think that, at any given time 'now', we can distribute evaluations to the differently tensed versions of the present-tense sentence which we are prepared to evaluate in some way at that very time (the present, in the example). If we are prepared to think of the present-tense sentence as defeasibly assertable now, then its past-tense version, uttered in a year's time, should now be seen as indefeasibly defeasibly assertable. Thought 2 is no more (or less) than one would expect from an understanding of the notion of defeasibility. It claims that a sentence is defeasible if we are, even while thinking it assertable, prepared to countenance the possibility that it would change this value at some future time.

I do not think that thoughts 1 and 2 can be made consistent, so I think that 'defeasible assertability' cannot be considered a plausible candidate for 'θ'. What this means is that the argument of 'Conclusive assertability and anti-realism', which, at the time, seemed so plausible, cannot be relied upon by the anti-realist. He cannot move from a consideration of his central semantic notion to a rejection of the metaphysical thesis of realism. Does my argument not also show that the anti-realist's semantics is in deep trouble? That, as they say, depends. As things now stand, it would seem that anti-realist semantics has made more commitments than it can consistently fulfil. I shall examine this, briefly, in the concluding section.

CONCLUSION

Two moves seem open to the anti-realist: he can try to describe a predicate which fills in for 'θ', but is not as strong as either realist truth or conclusive assertability and is not as weak as defeasible assertability; or he can claim that I misrepresented his original semantic goal. The second option needs some spelling out.

Recall that I described the ultimate goal of the recursive theory of θ as that of giving the content of sentences. It was this that led me to link the extension of θ with the truth predicate via the equivalence thesis. It is open to the anti-realist to block this link by insisting that his recursive theory of θ (when 'θ' is understood as 'defeasible assertability') does not aim to provide contents for sentences in this way. This road is open but it is, one feels, mysterious. Strawson sensed that such a move was being proposed and thought that this was, in itself, grounds for rejecting the semantic pretensions of anti-realism.[17] A more recent consider-

---

17 P.F. Strawson, 'Scruton and Wright on anti-realism, etc.', *Aristotelian Society Proceedings*, LXXVII, 1976/77.

ation of this option can be found in McDowell's 'Criteria, defeasibility and knowledge'.[18] Since I think that McDowell's argument has interesting parallels with the central contentions of this chapter it is worth inserting a note about them.

McDowell sees his main anti-anti-realist argument as epistemological: the anti-realist is seen as having unacceptable commitments with regard to the notion of what it is to know that p. This phase of McDowell's argument seems to me better seen as follows:

(1) The anti-realist must provide us with an explanation of how the theory of θ deals with contexts such as: x knows that p.
(2) In dealing with this context, the anti-realist, using the notion of defeasible assertability, ends up with a view of this context that is inconsistent with the intuitions that we have about knowledge.

Presented in this way, McDowell's argument is another variation of the argument that began with the conditional and took us through the truth-value link. As such, the argument is epistemological only in that the context happens to contain the word 'know'. (To see that this is not crucial, imagine that some other so-called 'factive' such as 'guessed' is put in place of 'know' in the argument.)

In more detail, McDowell's point 2 runs as follows. It is a consequence of 'x knows that p' that p is true. The anti-realist will see this second claim as indistinguishable from p is defeasibly assertable – if he accepts the whole background story about θ providing a theory of contents for sentences in the language. But, McDowell argues, it is incoherent to claim *both* that x knows that p and that p is defeasibly assertable. The latter claim seems to take away what the initial claim requires.

As I noted, this is only the first phase of McDowell's argument; he himself envisages a way of 'sidestepping' the argument. In essence, and from my perspective, this way consists in giving the anti-realist his special way of reading the entailment connection between 'x knows that p' and 'p', but this leads, in turn, to worries

---

18 J. McDowell, 'Criteria, defeasibility, and knowledge', *British Academy Proceedings* (1983).

about whether we have been given a theory of the content of claims to knowledge. Without some such notion of content, McDowell thinks the anti-realist has provided nothing to say to the sceptic and has, therefore, 'no room for anything recognizable as genuine knowledge'.

While remaining neutral to the force of McDowell's conclusion, one can see it as, in form, just what one would expect of the anti-realist as characterized in this chapter. Anti-realist semantics, I have argued, requires either the introduction of a more truth-like truth predicate, or the abandoning of the idea that a theory of θ is a theory of contents. It would be interesting to see how the first of these options could be achieved, but very difficult to imagine that the result would be satisfactory; the notion of truth involved is very likely to be claimed by the realist very soon after its birth. The second option is not one about which this chapter has expressed any views. If McDowell and Strawson are right, this option is no more acceptable than the first. However, my interest has *not* been in the question of whether the anti-realist can provide a semantics using the notion of defeasible assertability. Rather, I have been exclusively concerned with the bearing of this project on the metaphysical thesis of realism. It seems quite clear that the argument described in 'Conclusive assertability and anti-realism' does not go through if the theory of defeasible assertability is not also seen as a theory of content. With this road from meaning to metaphysics blocked, it is hard to see another; moreover, unless one is found, it is not unreasonable to take the conclusion of this chapter as a reason for finding the project of anti-realist semantics less interesting and, perhaps, less plausible.

AFTERTHOUGHT

The main point of the previous section was to investigate the effect of severing the connection between the theory of θ and a theory of content on arguments connecting semantics and metaphysics. A natural way to understand this effect was that it ruled out the central semantic notion as a possible candidate for truth surrogacy, and this had the further effect of preventing any move from the use of this notion in semantics to its anti-realist pretensions in metaphysics. There is, however, another way of viewing the matter which I find both intriguing and dark; because it is intriguing I present it here and because it is (to me) dark, I present it without further discussion and as an afterthought.

One might think that the real effect of the anti-realist's moves in regard to the conditional and other contexts, and in regard to content, was this; it made it impossible for the realist to coherently *state* his position in the first place. Recall that in the argument of 'Assertability and anti-realism', the realist position was put this way: truth is not coextensive with epistemic notions such as assertability. Perhaps one should see the anti-realist position as claiming that there is no way in which this can be understood without lapsing into incoherence. Of course, the realist (such as McDowell) can see his own position as, roughly, this: given the *intelligibility* of realism, anti-realism comes out as incoherent (or, at least, in conflict with a number of things we very much want to preserve – things like the truth-value link, or the entailment relations between 'x knows that p' and 'p'). If there is anything in this thought, then the real position is that realist and anti-realist have less to say to one another than is currently supposed. Perhaps this seems something for which, if it were taken to heart, we should be grateful.

8

How can we tell whether a commitment has a truth condition?

Simon Blackburn

BACKGROUND

This chapter explores a distinction within the class of commitments. The problem is how to discover which among our commitments are truth valuable. If an utterance expresses a commitment which is capable of truth value, then it itself has a truth condition; its truth condition is just whatever condition it is that needs to be satisfied for the truth value T to be assigned to it. Let us say that commitment to a proposition with a truth condition is *belief*, and call any other kind of commitment a *stance*. Then my interest is in the division between belief and stance. But to put the issue this way is not to prejudge it; it may turn out, for instance, that the division vanishes, or can be resurrected only as a division within the overall class of beliefs – between those for which one notion of a truth condition is correct, and those which deserve another.

However we end up expressing it, many philosophical issues hinge on whether there is *some* division here. Emotivists, instrumentalists, dispositional theorists of conditionals, instrumental theorists of the mental (and Kripke's Wittgenstein) all hold theories according to which many ordinary commitments are not properly truth valuable, or have no truth condition. They have a different function, that gives them something else – at best an assertability condition, perhaps. This also means that assent to them is not belief, but represents some other kind of state – the adoption or endorsement of a stance.

What is the motivation for the division? Often it will be metaphysical, and sometimes it will derive from the theory of understanding or from epistemology – how can we conceive of facts of *that* sort? and how could we know them? Although I thoroughly respect these motivations, I also think it important to stress others. For they can on their own give rise to the counter that they arise from an unduly restricted, prejudiced, view of facts, and knowledge. After all, from some perspectives it is easy to lose a sense that we understand the obtaining of any facts (those concerning space and time for instance), but we obviously hold corresponding beliefs. So perhaps we should not react too dramatically to the fugitive quality of any category of fact. Similarly, perhaps we should be epistemological liberals: we can understand and know wherever we can build theories, and we do that in all the disputed areas. Furthermore, the sceptic about the division may continue, we have all learned a fundamentally Kantian lesson about the way in which our own categories and concepts infuse our conception of the reality we inhabit – surely this lesson extends to cover necessities, values, mentality, meaning. Even if these are creatures of our categories, so is everything else, and it is arbitrary to confine reality to the facts trawled up by any one part of our conceptual net.

All this ignores an 'internal' explanatory reason for exploring the division, which is at least as powerful as those drawn from metaphysics and epistemology. This is that when we think about what a mind needs to do, we should antecedently *expect* there to be a need to express commitment in other dimensions than that of belief in fact. Our functioning is not the simple accumulation of data, but in part an active organization of them and reaction to them. So we must need to express ways we manage our data, or dispositions to draw inferences among them, or attitudes we hold towards them. Endorsing and ranking these dispositions, attitudes, etc. contrasts with simple possession of a piece of fact, or description of the actual way of the world. Consider, for example, assent to rules or conditionals, remembering the problem which Achilles faced with the tortoise. This fable is usually used to force a distinction between premises and rules of inference.[1] To complete this diagnosis we must see the tortoise's problem as treating acceptance of a rule as acceptance of a new proposition. The tortoise construed every new offering of Achilles as expression of another belief, which it duly accepted, or at least appeared to accept. But its assent never translated itself into a disposition to form other beliefs, nor into an endorsement of any such disposition. Hence Achilles could get it no nearer to the desired conclusion. So one way of describing the tortoise is that it misconstrued the nature of genuine assent to a conditional: if it is important to us to endorse and reject various systems of belief, or to make public and discuss dispositions to change systems which come about as a consequence of the acquisition of new beliefs, we will need a way of expressing these dispositions, policies, mandates and prohibitions. Given a need for such things, it may not even require metaphysical or epistemological argument to see commitment to conditionals as playing just that role.

The dispositions and mandates will of course need careful evaluation. Some will be better grounded than others, and the world will afford patterns of fact which make some obligatory and others less so; these commitments will need expressions enabling us to reason around them, work out their consequences, seek to better them. It may not be surprising if we find all commitments borrowing a propositional appearance so that this discussion can go well, and this foreshadows the major complication in establishing a reliable litmus test for the division.

It can be seen, from the way I have drawn it up, that this problem can equally well be approached by theorizing directly about propositions and truth, and by tackling it as a problem of propositional attitude ascription: how to separate things which are beliefs from those which are stances of other sorts. This is as it should be: well-developed areas where the nature of our commitments is problematic illustrate both strategies. For instance, moral realism is debated both directly, where the legitimacy of giving truth conditions to moral utterances comes under scrutiny, and indirectly, where it is some feature of commitment to moral views

---

1 Lewis Carroll, 'What the tortoise said to Achilles', *Mind* (1895).

which supposedly shows that they represent stances which are like or unlike other beliefs. But seeing the division as one within the nature of commitment does not make it any easier to locate it. It is not as though an individual can inspect the nature of his own commitments and pronounce with any authority on whether they represent stances or beliefs. You can announce to yourself or the world that you really *believe* in duties, gods, numbers, possibilities, conditionals, or equally that this is not belief but acceptance of an heuristic, or whatever, but you do not thereby establish the division. A theoretical distinction of the kind we are looking for needs a proper methodology, and untutored introspection does not provide it.

Commitments will typically get ordinary indicative expression. They can be called true. Some philosophers appear to think that this already settles it – that truth is so thin that it can be applied, by redundancy considerations, to any such commitment. This cannot be much of a point, since a thin theory of truth may have to consort with a thick theory of commitment, if we need more functional states than belief in the theory of cognition. And the example of rules and conditionals suggests that this could easily be the case. But in any case, is truth so thin that it can simply be purchased right across the board?

Do not think that the purchase is easy, effected simply by redundancy or 'transparency of truth' considerations. For, given that the division is well motivated, it could well have consequences – stances might show symptoms. Proposals fall under three heads. One might query whether a particular range of *cognitive attitudes* is explicable or legitimate, given the anti-realist starting point. Could we talk of knowledge, or discovery, or chances, for instance, in connection with stances (can morals be a matter of knowledge; can we doubt our stances?) Second, one might query whether a certain *syntactic form* is explicable or legitimate, given the starting point. Why do we treat expressions of stances as propositional? How do they function in indirect contexts? Finally, we might query whether a certain *logic* is explicable or legitimate for them. Why should we be committed to classical logical operations, laws such as bivalence (or even non-contradiction) given the anti-realist sympathy? Can stances have probabilities? A close investigation of the consequences of the division needs to speak to all these issues.

In principle, the investigation could result in any of four kinds of theory. We might find that in some area we practise non-propositionally: that, in some respects, we do not treat utterances as expressive of belief. To some extent I believe that this is so in the case of conditionals, although that is for later. Or, we may find that the surface phenomena are exactly as would be expected if we treat the commitments as belief. That can give rise to two obvious reactions: trust the phenomena and avoid the anti-realism, or trust the anti-realism and abandon or regret the phenomena. That is, regard them as embodying an error – the erroneous belief that the commitments in question possess genuine truth conditions. But the third reaction is the interesting one. This approach I call quasi-realism; and it aims to show that there is no error, and no reason to interpret the surface phenomena as favouring realism. It seeks to reconcile the propositional appearance with a stance-based theory. According to the quasi-realist, we can start with a stance-based view of what commitment in some area is – what it is to assent to a moral or modal or conditional or whatever commitment, and out of that *distil* a legitimate object of the attitude – a proposition to be believed, given a probability, said to be true or false. This is a kind of constructivism about propositions and truth. The constructivism has us say that if it is legitimate for us so to talk, this means that there *are* such propositions. Another way of putting it is that we invent a proposition to stand at a particular point, as an object of needed attitudes in a well-functioning cognitive economy, and the proposition put there is a kind of reflection of a stance. But then when we think of our ontology, we see no need for an aspect of reality to which these relate. Perhaps rather than invent an 'ism' to stand here, I should simply signal an invitation open to all: find out how many of the surface phenomena can be explained and made legitimate by a stance-based theory.

That, at any rate, is a programme. Where successful, it 'saves the phenomena' for anti-realism. It would reconcile a stance theory with a truth-conditional appearance, in cognitive attitudes, in syntax, or in logic. Quasi-realism thus does most service to anti-realists, who can be reassured that they do not need to regret the surface features of our thought which appear to need realistic explanation. But of course it would not compel anti-realism, since showing that P is consistent with Q is not showing that P, even when Q amounted to the principal reason against P. What will genuinely define a realist are thick, unearnable practices, which mean primarily at least practices of explanation.[2]

There is undoubtedly a tension between two ways of reacting to successes of quasi-realism. If stances behave so like propositions it follows that there is no mistake in talking of truth or falsity in connection with them. But is this just talking 'as if' there were moral, modal, causal, conditional truths, when in fact there is none? It can feel like it, but this is a bad way of expressing the end product. For it is not as if we had a notion of what it would be to come across 'genuine' causal, moral facts, but unfortunately have to content ourselves with talking as if we had performed this feat, when we have not done so. A quasi-realist may hold that *he* gives all the content there can be to sentences maintaining particular moral, causal, conditional truths. He can mean all that it is possible to mean by saying that a particular proposition, which reflects a stance, is really true or false. *The contrast with simple realism comes not in the things you end up saying, but in the theory which gives you the right to say them.*

It may help at this point to contrast two quite similar approaches to different categories of necessity – Quine on logical necessity, and Hume on natural. Each sees the modal vocabulary in terms of an 'essentially dramatic idiom': the expression of an attitude we take up, in the one case to propositions which achieve a certain protected status in our thinking, in the other case to regularities which we have come to take as fixed in our minds. But Hume is not properly represented as supposing that there are no causes, although we talk as if there were. He ends up saying that there are indeed causes, in the only sense which we can give that commitment. Similarly, there are values and virtues, laws and beauty: it is

---

2 This is urged in my 'Truth, realism and the regulation of theory', in *Midwest Studies in Philosophy, vol. V*, eds P. French, T. Uehling and H. Wettstein (Minnesota, 1980).

the explanation of our right to say so which is anti-realist.[3] On the other hand, Quine takes the projective theory of modality to be a relegation: it unfits the notion for serious science. Whose reaction is the right one? Notice that there are two very different aspects to Quine's position.[4] One is that he is centrally concerned to confine the real world to the world of physics; from this ontological perspective, he is right to say that there is no modality. This is the denial of real realism. Similarly Hume can say that in nature there is no (intelligible) causal nexus between events. But the second component in Quine's position brings the fundamental difference from Hume. Hume defends and enters into the way of thinking ('causalizing' – parallel to moralizing), which, in any case, nature demands of us. Quine, on the other hand, regrets the attitudes to propositions involved in giving them the status of necessary truths: modalizing is conservative (sometimes Aristotelian) and in any case potentially obstructive of scientific change. In this respect Quine stands to Hume on modality rather as Nietzsche does to Hume on ethics: it is the attitudes which he attacks. But Hume's reaction is possible and consistent: showing the origin and nature of the commitment need in no way undermine it.

If this is the end point, then we end up saying the things which were originally forbidden to the anti-realist – that there are causal, modal, conditional, moral truths, facts, or that we believe in them, with probability, knowledge, certainty. This sounds like queasy realism, especially if we are suspicious of 'real' realism – the belief that there is a coherent explanatory status for the disputed 'facts'. If nothing but images, ghosts and rhetoric exists on *that* side, it might be best to avoid the impression that there is a defined realist

---

3 It is difficult to overestimate the damage caused by missing this. A recent offender is David Armstrong, *What is a Law of Nature* (Cambridge, 1984) where a 'regularity theory' of causation is assumed to entail that we should say different, and unattractive things. Whereas in Hume, and its best development, what it does is to give a different account of the way in which we come to say the things we do.

4 Of course, there are many further aspects to the second part of Quine's position – the hostility to 'modalizing'. They include suspicion of use/mention confusion, suspicion that non-holistic theories of meaning are involved, as well as suspicion of Aristotelian essentialism.

theory to be *anti*. And in that case, everyone seems to be joining hands, and the distinctive contribution of anti-realism may seem to be undermined. But this is by no means so. As I said above, the distinctive contribution of projectivism plus quasi-realism lies in how we get there: by eschewing false metaphysical, or natural, explanations of our propensities, and substituting ones which enable us to see ourselves better. The theory lies not in the words we end up using, but in the hard-earned title to use them; it is the process, not the bare end point, which matters.

CONDITIONALS

There exist already approaches to propositional and quantificational logic which avoid explicit classical assumptions in their foundations. What is the basis for seeing particular formulas and inferences as mandatory or as having to be avoided? A classical approach cites the properties of truth and falsity. An anti-realist grounds the norms elsewhere – in whatever makes obligatory, or impermissible, a given structure of commitments, or a given practice of inference among them. For example, a classical probabilist says that prob ($-p$) and prob (p) must add to one because that is what probabilities or perhaps frequencies *do*; an anti-realist says that they must because if you adopt corresponding degrees of confidence, and thence betting rates in any other way, you stand to lose whatever happens. Incoherence in commitments generates the norms for a logic without supposing that the commitments describe some part of the world, but only provided that we have a firm concept of the consequences of assent to them.

A commitment expresses a state of mind – a belief, disposition or attitude. Let us call this its *assentability* condition. (This is better than the usual term 'assertability condition', for that conflates two issues. There is the issue of assent, and there is the pragmatic issue of when it is felicitous to express that assent, or to express it with a particular vocabulary.) But of course, assent has to be controlled: there will exist *standards* on the basis of which particular commitments may properly be entered into. For example, a disposition to infer propositions like Q from propositions

Commitment and truth condition

like *P* will be to some degree improper if it (often, occasionally or even possibly) leads from truth to falsity. Now, if quasi-realism works across the board, when we assess commitments and their standards we will have the right to talk exactly as if we are assessing a proposition for truth. So quasi-realism would close the gap between allowing that an utterance has a disciplined assentability condition, and supposing that it has a (thin) truth condition. It will favour the *passing assumption* (PASS), since it is the prime point at which we pass from talking in terms of assent to talking in terms of truth:

PASS: degree of assentability can be construed as probability of truth.

Of course, in an area in which he is operating, a quasi-realist will suppose that PASS *insinuates* a concept of truth, not that some antecedent notion of truth exists, and can be used to dictate when we should assent.

PASS is not a bland doctrine. In the theory of conditionals, many writers have accepted that there are decisive formal reasons for regarding the conditional as itself lacking truth value but possessed *only* of something less – assentability conditions, in my terminology. Whereas a quasi-realist can perfectly well tolerate putting things this way if it expresses, say, a thick metaphysical worry (about the existence of genuinely conditional facts), it is obviously more surprising if it comes out of abstract, formal or logical considerations – out of thin air, as it were.

The fact that it does so does no disservice to anti-realism about conditionals, of course – it may force a non-truth-conditional theory upon us – but it would give a good and rare example of a consequence of this theory for logic.

Before engaging the technicalities, I shall mention one more general aspect of anti-realism about conditionals. Although this chapter confines itself to the indicative conditional, it seems to me that the case is overwhelming for unifying the theory of indicative and so-called counterfactual hypotheticals. (The differences between them that matter to logic are, I think, mainly attributable to different temporal indications carried by the grammar.[5] But anti-realism then leads to difficult problems of conceiving of the 'stripped' world – the Humean or other ontology which leaves the bare facts which underlie or 'ground' our inferential dispositions. At its worst, we might suppose that all properties are dispositional; dispositions are identified by counterfactuals – so what world is left? I do not know how to answer this question. (I also think that any escape which comforts itself with the idea that dispositions are somehow grounded categorically is illusory. Which categorical properties are non-dispositional?[6]) But before leaping back to realism, it is worth pausing to wonder how that helps. For the usual realist theory of counterfactuals sees their truth as consisting in the distribution of properties in shells of similar possible worlds that surround the actual world. But that theory faces just the same problem. The actual world needs its own nature, quite apart from its surroundings: what is *it* in itself, so much as to have a place in relation to other similar entities? If the anti-realist has problems of stripped ontology, so does the realist.

The arguments to come deny that there can exist a connective $\to$, forming sentences of the form $A \to C$ which both have a certain assentability condition, and express propositions. If you have the assentability condition, goes the argument, you cannot regard this sentence as capable of truth and falsity. Or rather, you cannot in the presence of PASS. The arguments deny that the assentability condition in question can be regarded as a probability of truth.

The assentability condition is standard for conditionals, and was first made prominent by Adams, and summed up in what is sometimes called Stalnaker's thesis, that the probability of the conditional is the conditional probability.[7] What is a conditional

---

5 V. Dudman, 'Conditional interpretations of *if* sentences', *Australian Journal of Linguistics* (1984), section 27ff.
6 For a victim of this, see Gareth Evans, 'Things without the mind', in *Philosophical Subjects*, ed. Z. van Straaten (Oxford, 1980); see also Strawson's reply, p. 278.
7 E.W. Adams, *The Logic of Conditionals* (Reidel, 1975), p.3; R. Stalnaker, 'Probability and conditionals', *Philosophy of Science* (1970), pp. 64–80. Also to be noticed is R. Jeffrey, 'If' (abstract) in *J. Phil* (1964).

probability? A high value for a conditional probability C/A is construed as expressing (or perhaps endorsing) a disposition to accept C, with high degree of confidence, upon acceptance of A. Under idealized circumstances, this disposition could be measured by the value one would give to a bet, to pay $1 if C, given A, but to be called off if -A. The price one would pay for this bet measures one's degree of confidence in C, given A. Probabilists in turn equate this with a ratio of the probability of (A & C) to the probability of A (this move detains us later); doing so, we arrive at:

The definition: $A \to C$ is assentable in proportion to $P(A \& C)/PA$

I write this:

$$\text{ASSENT } (A \to C) = P(A \& C)/PA$$

For the rest of this chapter I shall call $A \to C$, whose assentability condition is defined in this way, an *Adams commitment*. But it ought at least to be noted that the definition is not fundamental, for a stance theorist of conditionals. It is the outcome of the theory itself, construing assent as expression of a conditional probability, *and* a further thesis about how that disposition can be equated with a ratio of non-conditional probabilities. If the going gets tough, this second aspect of the theory is not at all immune from query. For although since Kolmogorov there has been a tradition which makes the conditional probability equal the ratio as a matter of definition, there is another – de Finetti, Bayes and de Moivre – which sees it as a substantial matter to equate the two.[8] I return to this below.

Naturally, most writers have been centrally interested in whether Stalnaker's thesis is true. Certainly many conditionals seem roughly paraphrasable as 'mostly/usually/naturally, when A

---

8 B. de Finetti, *Theory of Probability* (Wiley, 1974), p. 136ff. For Bayes, see G. Shafer, 'Bayes's two arguments for the rule of conditioning', *Annals of Statistics*, (1982), pp. 1075–89; also 'Constructive probability', *Synthese* (1981), pp. 1–60.

(in the event that A, on it turning out that A), C'. If 'A' and 'C' are not self-standing propositions (as Dudman has shown they are often not), [9] this equation is particularly appealing. 'In those days, if Granny missed the bus, she walked home' is surely exactly the same as 'in those days, when Granny missed the bus, she walked home', and this in turn will be assertable in proportion to the ratio of cases on which, when Granny missed the bus, she walked home. Thus either assertion might meet the retort 'not always'. But this is not a direct refutation, whereas 'no, she hardly ever did' would be. Even when we have a simple hypothetical, if we think of the 'mostly' interpreted in some fairly airy probability space, the equation is still appealing. 'If the Green Party wins, it will do something about pollution' is surely assessed by imagining futures in which the Green Party wins, and if most, or better, all of the ways these would naturally turn out involve the party doing something about pollution, then the conditional is assertable. And of course, there is direct evidence from inferential behaviour – problems with transitivity, strengthening, contraposition – that this is an accurate model of the import of conditionals.[10]

Another nice property is that the dispositional theory accurately reflects our reaction to bizarre conditionals, which we only with difficulty force into the Protean bed of truth and falsity. Out of a context (such as a game), 'if the Alps are made of tertiary rock, then Russell had a sibling' strikes most untutored ears as simply *disengaged* from anything: one wants neither to assent nor to dissent. The dispositional theorist is beautifully placed to explain this, in terms of there being no unique inferential route that one wishes either to endorse or criticize, located by the expression. That is, outside a context, it is not clear which disposition to move is in question, for dispositions are defined over *kinds*, and the kind remains unspecified. Thus in a game where it is known that the two propositions have the same truth value, the move is known to preserve truth, which is one good point. But in the world, not all moves which are known to yield truth are good moves, for they may be the kind or form of move which is highly dangerous. We

---

9 Dudman, 'Conditional interpretations', section 3ff.
10 Adams, *The Logic of Conditionals*, chapter 1.

may think that all logicians can concentrate, but we do not endorse 'if all people who can concentrate are logicians, then all logicians can concentrate', just because of that: the invalid form shows that the disposition thus apparently endorsed is a bad one. But we can expect considerable vagueness and contextual relativity in recovering just one *kind* of move to endorse or not from the surface expression.

Conditionals are also freely ascribed truth values, and the proofs to come purport to show that Adams commitments cannot be regarded as true or false. Should this surprise us? One might mistakenly argue as follows. Probabilities are elusive things. But at least, if ordinary probability judgements are true or false, ratios among them will take definite values, and if that is so, then a commitment to a value of the ratio being in a given range ('high') would itself be truth valuable. It might suffer from vagueness, or it might even need 'indexes' attached, to pick out some definite probability space in which to interpret it. But these provide no principled obstacle to truth values. The real question is: is an Adams commitment equivalent to such an assertion?

Apparently not. Suppose firstly that 'is true' is transparent inside probability contexts, so that if $A \to C$ is assessable for truth, $P(A \to C$ is true$) = P A \to C$. And second, a probability of 0 corresponds to certain falsity, and a probability of 1 to certain truth. Dorothy Edgington has pointed out that, given these, the truth of $A \to C$ cannot be equated with the truth of 'the ratio is sufficiently high.'[11] For if 'sufficiently high' were put at $1 - e$, then on this proposal, when the ratio is *certainly* more than $1 - e$ but less than 1, there are contradictory conditions on $P(A \to C)$. The ratio remains less than 1, but '$A \to C$' would be *certainly* true; conversely, if the ratio is certainly less than $1 - e$, $P(A \to C)$ might remain quite high, but $A \to C$ would be certainly false.

The best way of resisting this argument would be to incorporate 'degrees of truth' for conditionals, corresponding to the degree of probability. There is independent evidence that this is a needed step in any case. Thus an elegant way to block the Sorites paradox is to introduce an intermediate range of such degrees of truth. In

11 In correspondence.

the case of vague predicates, the degree to which an object falls under a concept is semantically relevant, and the value given to 'if a man of height n inches is small, then so is a man of $n + 1$ inches' should reflect this. In the middle ranges of height, it is not false, but only true to a certain degree, and with each successive step the degree of truth of the conclusion drops. At the end of the Sorites the proposition detached is wholly false, but the paradoxical air is explained by each individual step being almost wholly true. In a logic reflecting these ideas, $\rightarrow$ elimination will only be valid if the degree of truth of the consequent is as great as the degree of truth of the antecedent.[12] In general it is a mistake to think of probabilities as degrees of truth, for intermediate probabilities attach to propositions which for independent reasons can be seen as wholly true or wholly false, but the suggestion is that in the case of conditionals, this assimilation is desirable.[13]

Still, we express our endorsement of these dispositions (those expressed by assenting to conditionals) by talking of truth, and we express wavering or partial confidence by talking of probability. It is certainly true that Edgington's argument may make us doubtful whether we have a 'model' of the truth of an Adams commitment. We have only shifting ratios, but no cutoff points. This may mean that such talk of truth or falsity as we go in for is superfluous, and, in its suggestion of just two values, logically misleading. But it is often part of quasi-realism's strength that there is no model or *reductive* account of the commitments in question, or of what 'their truth consists in', so that we have to approach talk of truth via talk of assentability and standards for it. So it may be that we can yet explain and make legitimate some talk of truth construed in this way.

If we do not, we must deny that $A \rightarrow C$ is evaluable for truth and modify PASS by restricting it to propositions which, for other reasons, have been accorded truth conditions. Of course, it is still

---

12 G. Forbes, *The Metaphysics of Modality* (Oxford, 1985), p. 169. The formal system Forbes favours is that of J. Goguen, 'The logic of inexact concepts', *Synthese* (1969).

13 The general claim is put forward in John Lucas, *The Concept of Probability* (Oxford, 1970).

possible to identify conditionals with Adams commitments. This is done by van Fraassen, Ellis, Edgington and Appiah, all of whom deny that conditionals are truth valuable.[14] Or, we can suppose that conditionals have truth conditions, but that for some other reason assentability does not go by probability of truth. This is the reaction of Jackson and Lewis.[15]

Perhaps we have already said enough to make it apparent why Adams commitments are not truth valuable. But before accepting this, I want to explore two more arguments to the same conclusion. The first is due to Carlstrom and Hill, and the second is the more familiar, famous argument due to Lewis.[16]

CARLSTROM AND HILL'S PROOF

Definition 1: A partial truth function of two truth values, expressed by a connective →, is strictly partial iff there exists at least one ordered pair of truth values such that, if A has the first value, and C has the second, '$A \to C$' can be either true or false.

Definition 2: A two-place probabilistic connective is a connective '→' such that there exists a function f for which, for every probability function P,

$$P(A \to C) = f(P(A), P(A \& C))$$

---

[14] B. van Fraassen, 'Probabilities of conditionals', in *Foundations of Probability Theory etc.*, eds W. Harper and C. Hooker, (Reidel, 1976); B. Ellis, *Rational Belief Systems* (Basil Blackwell, 1979); A. Appiah, 'Conversation and conditionals', *Philosophical Quarterly* (1982); 'Jackson on the material conditional', *Australasian Journal of Philosophy* (1984).

[15] D. Lewis, 'Probability of conditionals and conditional probabilities', *Philosophical Review* (1976); F. Jackson, 'On assertion and indicative conditionals', *Philosophical Review* (1979).

[16] Lewis, 'Probability of conditionals'; reviewed by I.F. Carlstrom and C.S. Hill, *Philosophy of Science* (1978), p. 156.

Consider three possible worlds X, Y, Z. In these, the truth values are as follows:

	$A \to C$	A	C	P	P'
X	T	T	T	0.5	0.5
Y	T	$	%	0.5	0
Z	F	$	%	0	0.5

In P, X and Y have (roughly) the probability of 0.5 each, and Z is very unlikely; in P', X and Z have roughly the probabilities shown, and Y is unlikely. Symbols \$ and % can represent any truth value we wish, other than \$ = % = T. The proof goes as follows:

Proof: since $\to$ is a probabilistic connective, we are now trapped in a *reductio*. On the one hand, $P(A \to C)$ must be the same in each of these two functions. For by giving the probabilities that each of them gives to the truth values of A and C (and thus of $(A \mathrel{\&} C)$) in (all) the worlds either of them allows, we have fixed the value of $P(A \to C)$, and of $P'(A \to C)$, and these must be the same because this value is a function of the probabilities of A, C and $(A \mathrel{\&} C)$, all of which are the same in P and P'. On the other hand, the value has to be different, because the probability of $(A \to C)$ ought to be 0.5 in P', and near 1 in P. So:

Theorem: no strictly partial truth function of two truth values is a two-place probability connective.

Is this proof acceptable? Well, what are P and P'? Suppose they are the probability distributions of two different (coherent, responsible) subjects, called P and P' respectively. How did they get into this fix? A conversation might be as follows:

CONVERSATION

SWB: At least you two will agree about prob $(A \mathrel{\&} C)$/prob C.
P: Sure. One thing we can be pretty certain of, is $A \to C$.

Commitment and truth condition 217

P': Not at all – I give it about 50-50.

SWB: How come? Look, you agree that there is a 50 per cent chance of $A = C = T$, and a 50 per cent chance of A being \$ and C being %, so you agree about the chance of A, the chance of C, and the chance of A & C. Hence, you agree about prob $(A$ & $C)/$ prob A. Hence you agree about prob $A \to C$ because that is what prob $A \to C$ is.

P': Well, it looks as though we ought to, but it so happens that we don't, because he rules out Z and I rule out Y.

SWB: You two are irrational. You each suppose that you have a degree of freedom left, which in fact you haven't. You think that there is a *further* stance to take, on whether $(A \to C)$, so that you can rule it in or out with more or less confidence, when you have *already* taken up positions which constrain what you have to say about prob $(A \to C)$.

P & P' *in chorus*: Don't you admit that X, Y and Z are possible? And if they are possible, why can't we put probabilities on them? And why can't one of us favour the fact – for it is to be a fact or not, if only a thin one – that $A \to C$, while the other does not?

SWB: Perhaps this a real (rare) instance of what van Fraassen was getting at with that otherwise obscure charge of 'metaphysical realism' (see below). You think, wrongly, that because one can say that $A \to C$ has a truth value, it also introduces a fact about which we can speculate, or that we can attach probabilities to it, *independently* of what we do elsewhere. Your image is this: you know what to say about the probabilities of the atomic constituents, and their conjunction. But you don't know how likely is the world in which God has put the fact that $A \to C$ snug in its little box somewhere, or how likely it is that He has not. You have given yourselves a quite fallacious subject for freedom of opinion or scepticism. What you ought to be saying is: we agree, and indeed know, how probable $A \to C$ is, given that we agree to know the probabilities of the truth values involved. We *could* be wrong about $A \to C$, but only if we turn out wrong in one of the proability assessments. We could improve out estimate of prob $(A \to C)$, but only by improving our assessments of prob $(A$ & $C)$, or of prob A.

P & P': Aren't you forgetting that $A \to C$ is supposed to be truth valuable, and a partial truth function?

SWB: No. Given the definition, what we are to *say* about the truth of $A \to C$ must depend upon what we are to say about the probabilities. A high enough correct probability ratio for $A \& C/A$ is the norm to aim for. Then you can get cases where A is \$ and C is % and the ratio is very high, and you can get cases where A is \$ and C is % and the correct ratio is very low. In the one case it will be correct to call it true that $A \to C$, and in the other not. So $A \to C$ is in good standing as a partial truth function.
(End of conversation.)

Since P and P' each had an *irrational* attitude, the most the theorem can be read to show is that no partial truth functor is the two-place probability connective expressing the commitments of irrational subjects.

Now this illustrates a central tactic of quasi-realism. It tries to earn its legitimate, thin, conception of truth by concentrating upon the procedures which are to be properly used in assessing, improving, debating, commitments. To use a parallel, according to me, P and P' display the same mistake as someone who acknowledges that moral commitments express attitude, and acknowledges some constraint on his attitudes, but then goes on to think as if moral truth were something else yet again. I actually think this psychology can exist. For instance: someone might admit that proper moral attitudes were constrained by a supervenience demand, but go on to express doubt about whether the moral 'truth' is, and this would display a false metaphysic of moral truth.

LEWIS'S TRIVIALITY PROOF

The crux is the thesis I shall call COND:

COND: in all acceptable probability functions,

$$P\ A \to C/B = P\ C/A \& B$$

Proof:

ASSENT $(A \to C) = P\,A\ \&\ C/P\,A$	the definition
For all Q, ASSENT (Q) = prob of truth Q	PASS
And prob of truth Q = prob Q	transparency
So $P\,A \to C = P\,A\ \&\ C/P\,A$	

This is just construing ASSENT as a probability function. We now suppose that there exists a new probability function, P', representing the result of conditionalizing upon B. We suppose further that this is defined over all propositions. So:

$$
\begin{aligned}
P'\,A &= PA/B \\
P'\,C &= P\,C/B \\
P'\,A\ \&\ C &= P\,A\ \&\ C/B \\
P\,A \to C/B &= P'\,A\ \&\ C/P'\,A \qquad \text{(by the definition)} \\
&= PA\ \&\ C/B\ /\ PA/B \\
&= P(A\ \&\ C\ \&\ B)/P\,A\ \&\ B \\
&= P\,C/A\ \&\ B
\end{aligned}
$$

This proves COND and, once it is accepted, the rest is silence. For using standard probability theory we can:

Expand $P\,A \to C$ into $P((A \to C)\ \&\ C) + P((A \to C)\ \&\ -C)$.

Express the probability of conjunctions as the conditional probability $(P\ (X\ \&\ Y) = PX \times PY/X)$:

$$= P(A \to C/C).PC + P(A \to C/-C).P\!-\!C$$

But from COND this is:

$$P\,C/A\ \&\ C.PC + PC/A\ \&\ -C.P\!-\!C = 1.PC + 0.P\!-\!C$$

and we have the Lewis *reductio*, that $P\,A \to C = P\,C$.

The result is of course quite inconsistent with the motivation behind the $\to$ function in the first place, which was to define a conditional probability; under this result, the conditional probability has just collapsed into the initial probability of C. And Lewis goes on to display the unacceptable ('triviality') consequence of this. That is, there cannot be three possible but mutually inconsistent propositions in a language of which this is true.

Lewis's result seems to come out of thin air. Part of its power comes from the difficulty of seeing quite which steps are, in principle, vulnerable. It may help to have a slightly more perspicuous proof of COND, due to Stalnaker,[17] in front of us:

Proof: As before, P' is the probability function arrived at by conditionalizing upon B. Then there are two distinct ways of evaluating $P'(A \& C)$:

$$P'(A \& C) = P(A \& C)/B$$
$$= P(A/B) \cdot P\ C/A \& B$$
$$= P'A \cdot P\ C/A \& B$$
$$P'(A \& C) = P'A \cdot P'\ C/A$$
$$= P'A \cdot P'(A \to C) \quad \text{(by the definition)}$$

Hence, equating these and dividing by $P'A$, we get COND:

$P'(A \to C) = P\ C/A \& B$ as before.

The effect of COND is to roll iterated conditionals into one: $B \to (A \to C)$ is evaluated as $(A \& B) \to C$. This of course clearly gives us a probability of 1 for $C \to (A \to C)$, and of 0 for $-C \to (A \to C)$, and this perhaps makes it easier to see why Lewis's result will emerge. It also suggests that there ought to be *a* way of avoiding it. There ought to be a way, it would seem, of evaluating Adams commitments relatively independently of whether we *actually* know C, and take it into account in our reasonings. For it need not be so that the 'probability space' in which we assess the commitment is entirely determined by actuality. That is, although we may suppose that actually C (or $-C$) we may still wish to assess whether $A \to C$, in a 'space' which leaves that open. This is merely another way of putting the point made above, that a particular

---

[17] R. Stalnaker, 'Stalnaker to van Fraassen', in Harper and Hooker (eds), *Foundations*.

disposition to arrive at C from A may not gain endorsement even when C is true – not if the disposition is one to perform a dangerous *kind* of move.

The point may be put like this. We have seen that, on a non-propositional account, assent to $A \to C$ would be expression or perhaps endorsement of a disposition to infer C, upon learning A. What then can $B \to (A \to C)$ be? We face the Geach–Frege problem of construing an occurrence of a fundamentally non-propositional element in what we take to be a propositional context.[18] But as with the same problem in other areas, there is an answer. In a quasi-realist construction of moral contexts, 'if it causes harm, then lying is wrong' is also an endorsement, in this case of a sensibility which is so organized that the attitude identified by the consequent follows upon the belief identified in the antecedent. The parallel here will be to endorse cognitive systems so organized that the disposition identified in the consequent follows upon the belief identified in the antecedent. But this endorsement can be quite different from endorsing a system which is disposed to infer C from $(A\ \&\ B)$. For example, on acquiring the belief that $-C$, I would not normally become 100 per cent *against* dispositions to infer C from A, or from the addition of A to an arbitrary stock of belief. And on acquiring the belief that C, I need not become immediately *for* dispositions to infer C from A, or from the same addition of A.

Yet as a consequence of COND, we derive that $PA \to C/-C$ is 0. Now this clashes with the point I have just made. My commitment to 'if Regan weighs 100 kg, then he weighs an even number of kilograms' just does not alter, if I am told that in fact he weighs 73 kg. Imagine me coming up with the conditional, and you saying 'Ah, but aren't you forgetting that he weighs 73 kg' or 'but now see what you would say if we make the supposition that he actually weighs 73 kg.' My commitment to the conditional remains, and would remain even if I learn that neither he nor anybody else weighs so much. Let's call this a $-C$ *resistant*

---

18 P. Geach, 'Assertion', *Philosophical Review* (1965). For a discussion of the impact of this argument on moral contexts, see my *Spreading the Word* (Oxford, 1984), section 6.2.

conditional: I would say that $A \to C$ is still highly credible, even if I learned $-C$. This is an example where the conditional is logically true, but there are perfectly adequate examples where the conditional is contingent, but highly assentable, and resistant to $-C$. If I put my hand on this stove I will burn it, and my commitment to this quite survives my confidence – certainty – that I am not going to burn it. All that is required, in general, is that the disposition endorsed by commitment to $A \to C$ should be unaffected by the kind of thing which alters confidence in C. Mathematics is unaffected by Regan's weight. Conditionals held, for example, on grounds of well-established natural law will equally resist $-C$. Similarly there is the converse case. I am sure that C: nothing substantial will be done in the near future about industrial effluent. But I do not believe that $(A \to C)$: if the Green Party wins the next election, nothing substantial will be done about industrial effluent. This is a C resistant *rejection* of a conditional. In short there ought to exist rational assentability functions in which attachment to $A \to C$ is unaffected by certainties of A, and of C. (After all, this is why the things are *conditionals*: it is often just irrelevant to assessing whether $A \to C$, to start talking about the certainty of C or of $-A$.) Put functionally, the endorsement of the disposition, expressed in Adams commitment or in conditionals, need not be determined by actuality. (Of course, there is room for indeterminacy here. Someone might want to endorse a disposition which comes up with the right result on a *particular* occasion regardless of its falsity-yielding general nature. We *can* hear ourselves saying: if Regan weighs 73 kg then (dammit!) if he weighs 100 kg he weighs 73 kg.)

A possible line is to suggest that, in these examples, the object of interest has changed from the original indicative conditional to a related counterfactual. Certainly subjunctive expression becomes quite natural when we think about knowing that C is false. But the original indicative conditional was perfectly correct – the assent was absolutely proper – in spite of that. The person saying that if Regan weighs 100 kg, then he weighs an even number, or that if I put my hand on the stove I will burn it, is not *refuted* by evidence that the consequent is false. Nor is he saying something which, in that circumstance, we simply cannot evaluate! Of course we can, and of course he was right. This will raise the technical question of whether the mathematical ratio is in fact an adequate measure of endorsement of dispositions, or it may mean that we need an arithmetic of infinitesimals. In any event, the examples show that we would not expect to treat indicative conditionals, or Adams commitments, in accordance with COND. How then to avoid Lewis's proof?

Before turning to that, notice that not all conditionals are $-C$ resistant. Here is an example. I believe that if it rained, the picnic was to be cancelled. And I think it probably rained. But if I were to learn, to my surprise, that the picnic was not cancelled, this would shake my commitment to the conditional. I mightn't say that any more – it becomes unassentable for me. For these conditionals, one would take the other tack. One would say: 'Given what we've learned, there's no chance of C, so *either* $-A$ (it didn't rain after all) or $-(A \to C)$. Perhaps after all they went ahead in the rain.' The same freedom is apparent when we turn to the antecedent A. Some conditionals are stochastically independent of their antecedents, as we have seen. But not all. I may think it is not raining, but that if it rains the picnic is to be cancelled. I may also have other beliefs – for example, that if the picnic is even likely to be cancelled there will be a great deal of telephoning and fuss. When I look out of the window and find that it is raining, my commitment to the conditional diminishes: in the light of the evidence that there has been no telephoning and fuss, I may become insecure again. In possible worlds of talk, I evaluate the conditional in what I take to be the probability space of 'near' possibilities in which A. Learning that mine is actually an A world may alter what I think about that space.

The crux, then, in escaping the proof of COND lies in noticing an ambiguity which arises whenever we are asked to evaluate a proposition 'confining ourselves' to B, or supposing that B. This can mean: remembering, or taking for granted, that actually B. Or it can mean: discarding possibilities under which $-B$. The ambiguity is sometimes benign. But in the case of conditionals, or other propositions where spaces of possibilities are in play, it emphatically is not. Its impact on the proof is quickly seen. What am I to think about $A \to C$ if I suppose $-C$? What am I to think about it if

I suppose C? As we have seen, sometimes I *do* suppose $-C$ – in fact, I am sure of it – but still assent to $A \to C$. What we actually do is to think in terms of an abstract space of possibilities, and ask 'in how many cases' (i.e. what proportion of times) when A is true is C true? What proportion of times, when Regan weighs 100 kg, does he weigh an even number of kilograms? Every time. Would you say this, even remembering that he actually weighs 73 kg? Yes. What proportion of times, when you put your hand on the stove, do you burn it? Every time. Would you say that, remembering that you are not going to burn it? Yes. Weighing up the space of possibilities, we do *not* restrict ourselves to those which conform to (merely) *actually* true assumptions or suppositions. We do not do this *even* if these are given to us as certain. Thus 'How many times (in the worlds in which he weighs 73 kg) does Regan weigh 100 kg and an even number of kilograms?' is a question of sorts, perhaps, and it gets the answer zero. But it is not the question naturally considered when we are asked to evaluate the conditional 'if he weighs 100 kg, then he weighs an even number', *even supposing* that he weighs an odd number. In fact, as I have already remarked, since knowing Regan's weight has no impact on my adherence to arithmetic, making this supposition does not alter attachment to the conditional.

So evaluating conditionals 'on a supposition' can mean one of two things. It could mean that we allow the supposition that B is actually true to affect the relative proportions we suppose appropriate. Sometimes, as we have seen, the supposition has no effect. The supposition is made that we are *actually* at a B world, and we envisage what to say about the ratios in the light of that. But this does not mean that we restrict ourselves to B worlds as the only ones relevant to assessing the ratios. We restrict ourselves, on the contrary, to the A worlds (if A . . .). If B would not be true if A were, then we evaluate the conditional 'on the supposition that B', *allowing ourselves to consider worlds in which B is false*. I suppose that in the actual world, nothing will be done about pollution. But when I consider 'if the Green Party win, they will do something about pollution', I think of ways and ways things would turn out if they win, and come to a verdict in the light of that. I do not restrict myself to worlds in which nothing is done about pollution, just because of the supposition about actuality. And if you heard me assert the conditional, and then said 'yes, but remember that nothing will actually be done about pollution – now take that into account', nothing changes. The conditional is assertable because of standing dispositions or policies of the Green Party, and these exist regardless of whether they are bound to lose.

Evaluating conditionals 'on a supposition' on the *other* reading means something quite different. It means restricting ourselves to proportions among the supposed B worlds. As I shall shortly explain, the model of unfolding games of chance encourages this reading, and it is on this reading that we have to take $P\,A \rightarrow C/C$ to be one, and $P\,A \rightarrow C/-C$ to be zero. But this reading is not forced upon us by the assent conditions of $A \rightarrow C$.

So the crucial move in Lewis's deduction is now apparent. The expression we get for $P(A \rightarrow C)/B$ is expanded exactly *as if* the '/B' locution confined us to B worlds, when in fact it does not. The effect is predictable: confining our ratios to those obtaining in B worlds is equivalent to evaluating $A \rightarrow C/B$ in exactly the same way as if we were evaluating C/A & B, and the result follows.

CONDITIONALIZING VERSUS EMBEDDING

Because of these considerations, B, the proposition conditionalized upon, may have a different impact on the elements A, C and on $A \rightarrow C$. For atomic constituents, the probability function P' is indeed one which arises when we 'confine ourselves' to B worlds and to things which happen or may happen consistently with B. But when the disposition is assessed in the light of ours being a B world, this is just what we do not do. Is this enough to forbid us from regarding Adams commitments as kinds of proposition? The usual reaction to Lewis's proof is to deny that Adams commitments are propositional, or in other words, evaluable for truth and hence probability. Of course, it is not clear how that helps: if ASSENT behaves much like a probability function, it will not help at all. The idea is that Adams commitments will not occur in the right embeddings, so that $B \rightarrow (A \rightarrow C)$, or $P(A \rightarrow C)/B$ will not be defined for them. But Adams commitments ought to permit these embeddings, for dispositions need assessment in the light of different suppositions, just as ordinary beliefs do. Some notion parallel to conditionalization must be allowed, whether or not ASSENT is construed as a probability. Will it be real conditionalizing?

Since a lot now hinges on this notion, it is important to be clear what it means. Conditional probability has its original home in the unfolding of events in structured games of chance. Within such an arrangement there exists what the statistician Glen Shafer calls a protocol: enough structure is fixed to give the rational subject an opinion on the odds he would post for a proposition (Nathan will throw an eleven) upon acquisition of information (Nathan has thrown a six).[19] Eliciting conditional probabilities is eliciting opinion on what odds to post *if* information about the subsequent event is included in the basis of assessment. Within such a structure antecedents will roll together. $B \rightarrow (A \rightarrow C)$ (if she plays the ace, then if he plays the King I shall have to discard . . .) evaluates as $(A \& B) \rightarrow C$. As events unfold we will confine our future reasonings to probability spaces set by what has actually happened. In this circumstance COND is acceptable, and the ambiguity I have stressed is benign. But it does not follow that this is always so.

Conditional probabilities may not be too thick on the ground. There exist good reasons for requiring that a rational subject stand by such odds, once elicited, in that once information Q does come in, his subsequent probability for P should be what he originally gave as his conditional probability, for agents who systematically default upon the original odds can be made to lose whatever happens.[20] But there exist no good reasons for requiring that an agent should have an opinion (be prepared to post particular odds) for a conditional probability for any old pair of propositions. I might just not know what I would say about C given information B. I might neither have nor wish to endorse any disposition to take B in one particular way. I may not see any unique kind of reasoning to tell me where to move from B. I might need to know what else is supposed to have happened as well as the arrival of B.

19 G. Shafer, 'Bayes's two arguments'; 'Constructive probability'.
20 P. Teller, 'Conditionalization and observation', *Synthese*, (1973).

In short, we are in effect thinking in subjunctive terms – 'were one to learn B, *this* would be the right thing to say about C – and often no verdict can be given. These indeterminacies are ruled out in structured games of chance – this is what is meant by there being a protocol – but they are not ruled out in the full world. Indeed, indeterminacy at this point is responsible for the standard paradox of conditional probability (Freund's paradox of the two aces, or the paradox of the three prisoners).[21] In such paradoxes there are two equally proper ways of looking at the acquisition of new information, but they have different consequences for the probabilities. Thus in the three-prisoner version, I and two other prisoners know that two of us will be shot on the morrow. I sidle up to the guard, and ask: will one of the others be shot? 'Yes' he says (merely confirming what I already know), and adds as an afterthought 'Fred will'. Looked at one way this is good news, since I am left with a 1/2 chance of being shot, which is better than 2/3. But how can it be, when I already knew that some proposition of that form was true, and it is indifferent which? The solution must be to insist that there need not be any one right way of taking this acquisition of information. It depends on what can be discerned behind the guard's releasing just that proposition, and in the absence of an antecedent structure, or protocol for the acquisition of this information, no way of taking it is uniquely right.

So we should not let the mathematics delude us into thinking that conditionalization is going to be a well-defined operation interpreted over any pair of propositions. And conditional probability has other curiosities which may be relevant. I have already remarked that the arithmetical ratio may come under suspicion as a measure of the endorsement of the disposition expressed when we assent to a conditional probability. Certainly, the need for careful interpretation of conditional probabilities is quite hidden if we imagine conditional probability *defined* by the usual equation

---

21 J. E. Freund, 'Puzzle or paradox?', *American Statistician* (1965); F. Mosteller, *Fifty Challenging Problems in Probability with Solutions* (Addison-Wesley, Mass., 1965). Also I. Copi, *Introduction to Logic* (Macmillan, New York, 1968), p. 433. Discussions of the paradox occurred in *Philosophy of Science* from 1972 to 1976. My reaction is that of Shafer.

prob (A/B) = prob $(A \& B)$/prob A

for this suggests that the notion is no more perplexing than attribution of probability to conjunctions. Indeed it may not be, but the illumination is brief if we remember how probabilities of conjunctions are introduced. To avoid the fallacy of supposing that in general prob $(A \& B)$ = prob A × prob B, we have to build upon an antecedent understanding of conditional probability anyhow, meaning that in the *ordo cognoscendi* this equation comes first:

prob $(A \& B)$ = prob (B/A) × prob A

Probabilities of conjunctions do not stand to probabilities of their components in the same transparent relation that conjunctions do to theirs! In fact, the matter is even worse than this. For, as is pointed out in Huw Price,[22] there are cases where it is much more evident that we have a conditional probability, than it is that there are any absolute probabilities. I believe that if it is raining in Moscow, then the Kremlin roof is wet. But I have no subjective probability, or particular degree of confidence, that it is raining there, or that the roof is wet. What I do have is a standing disposition to adjust assignments of the one probability in the light of the other. Any way of firming up the first probability carries a consequential effect on the second. But the inferential disposition is in much better standing than any *actual* absolute subjective probabilities whose ratios could be alleged to define it. The disposition has the fundamental psychological reality, not the elements of the ratio.

With this in mind, we can ask how similar the difficult embeddings, with Adams commitments, are to conditionalization. If I am asked what chance I give to X/Y, what I first do is turn in my head what one ought to say about X, upon learning Y. I hypostatize the additional state of information that learning Y would create, and decide what it does to the assentability of X. This corresponds to pondering the question: what to think about

---

22 H. Price, 'Conditional credence', *Mind* (1986).

X, if we make the supposition that Y? Now this thought process occurs when X is itself an Adams commitment. I believe that if my total corresponds to that in today's *Times*, I will win a lot of money. But if I learned a lot of things that commitment would become less assentable. So if I now ponder what to say about the conditional, on the supposition that some one of those things is true, I can given it a lower assentability. If I learned that *Times* employees rig the way they deal with queries, I might abandon that conditional. If I do not learn this depressing fact, but merely start to give it a higher chance of being true, then again that has an impact on the assentability of the conditional. Since this thought process conforms exactly to our explanation of what attributing a conditional degree of confidence is, it seems then right to say that, in my subjective 'assentability function', ASSENT $(A \to C)/B$ is low. The assentability of the conditional 'if this government is re-elected, inflation will stay down', may be high. However, that would alter if we also suppose B: this government has secret plans to overheat the economy after the next election. On that supposition, the conditional changes plausibility dramatically. The same argument will go through for $\to$, regardless of whether Adams is right about conditionals. If we just took directly the probability ratio, $P(A \& C)/PA$, then clearly there is an intelligible question not just of the value we give it, but of what we would say about it under the supposition that B. So it will not be a satisfactory response to Lewis to simply deny the propriety of the contexts in which $A \to C$ gets put.

One could concede the brute facts about embedding, but resist interpreting them as equivalent to conditionalization. One could admit that evidence leads us to alter our assent both to conditionals and to Adams commitments, and that in advance we can consider what the evidence would or would not do. But conditionalization is not the only way to 'model' change of commitment on addition of evidence, and, in default of other reason to regard $A \to C$ as itself truth conditional, we cannot assume that it is happening in these cases. I agree with this. But we cannot assume either that it is *not* happening because so far the needed contrast between ASSENT and probability has simply not emerged.

Are the dynamics different in the case of Adams commitments (probability ratios)? Is the value we give to a conditional 'assentability' not that which we would give if it were a proposition whose probability we were imagining to be affected by evidence? This is held by van Fraassen, who calls it denying metaphysical realism. He says (endorsing a way of putting it due to Stalnaker) that the way to escape Lewis's proof is to realize that there is a suppressed 'metaphysical realist' assumption, namely 'the proposition expressed by a conditional sentence is independent of the probability function defined on it.'[23] Certainly, if we deny that, we break the proof of COND. There will be no certain way of expressing the assentability, or probability, of this *new* proposition as a function of what was true of the old ratio. But of course by itself the explanation is entirely mysterious. On the face of it there is no shift of proposition at all. We are surely interested in the same commitment, and what we would say about *it*, given further evidence (would you still say *that* if I tell you that employees rig the lottery?). The question that bothers us might be, for instance, whether if Henry comes the party will be ruined, and this single topic retains its identity through all the additions and diminutions of evidence. A better diagnosis (but one which has nothing to do with metaphysical realism) might try to see the conditional as containing a concealed indexical element, for instance indexing it to some possible world, or space of such worlds, and arguing that the index changes as evidence accrues. But it is much better to get the same effect without incurring the cost of shifting content. We get the effect because the background against which we are evaluating the inferential disposition changes, and this is itself sufficient to explain why COND fails as a general principle.

In supposing that there is a unique function taking us from one probability distribution P to another P', 'remembering B', we are supposing that what we are to say about $A \to C$, given B is defined in terms of what we are to say about A, and C, remembering B. And this is just what is not so, for the reasons I have given. So the escape from Lewis's proof lies, as it must do of course, in disallowing that the class of admissible probability functions is closed under conditionalizing (for Lewis proves a *theorem* for a

---

23 Stalnaker, 'Stalnaker to van Fraassen', p. 302; van Fraassen, 'Probabilities of conditionals', p. 307.

language in which there is a total conditionalization function). The work lies in showing that this absence of a function is not an argument against treating $A \to C$ as propositional, but only as a kind of proposition which admits a different behaviour in the relevant embeddings. Since conditionalization should not even be expected to be well defined over all propositions, this is not itself an argument for refusing to treat $A \to C$ as propositional.

Probability changes of $(A \,\&\, C)$, as already argued, are downwind of what we think about the conditional probability – the probability of one conjunct being true if the other is. Now in Stalnaker's proof, $P'(A \,\&\, C)$ represents what to say about $(A \,\&\, C)$, given B. This is rightly expanded in the second way, to $P(A/B) \times P'(A \to C)$. But on the reading of conditionalization of Adams commitments that I have been exploring, it is not rightly expanded the first way. For the new probability function may not treat C/A in any way represented as a function of their value in the old function P. $A \,\&\, C$ is on the 'infected' side of things, where the impact of B cannot be assessed as a function of its impact on the atomic constituents. Is it right to blame PASS? It seems not. It was not the view that conditionals, or Adams commitments, have *probabilities* which gave this line of the deduction, but a particular view about how those probabilities should behave under conditionalization. Remember, as I urged above, there is no particular reason to expect prob (A/B) to be well defined for all undoubtedly bona fide propositions. The well-ordered mind need have no measurable dispositions at every point. So it would not by itself be an argument against PASS if we found no general way of defining a conditional probability for conditionals, in terms of P' – the conditionalized probability function which gives values for their constituents. Of course, it is possible to see how in the cases in which there exist protocols the rolling together of the antecedents occurs. But this does not give us the general identity which the proof needs. Once we have seen how and why this occurs, PASS is unscathed.

What is at stake in seeing $A \to C$ as behaving logically *like* a proposition-forming operator, if the basic philosophy sees it otherwise? Perhaps not too much. Our propensity for propositional forms of expression is fairly easily explained. Dispositions and attitudes demand justification and discussion: there is correctness and incorrectness, improvement and deterioration here as there is in belief. Discussion is conducted by focusing upon a unit of acceptance or rejection – a proposition – and this is apparently what we do, here, as when we moralize, or modalize. At least, that is so if it is right to identify conditionals with Adams commitments. I have not directly defended this: the question of the propositional appearance of Adams commitments is interesting whether or not Stalnaker's thesis is true. In fact, I have independent reservations about whether it is true, but they are not germane to this issue.

The upshot is that there is enough doubt about conditionalization to destroy the idea that there should be any well-defined function carrying P into P', for conditionals as well as atomic propositions. Since that is so, the propositional nature of conditionals, construed as Adams commitments, need not be impugned: their behaviour in these indirect contexts does not betray their non-propositional origins. One might indeed react to all this by saying that $A \rightarrow C$ has no truth conditions after all. But it can behave as if it does: it can mark an objective commitment, one that people can fail to know, about which improved opinions are possible, which added to other sets of commitments quite changes their consequences, and which can be argued for and from. I have not discussed all the arguments bearing on the extent to which conditionals, and Adams commitments, emulate propositions.[24] But for all that the two discussed arguments to the contrary show, there is no mistake in treating such a commitment as capable of truth, falsity and probability. There may not be much gain in doing so, but the fact that we do so (to the extent to which we do) will not refute an anti-realist theory of the commitments we have.[25]

---

24 Further considerations are given in Allan Gibbard, 'Two Recent Theories of Conditionals', in *Ifs*, ed. W.C. Harper, R. Stalnaker, and G. Pearce (Reidel, 1980).

25 I am grateful for conversations and correspondence with Anthony Appiah, Dorothy Edgington, Geoffrey Hellman, Frank Jackson, Glenn Shafer, and Charles Travis, which helped to mould this paper.

9
Facts about truth bearing and content
Charles Travis

Conversing requires, it seems, what seems often to be provided: that there be facts about what is or was said in words and when this would be so. If you understand my words, 'My suit is brown', then you take yourself to know what to expect of the suit if it is as said to be. So you take it that there is something one can expect, and hence something required of the suit for it to be as said to be in my words. If the suit fails to meet this requirement, then my words failed to fit it. Hence there are, on the one hand, facts about what I said to be so, and on the other, facts about what is required for that to be so. At least, such seems to be the rule. *Mutatis mutandis* for words of a language, such as the English 'is brown'.

On the other hand, when a philosopher asks what could make it a fact that things are (or are not) as words say them to be – that things pass or fail to pass requirements for this which the words impose – he appears to come up empty handed. How is such a situation possible? One way is that there are no facts about what words require for fitting things, our intuitions notwithstanding. Another is that there is a maker of such facts which the philosopher overlooked. In what follows, I want to discuss an idea on which neither of these possibilities is realized. The idea is Wittgenstein's. It leaves ordinary intuitions intact, but not by pointing to a fact-making factor which the philosopher had overlooked. It is not compatibilist. It does not offer some non-obvious analysis of what the plain man really means when he speaks or thinks in the ways alluded to above, much less some sense in which the philosopher would really be right in taking it that there were no facts about content and what it requires. The idea at first approximation is that nothing is required to make facts about content obtain except our taking such facts to obtain. But for making this idea convincing, more than a first approximation is called for.

UNDERSTANDING AND TRUTH BEARING

Wittgenstein sets out his idea not directly in terms of content, but rather in terms of truth, or more precisely, being a *truth bearer*. The relevant passages are *Investigations* 136 and 137.[1] Truth bearers, as the term is used here, are words to which the notions truth and falsity apply – words which are to be evaluated as to truth, or which say or said what might be true or false. 'Snow is white', for example, is generally held to do this, whereas – on some views – 'Noodles taste terrible', does not. Given the idea of such a difference, the question might arise: what confers the status of truth bearer on something?

In 136, Wittgenstein describes a picture on which this last question has a certain sort of substantive answer:

> Now it looks as if the definition – a proposition is whatever can be true or false – determined what a proposition was, by saying: what fits the concept 'true', or what the concept 'true' fits, is a proposition. So it is as if we had a concept of true and false, which we could use to determine what is and what is not a proposition. What *engages* with the concept of truth (as with a cogwheel), is a proposition.

('Proposition' is Anscombe's translation for *Satz* – on Wittgenstein's use of it a notoriously difficult word to render into English. 'Truth bearer' is a non-colloquial but I hope somewhat less misleading way of rendering what Wittgenstein was after).

Wittgenstein terms the above a bad picture: 'It is as if one were to say, "The king in chess is *the* piece that one can check." But this

---

1 Henceforth all references to numbers will be to passages in the *Philosophical Investigations*.

can mean no more than that in our game of chess we only check the king.' He then offers a better picture as follows:

> And what a proposition is is in one sense determined by the rules of sentence formation (in English for example), and in another sense by the use of the sign in the language game. And the use of the words 'true' and 'false' may be among the constituent parts of this game; and if so it *belongs* to our concept 'proposition' but does not 'fit' it. As we might also say, check *belongs* to our concept of the king in chess (as so to speak a constituent part of it).

On the bad picture, there is something about words, or what they say, which makes them things to be evaluated in terms of truth and falsity. Whatever had this 'something' could not but be a truth bearer. On the better picture, words are a truth bearer (or not) because that is what we treat them as being (or not), not in virtue of any other fact. To say that a given property of words depends on how we treat them is to say, at least, that in that respect there is more than one way the words conceivably could be treated – so as to have the property in question, or so as to lack it. In this case, the thesis would be that given words could be treated as a truth bearer, and so be one, or as not, and so not be one, while the other features of the words and of what they say remain the same.

The plausibility of the thesis depends, *inter alia*, on what it is for us to treat words as a truth bearer, or for that to be part of 'the use of the sign in the language game'. I suggest the following as a useful way in which this idea could be interpreted. There are, to begin with, various ways of understanding given words. Consider, for example, 'Mary had a little lamb'. This might be understood either as saying something about meat eating, or as saying something about pet keeping. On a given speaking, the words may be to be understood in the one way and not the other. They may, for example, say something about meat eating, and not about pet keeping. In any case, whether the words did say the one thing or the other (if either) depends on how they were to be understood. The above sorts of features of words contrast, for example, with the feature of having been spoken at 3 p.m. If given words were spoken at 3 p.m., then that is a feature of them regardless of how they were to be understood. One cannot confer on these words the property of having been spoken at 4 p.m. simply by getting them to be to be understood in the right way. Conversely, if it is recognized that having been spoken at 3 p.m. is a property of this sort, then one cannot get words to be to be understood as having been spoken at 3 p.m. For a choice between ways of understanding in this respect would be a pointless one, with no bearing on the words having the property in question.

The suggestion is, then, that a large part of Wittgenstein's better picture of truth bearing can be rendered as follows. That words are a truth bearer or not is part of what is to be understood, that is, part of a proper understanding of them. Being to be assessed as true or false or not is a respect in which proper understandings of words may differ; hence, to that extent, a respect in which words need to be understood in one way or another. In more intuitive terms, part of what is to be understood about the given words, 'Mary had a little lamb', on a par with understanding that something is being said about meat eating, is that something is being said which is either true or false (or at least which is the sort of thing that might be the one or the other). A choice of understandings *here* is no pointless gesture. It may fail to confer the property of being true or false on the words in question. But where things go well enough, it may also succeed in this.

To say that whether words are a truth bearer depends on how we treat them may be to state a terrifically unexciting thesis. For it may mean no more than that such depends on what we treat the words as saying. If they say the right sort of thing – for example, that Mary ate some meat – then they are either true or false, and if they say the wrong sort of thing, then they are not. But such clearly is not the intention of 136. The idea there was that we cannot, simply by recognizing other features of what was said, recognize whether it is the right sort of thing to make words bearers of truth and falsity or not. This thought is captured on the present rendering. For words would not need to be understood as saying what was either true or false – such would not distinguish one way of understanding words from others – if such were simply guaranteed by other distinguishing features of the way in which words were or are to be understood (features, say, of what it is they were saying).

The thought, then, is that being taken to be understood as saying something either true or false is an independent feature of an understanding of words. One might make the following comparison. For a given understanding of 'Mary', 'Mary had a little lamb' might say someone to have eaten some meat, or it might say someone to have kept a pet. Such features of an understanding of those words are independent of how 'Mary' is to be understood. (They depend, of course, on a proper understanding of 'had a little lamb'.) Similarly, given a proper understanding of 'Mary' and of 'had a little lamb' (e.g., that it speaks of meat eating), and of the structural relations between the two (e.g., that 'had a little lamb' says the referent of 'Mary' to have done what it speaks of), the possibility still remains open of understanding the words in either of two ways: either as saying something either true or false, or as not. If we fail to recognize both possibilities, that is only because it is a deeply engrained part of our language game – that is, of the expectations and understandings with which we meet those words – that we understand them as saying something either true or false. The fact remains (on the thesis) that this is only one of a variety of possible ways of understanding them.

This thesis of the independence of truth bearing from other aspects of an understanding may be helped somewhat in plausibility by two comments on understanding it. First, some of the terms in which an understanding might be described – 'report', 'order' and 'guess', for example – describe the force of words. Force is a matter of the general purposes to which, it is to be understood, given words may be put, and hence intimately connected to the terms in which those words are properly assessed. In fact, force makes its presence known precisely in the fact that it may distinguish between understandings of a whole, with fixed understandings of its parts, and just so as to settle whether a given term of evaluation is applicable or not – 'kept', for example, if the question is whether the words in question were a promise. It would not be surprising, then, if some force describing terms did presuppose or imply that the words to which they apply are properly assessable as true or false. 'Report', perhaps, is an example. So the present independence thesis had better not be denying that describability in such terms may settle that something is a truth bearer. On the other hand, if 'report' is an example of this sort, then it contrasts in this respect with 'say'. If someone says, 'Noodles taste terrible', for example, then we may take him to have said noodles to taste terrible, even if we also take it that such things are neither true nor false but, for example, mere expressions of taste. The independence thesis is that there are not particular sorts of things to be said whose nature requires that they be assessable as true or false or bear a force on which they would be. In so far as some such thing may be assigned a force on which it is assessable as to truth, it is also at least conceivable that the same thing may be said but with a force that does not require or even admit such assessments. If a report *must* be true or false, then what bears the force of a report might also bear some other.

Second, it must also be recognized that the semantic contribution of any part or device to a whole in which it figures *may* be described in terms of truth *if* it is taken as given that the whole in question is, in fact, a truth bearer. For example, the contribution of a predicate such as 'had a little lamb' to a truth-bearing whole such as 'Mary had a little lamb' might be described, roughly, by saying that it is such as to make the whole true just in case the subject of its predication (here, the referent of 'Mary') is as it says something to be. Where it is not taken as given that words are a truth bearer, however, such references to truth may be replaced by references to the general terms of assessment which are applicable to the words in question, whatever these may be. For example, we may still describe 'tastes terrible' in 'Noodles taste terrible' as predicating something of noodles, but, depending on the exact status of this whole, we might describe this contribution by saying that the whole expresses a reasonable taste, just in case what is expressed in 'tastes terrible' is something it is reasonable to find of noodes. We can also recognize that if the whole were (or is) either true or false, then that same contribution would be such as to make the whole true, just in case what is (here) said to be so of something in 'tastes terrible' (whatever that may be) is so of noodles.

The thesis, then, is that there is nothing about what is said in given words that requires that they be treated as a truth bearer other than their being understood to be such. Undoubtedly, the thesis itself still admits of various understandings. Working out the details of the most plausible one could be a consuming task. Given the applications now in view, however, it will do to grasp something about the intuitive idea behind the thesis. This is best done, perhaps, by means of illustration. If we begin by thinking of the thesis as applying to words like 'Mary had a little lamb' or 'Snow is white', it may seem quite a bit less than plausible. How could words say what those words do without being to be assessed as to truth? Things might look different, however, if we look at words like (1) and (2):

(1) Hugo needs a cleaning lady.
(2) *Mépris* is a good film.

In each case, there are reasons both for and against taking the words to say what is either true or false. Sentence (1), for example, speaks of needs. This appears to be a matter about which, in general, there are facts. Consider (3) and (4):

(3) My car needs a new clutch.
(4) A number other than two needs to be odd to be a prime.

If my clutch is in good working order, then it is not true that I need a new one. If my mechanic tells me that I do, he is simply being dishonest. It is no argument against (3) being either true or false that my car may not need a new clutch, regardless of the condition of the present one, if I plan to put it up on blocks and exhibit it. If such holds for clutches, then why not also for cleaning ladies? Against (1) being a truth bearer, on the other hand, there is an apparent irresolvability to disputes over its truth. Someone might maintain, for example, that (1) is false since, by rising earlier and working harder during the day, Hugo could keep the apartment tidy himself (though doing so would make him industrious indeed by normal community standards), or because keeping an apartment tidy is, after all, not very important. What could show conclusively that such a view was simply mistaken?

Neither of the conflicting considerations above is, I think, conclusive. Which is to say that we have no definite answer to the question of whether (1) is a truth bearer. The result is significant.

For we can certainly be said to know what (1) means, and to understand the words if spoken to us. But now it seems that everything we know about what the words mean is compatible both with their being a truth bearer and with their not being one. If this is so, then I think we can imagine two communities, both of which share our understanding of (1) as far as that goes, but which differ from each other as follows. One community takes it for granted that (1) is to be understood to say what is either true or false, and does understand it accordingly. The other community takes it for granted that (1) is not to be so treated, and does not so understand it; this community might construe (1) as an expression of attitude, for example. Neither community would quite be us. But either could be us as we might have been were we impressed a bit more strongly by the considerations in one direction or those in the other. And, if the independence thesis applies in this case, neither community could be accused of having got the facts about (1) wrong. For, independent of the respective ways in which they do understand it as used by them, there is no fact of the matter as to its 'really' being a truth bearer or not.

There is another side to the present coin. Given that each community treats (1) as it does, there may be further things to be said truly within that community about the proper understanding of (1), where these things differ from what could be said truly either in the other community or by us. Consider the various situations in which Hugo might find himself. On the assumption that (1) says what is either true or false, we may suppose that these situations arrange themselves into those that make (1) true, those that make (1) false, possibly with gradations in the clarity with which they do so, and perhaps those that are such as not to decide things one way or the other. Given that there is such an arrangement of cases, there may be definite things to be said about which arrangement this would most reasonably be taken to be. Such things might then be taken correctly, within the first community, as part of a description of the proper understanding of (1). Suppose, for example, that on the most reasonable arrangement, given that there is one, Hugo's actual situation would fall in the class of situations which would make (1) true. ('It's true of Hugo if it's true of anyone'.) Then, within this community, (1) may be taken correctly as to be understood as saying something true of Hugo in his actual situation. Similarly, if situations arrange themselves, on this way of doing it, according to certain general principles, then these principles of arrangement may be taken to be part of a proper understanding of what (1) says.

Suppose now that (1) is neither true nor false but, say, merely an expression of attitude. There may still be situations in which it (or its denial) is an absurd or unreasonable attitude to take. For example, normally the attitude expressed would be quite out of place if Hugo already had a cleaning lady. The rule, however, will be that situations do not arrange themselves in the way envisioned above. With exceptions, perhaps, whatever situation Hugo finds himself in, it will be one towards which one might take the attitude expressed in (1), or towards which one might take its contrary. Though someone who takes the one attitude or the other might be accused of all sorts of things, he could not be accused of having got the fact of the matter wrong. For, if (1) is no more than an expression of attitude, it cannot be properly understood as saying what simply does fit Hugo's situation, or as saying what simply does not. Such is a rough description of what could be said truly within the second community about the proper understanding of (1) – at least as long as they remain entitled to construing the status of (1) with regard to truth bearing as they do. As for us, if I am correct in thinking that we make the assumptions of neither of the two communities, we are entitled to neither of the above two sorts of descriptions of content.

Two subjects have so far been under discussion: first, being assessable as to truth or falsity (in present terms, being a truth bearer), and second, being to be understood as so assessable. The thesis under discussion so far relates these two subjects. It is that to be a truth bearer is to be so to be understood. Thus, saying something either true or false is something words may be to be understood to do or not, in the same way that some words may be to be understood as speaking of being red. Both of these subjects are to be distinguished from a third, namely, whether words are in fact either true or false. The distinction in the case of understandings rests on the general point that a proper understanding of words may have them as doing something which, as it turns out, they cannot be taken to do. A predicate, for example, may be to be understood as speaking of a property of a certain sort where, as science occasionally shows us, there is no property of that sort to be speaking of. But the point is most easily illustrated in the case of names. 'Hugo likes noodles', on most speakings, is to be understood as saying of someone that he likes noodles. In that sense, 'Hugo' is to be understood as naming or meaning someone in particular. For all that, it could turn out for some such speaking that there is no one who was said in it to like noodles, and thus no one that 'Hugo', in it, meant or named.

If 'Hugo' is taken as it was supposed to be on its speaking, then it will be treated in ways in which there is one individual who is correctly given the role of the one named by the name; any other individual would be incorrectly assigned such a role. Where we take it that there is a reasonable (and most reasonable) assignment of this role, and considerations which make it so, we do treat the name in accordance with what was given to be understood about it. We take it to be a fact, for example, that it was said of someone that he likes noodles. We can become convinced, however, that we cannot maintain such treatment – perhaps that nothing is reasonably taken to make any actual individual a plausible candidate for the role of the one named, or that there are equally strong reasons for assigning the role to any of a number of distinct candidates, or that wherever there is a reason in favour of some candidate's being assigned the role, there is equally strong reason against this. In such a case, we may still recognize that 'Hugo' was to be understood to function as a name, but will conclude that it does not in fact name anything. The words in question may then be regarded as a failed attempt to say that someone likes noodles.

The situation is quite similar with being either true or false. If words are to be understood to say what is either true or false, then it is to be understood that there are, or may be expected to be, facts which count in favour of their truth or facts which count in favour of their falsity or both, and that the facts in the one category will outweigh those, if any, in the other. The general supposition is that words are to be treated as it was given to be understood that they were to be, if (reasonably) possible. So, if there is a reasonable (and most reasonable) way of assigning statuses as reasons for and against the truth of the words in question to the facts that there are, so that the above supposition about distribution of reasons is maintained, then we will take it that the words in question are either true or false, according as they are shown to be on that way of distributing statuses to facts. Occasionally, however, we must conclude that there is no such way. Sometimes (as with some semantic paradoxes, for example) we might even conclude that there could not be any such way. Anything which we can recognize as counting in favour of (or against) the truth of words in question we find to be counterbalanced by an equally powerful consideration on the other side. Such need not compel us to find a different way of understanding the words in question. They may still have been to be understood as saying something to be so – just as 'Hugo likes noodles' was to be understood as saying something of someone – and hence as saying what would be either true or false. Given the right sorts of facts to which to distribute statuses, they might even have turned out to be the one or the other. As things are, however, they must be regarded as a failed attempt to say something with a truth value.

So far, we have discussed the relation between what is to be understood and being either true or false. But it is clear that similar remarks apply to being a truth bearer and being either true or false. Something – 'The ball is red', for example – may be taken to be *assessed* as either true or false. We may even know (some of) what it would be like for it to be the one or the other (as we take ourselves to know what it would be like for the ball to be red). But on any reasonable assignment of status to the facts as they are, every reason for saying the ball is as said to be (red) is exactly counterbalanced by one for holding that it is not, and vice versa. *Mutatis mutandis* for reasons for holding the words true and those for holding them false. If words are a truth bearer in the present sense, then compelling reasons are required to conclude that the words are neither true nor false. Still, in exceptional cases, at least, such might happen.

In 136 Wittgenstein says, 'To say that check did not *fit* our concept of the pawns would mean that a game in which pawns were checked, in which, say, the players who lost their pawns lost, would be uninteresting or stupid or too complicated or something of the kind.' The comparison is with saying that given words do not (or do) fit the concept of truth, where this is not merely a remark about how they are to be understood, given the way we in fact treat them. We have now described one way in which the comparison might be drawn. Where words are a truth bearer, or so to be understood, it may turn out to be too stupid or complicated or whatever (for us, at least) to go on maintaining that they are in fact either true or false. Of course, there will always be some assignments of statuses to the facts that there are on which the words would turn out to be true or to be false. But it may become uninteresting or whatever for us to maintain that any of these could be reasonable, or that some one or another of them must be right.

There is a second comparison to be drawn. Suppose that we know or expect or are convinced of given words W that if they were subject to evaluation as to truth, there are no facts that could show them to be true or show them to be false in ways convincing to us. So the situation described above, which may sometimes arise unexpectedly through non-co-operation on the part of the world, is one which we expect in advance for W. Then we may conclude that it is stupid or pointless or whatever to regard W as subject to assessment as to truth – that is, as a truth bearer – and may therefore refrain from doing so. In fact, where such expectations are shared, it will be difficult to get W to be taken to be understood as saying what might be true or false, just as, where it is known that 'Hugo' could not be referring to anyone, it is difficult to get 'Hugo likes noodles' to be understood as saying of someone that he likes noodles. Suppose, for example, that we are convinced that no facts could ever resolve our disputes over whether Hugo needs a cleaning lady, or that there could not, as a rule, be facts which we could agree to settle such issues. It could still be maintained that there is a fact of the matter – perhaps one that we are inherently blind to – so that (1) is after all either true or false, despite the persistence of our disputes. But we might find it stupid or pointless to maintain this. If we are agreed in that, then we will not understand (1) as saying something such as to be either true or false. In which case, as used by us, it will not do so.

Let us return to the two contrasting communities described above. We said that neither, in treating (1) as it does, could be accused correctly of getting the facts wrong. Neither believes falsely that (1) expresses what might be true or false, whereas the fact is that it does not, or vice versa. But with the above comparison, Wittgenstein suggests another sort of criticism to which either sort of community might be subject. If regarding (1) as a truth bearer leads to the persistence of stupid and pointless disputes within the first community, or if there are no disputes there but also no rationale for whatever agreement there might be, then that community might be accused of regarding (1) in a stupid or pointless way (or something of the sort.) Our evaluations of their disputes and agreements may thus lead to further evaluations of their understanding words such as (1) as they do. The second sort of community might be subject to a reverse sort of criticism. Suppose we find that if (1) were subject to evaluation as to truth or falsity, then, under most circumstances, at least such evaluation would run smoothly and yield positive results. On the assumption that there are situations which would make (1) true of Hugo, and those which would make (1) false of him, there is, we find, an eminently natural and effective organization of situations into those that do the former and those that do the latter (with the usual gradations in clarity, etc.). Then we may find that there is something this second community is missing in treating (1) as they do, and that it is pointless or stupid or whatever for them to do so.

Such a view of the matter allows for very clear cases of pointlessness. It would be pointless beyond question, though not impossible, to regard 'Mary had a little lamb', for example, as a mere expression of opinion rather than as a truth bearer, given the ease with which we would normally get results as to truth or falsity on the latter way of treating it, and given the usefulness of such results, on occasion, in our lives.

Suppose one wants to be a 'value realist' – for example, about the excellence of films or of wines. So one wants to maintain, *inter alia*, that words like (1) express what is either true or false – *ceteris paribus*, at least. On the present view of truth bearing, there are at least two things such a view might come to. First, it might be a view about the proper understandings of words: words like (1), as used by us, are in fact to be understood as saying something either true or false. Such a view would be adjudicable in the same way as we adjudicate any view on the proper understandings of words – for example, as we decide whether given words 'Mary had a little lamb' said something about meat eating or something about pet keeping. Second, the view might amount to a recommendation. Treating words like (1) as truth bearers runs smoothly; as a rule we would get positive results as to their truth or falsity. And to treat them otherwise would be to miss something, for such results, where obtainable, may have great importance in our lives. To say that there may be no further fact of the matter than this is not to belittle such a thesis or to suggest that it is not of the greatest importance, philosophical and otherwise.

In summary, whether given words are either true or false depends on two issues. The first issue is how the words are or were to be understood. For it may be to be understood of words, as part of their proper understanding, that what they are saying is something either true or false. That words are understood in this way may be what distinguishes one understanding of them from another. Given that there is such a way of being understood, words will be so to be understood if that is the most reasonable way of understanding them, given all the facts about them which might incline one to understand them in one way or another. That words do (or do not) say something either true or false is not entailed by any of their other properties, besides that of being (or not being) to be understood to do so. (Nor need this property be *entailed* by others.) Given that words are so to be understood, the second issue about them concerns what happens when evaluations as to their truth or falsity are carried out. The words may be more reasonably regarded as saying something true than as saying something false, which in turn *may* have an effect on what they are most reasonably regarded as saying. On the other hand, correct evaluations *may* be incapable of yielding either the result that the words are true or the result that they are not. Such may provide reason for concluding that the words are *not* to be understood as saying what is either true or false. The first issue is not wholly independent of the second. But in some cases – such as contingently arising liar paradoxes – the right conclusion may simply be that the words do not succeed in doing what they are to be understood to do. In that respect, at least, taking something to be so, even where it is so to be taken, is not enough to make it so where the issue is what words say.

Notice how the above provides an example of how facts of a given sort may lead a life of their own. As it happens, we have a notion which we take to apply to some things and not to others. In this case, the notion is that of saying what is either true or false, and a reason for taking it to apply to some things, at least, is that it is to be understood to do so. When it comes to working out to which things the notion would apply and to which not, assuming that it does apply to some things and not to others, there are enough particular cases which are clearly enough classified one way or the other. There are enough of our words, in this case, about whose status, given that there is such a thing as being a truth bearer or not, no reasonable person would disagree. But no further proof than this is required for there to be facts about what possesses the property that the notion is of, and what does not. Again, *taking* there to be facts of a certain sort does not quite make this so. But when such meshes with a reasonable enterprise of saying what the facts are, given that there are such – in Wittgenstein's terms, one which we find neither too stupid nor pointless nor difficult – the pointfulness of the enterprise is all the proof there could or need be that we made no mistake in taking there to be facts of the sort we did.

NAMES

So far, we have applied a thought to the bearing of truth values. The thought would seem to have other applications as well. About names, for example, one might say the following. What makes a word a name is the fact that it is part of the language game to treat it as such. No *other* properties of the word *make* it a name or not, or make it fit or fail to fit our concept of a name. To say that a word *could not* be a name, where this does not merely mean that that is not in fact how we treat it, could only mean that treating it as a name would be too stupid or uninteresting or complicated, or something of the sort.

We have interpreted the thought in terms of proper understandings. Continuing to do so, we may say: it may be part of the way in which a word is to be understood – part of what there is to be understood about it – that it is to be understood to be a name, or to be doing what a name does. Such is part of what there is to be understood about a name, and, where it is not to be understood, the word in question is not a name. To say that words may be to be understood in one way or another in this respect is, once again, to say that having the property – being a name or doing what a name does – is not brought about by other features of the word in question, whether features of its proper understanding or otherwise.

Features of a word other than features of how it is to be understood might include such things as having been spoken by someone who winked twice while doing so, or by someone with someone in mind while doing so. Some may have theories linking such properties with that of being a name, or even with doing what a name does in a particular way – for example, naming so-and-so. Such theories would certainly run counter to the trend of Wittgenstein's thought, in 136 and elsewhere. But since there are enough other things to discuss here, I propose to leave properties of this sort to one side for the moment.

To see what it is to be a name, we might ask what salient properties a word has in virtue of being that. A conspicuous one is this. If a name does what it aims or purports to do, then there is someone or something it names. It will mean that person (or thing) and be to be understood to do so. If 'Mary had a little lamb' says what it aims to, then there will be someone whom it says, in the relevant sense, to have had a little lamb. 'Mary' will then name that person, and will be understood to do so, properly construed.[2] The present thought, then, is that these are properties that a word may

---

2 The last sort of property is not innocuous, and it is not totally beyond controversy that names have it. I think they do, and I think Wittgenstein thought so. But I will not argue either point here. Let us just see how the Wittgensteinian thought develops, given that this is how names work. As we shall see, what it takes, on the thought, for names to have such properties is roughly no more than that we take names to have them. And the evidence is that (outside of philosophy) that is what we do.

be to be understood to have. The word will be so to be understood if it does have these properties. For no other features of it or its proper understanding could bring it about that it had them. It is this aspect of a way of understanding a word in which its aiming or purporting to do what a name does (in present respects) consists. And being so to be understood will confer the properties in question on a word, provided it is not too pointless or stupid or whatever to treat the word, in accordance with its proper understanding, as having such properties. All of which is to say: it is a feature of a name that it is to be understood that there is someone whom it is to be understood to mean. Such accord with descriptions we would ordinarily take to fit. One might say, '"Mary had a little lamb" was to be understood to be saying of someone that she had a little lamb'; hence, 'It was to be understood that there was someone that "Mary" was to be understood to mean.' It remains to be seen how such remarks might have the deeper significance that the present thought ascribes to them.

Part of the Wittgensteinian thought is that being a name, and so having the above properties, is independent of other features of how a word is to be understood. Hence the need for understandings of the sort just pointed to above. We can see better what this independence might come to if we compare the thought with a thesis of Leibniz's.[3] Leibniz distinguished between two sorts of concepts, which we might call *individual* and *general*. A general concept is one such that, if it does apply to a given individual A, nevertheless there might be or might have been some individual B, distinct from A, such that the concept applied to that individual. The concept of being red would be an example of this. An individual concept is one for which the above is not so. So if there is an individual A, such that the concept applies to it, then the concept could not apply or have applied to any individual other than A. If there is an individual concept of being Wittgenstein, for example, then to fall under it would be to be Wittgenstein. Hence nothing other than him could fall or could have fallen under it. Leibniz's thesis was that no individual concept is equivalent to any set of general ones: specify such a set, and those concepts could

---

3 See the *Discourse on Metaphysics*, section 8.

apply to something without the individual concept doing so, and/or vice versa.

Leibniz did not state his thesis in terms of names. But it may be applied to names via the observation that the fact that there is someone whom a name N is to be understood to mean is equivalent to there being some individual concept the name is to be taken to express. For suppose N is to be understood to mean A. What is required for being the one it means *on that understanding* is precisely being A.[4] And on the understanding in question, N is to be understood to impose just this requirement. But then N is to be understood to impose a requirement which is just that for satisfying some individual concept, namely a concept of being A. That concept is, then, a concept of what is to be understood to be required for being the one N means. There is, then, something to be understood about N – something about whom N means – which is fixed by an individual concept, and not, on Leibniz's thesis, by any set of general ones.

Leibniz's thesis, applied to names, says, first that where a name does name, there is a requirement imposed by its proper understanding which is distinct from any requirement which any set of general concepts impose for their satisfaction. Suppose, then, that an understanding of a word is specifiable in part at least in terms of general concepts. There are then two possibilities. First, these general concepts may be understood to exhaust what is required, on a proper understanding of it, for correct application of the word. Second, they may be understood to be non-exhaustive in this respect – pointing to the one the name names in one way or another, perhaps, but not stating the requirement for being the one the name names. If they are understood as exhaustive, then the word is not being understood as a name. And if there is nothing further to be understood about how it is to be taken, then it is not a name. If the general concepts are non-exhaustive, then there must be something further to be understood about the word in question. Non-exclusively, either there is some individual concept such that

---

[4] It could not, thus, be to be understood to mean A, but mean a distinct B, though the right (or wrong) facts about A and B might bring it about that it was not, after all, to be understood to mean A.

this further aspect of an understanding is specifiable in terms of it, or at least it is to be understood that the word requires, for applying to what it does, what is required for satisfying *some* individual concept. To understand a word in this way is to understand it as a name, at least in those respects mentioned above.

Leibniz's thesis does not require that names are not to be understood in terms of general concepts. It requires only that in so far as they are so to be understood, such an understanding is not exhaustive. It must also be taken to be understood that what is required for satisfaction of the general concepts in question is distinct from what is required for being the one the name names: the one requirement could be satisfied while the other is not. Such constrains the role that general concepts could play in identifying the one the name names. But it does not exclude their having one. What general concepts specify about an understanding might be used in any of a variety of ways. Being the understanding of a name excludes uses on which the name is to apply to just what satisfies those concepts. But the variety in uses for what general concepts specify makes being a name compatible with having such further aspects of understanding or not.

Translating back from Leibnizian terminology, we get part of the Wittgensteinian thought. If N is a name, and does what a name does, then either it is to be understood that there is someone N is to be understood to name, or, for some individual A, N is to be understood to name A. No other features of an understanding can make it one with those features of the proper understanding of a name. Conversely, if a word is to be understood in this way, then it will function as a name regardless of other features of how it is to be understood. In particular, it is neither the case that a name must be, nor that it cannot be, to be understood *inter alia* in descriptive terms. (Wittgenstein 79, for example, might be read as proposing just this view.)

Another side of the Wittgensteinian thought emerges if we ask how any word could express an individual concept. How could it be that the second half of the above disjunction holds: for some A, N is to be understood to mean A? Philosophers, Russell for one, have puzzled over this. The worry is that in so far as we have criteria for the application of a word, it would seem that these must be specifiable in general terms. For otherwise it would be mysterious how we could recognize when the criteria were satisfied. Russell sought special cases which escaped this general rule – cases where, in a sense, no criteria of application were called for. The Wittgensteinian thought, however, proposes a simpler answer. A word will express an individual concept if it is to be understood to do so – that is, taking it that there is some individual concept it expresses is taking it as doing what it is to be understood to be doing – and if treating it in this way is neither too stupid nor pointless nor anything of the sort. To suppose that a word expresses *some* individual concept is simply to treat it in one possible way of treating words. Such would be stupid or whatever if there failed to be clear enough answers to the questions which arose for us on that supposition. Such questions would concern which individual concept the word expresses on the supposition that it expresses one. In other terms, for various A and B, they would be questions about whether the word was to be understood to mean A or B. We may ask, for example, whether 'Wittgenstein', on a given use, was to be understood to mean Ludwig or Paul. If we fell into confusion when it came to answering such questions – if there were no answers which could be seen to be correct – then we should take it that the word in question did not bear the sort of understanding it was to be understood to bear. Such does happen for some names on some uses. We sometimes do conclude that, contrary to what was given to be understood, there is no one that a given name is to be understood to mean. But often enough it is clear enough what to say on the stated supposition. Where we can make the choices that thus need making, there is no further question as to whether there is someone the name is to be understood to mean. In other terms, in such cases, there *is* an individual concept the name expresses.

Just as nothing makes it the case that N is a name beyond the fact that it is to be understood to be such, so nothing makes it the case that N names T beyond the fact that such is a consequence of the most reasonable way of treating it given its proper understanding. That there might be some particular ingredient with the general property of making names name is an idea which Wittgenstein criticizes in 38:

Naming appears as a *queer* connection of a word with an object. – And you really get such a queer connection when the philosopher tries to bring out *the* relation between name and thing by staring at an object in front of him and repeating a name, or even the word 'this' innumerable times. For philosophical problems arise when language *goes on holiday*. And *here* we may indeed fancy naming to be some remarkable act of mind, as it were a baptism of an object.

Staring at a thing and repeating a name over and over is reminiscent of another mistake Wittgenstein mentions elsewhere (314), that of studying 'the headache I have now in order to get clear about the philosophical problem of sensation'. It is doubtful whether any philosopher has ever quite done either of these things, or, if some philosopher has, whether that fact in itself would be of any great philosophical significance. But the idea is clear enough. What the philosopher who studied his headache would be looking for is some ingredient which made it a headache, or which made the concept 'headache' apply to it. Similarly, the philosopher who repeats the name would be trying to observe not just the name and the thing named, but, as it were, the *naming* which the name does – some ingredient which binds name and thing together in the relation of name and bearer. The headache-making ingredient, if found, would be philosophically interesting if it were not merely something which conferred status on the philosopher's *present* headache, but an ingredient incompatible with something's not being a headache, and still better, if its absence were incompatible with something's being a headache. Similarly for the naming. An account of why 'Wittgenstein' names Wittgenstein, as long as it is merely that, is not what Wittgenstein's philosopher is looking for. To solve philosophical problems about naming, he wants to find in his particular case some ingredient incompatible with a name's not naming the thing in question (at the least). What he wants is a description in other terms of *naming a thing*; a specification of that state of affairs, other than that of a name's naming a thing, which would link a name with a thing in that particular way. And where philosophers seek such things, there is also often the suggestion that if no such ingredient can be found, then perhaps names really do not name things, or the things we take them to, or at least that there are no facts of the matter as to whether and what names name. (Here again, the Russell of 1918 will serve as one sort of example.)

Part of the story about 38 is that Wittgenstein holds the assumption on which the above sort of investigation would be interesting to be mistaken. Such is indicated by his emphasis on 'the' in '*the* relation between name and thing'. On Wittgenstein's view, there need be no essence of naming of the sort the above philosopher seeks, for an entirely general reason. For any concept at all, the features of an object or situation which make the concept apply to it need, and generally will, not be incompatible with the concept's *not* applying to something with those features under some circumstances or other. There need, and generally will, be no such features of an object. What is required in a given case is merely something which makes it more reasonable in the case at hand to take the concept to apply than to take it not to, given that there are those alternatives to choose from – that is, on the (defeasible) assumption that the one thing or the other is the case.

But what of the idea of 'language having a holiday'? The idea is that this is something that occurs where words are designed to be used in certain sorts of circumstances, where they make good sense, but are then used outside such circumstances – as frequently occurs in doing philosophy, Wittgenstein suggests. Such use of words outside appropriate surroundings would pose a particular problem if, for those words, the surroundings were needed to determine a complete thought or question or whatever for the words to express. For one model of this, we might think of the words 'It is now 3 p.m.' occurring in the middle of a textbook – on algebra, say – in such a way that there was no way of determining what 'now' should be taken to be (the time of reading, of writing, of printing, or what?). As the model indicates, such a problem would arise where any of a number of distinct things are expressible in given words on some speaking or other; for example, thoughts with distinct truth conditions, or questions with different conditions for being answered correctly. It might arise for the words, 'My suit is brown', for example, if there are different things that being brown is to be taken to come to for different speakings of those words. And the problem may be philosophically insidious to the extent that the variety of things to be expressed in given words may go unnoticed.

For language to have a holiday in the case of naming, there must first be a variety of like-sounding questions to be asked in asking why name N names thing T, or what makes it do so, or why it should be taken to do so, or whatever. On an occasion where such a question is posed, circumstances must then determine which specific question is being posed – or, as it were, which complete interrogative thought is being expressed. If the words for such a question were produced where no circumstances filled in such a complete thought, then no question in particular would be asked, just as nothing in particular is said in, 'It is now 3 p.m.' where there is nothing to fill in what 'now' is. Language would then be on holiday.

Such a variety of like-sounding questions would be distinguished from one another in what each requires for an answer, so that what would answer one such question would not answer some other. No such question has an answer, of course, if N does not name T, or ought not to be taken to do so. There is no explaining why N names T if it doesn't. But where such questions have answers, the answer to each question may be supposed to rule out some ways in which N might not have named T. But if such an answer is not to answer every such question, it cannot be expected to rule out every way in which it might have been the case that that was not what N did.

In these terms, it is clear what the staring philosopher is being accused of. Naturally enough, he does not want to confine himself to any one question out of the variety. For the answer to that would not in itself be philosophically interesting. It would not remotely resemble a theory of naming. So what the philosopher seeks is something that would answer every question in the variety – something which thus leaves open no way in which N might not have named T. But, the accusation goes, first, there is no such thing, and second, it is wrong to demand it. No such thing is required for it to be the case that N names T, or for us to know that it does.

Where a question why N names T has an answer which explains why, it must be true to say that N does name T. If, in given circumstances, a given thing would be asked in a question as to why N names T, and that thing has such an answer, then, in those circumstances, it is true to say that N names T. If there are a variety of like-sounding questions to this effect, then the answer to any one such will not answer every one. Which is to say that it is compatible with N's not naming T, were appropriate further facts to obtain. By the same token, where that is the question posed, these possibilities for N's not naming T would not count against something being an answer to the question, where that thing does not rule these possibilities out. Nor, by the link just forged, would it count against the truth of what would be said under those circumstances in saying N to name T. If for the philosopher's quest language is on holiday, there will be no way of seeing which like-sounding question he would or should be asking, and hence which substantive answer should satisfy him. But if he demands more for N's naming T than what must be the case where there are substantive answers to the particular questions that there are to be posed, then, by the above reasoning, he demands more than is required for the truth of what there is to say in saying N to name T. But what is more than required is not what would fit his conception of an essence of naming.

Suppose that Hugo says, 'Sam is coming to dinner.' Suppose we understand his 'Sam' to mean one Sam Goode, a good friend of Hugo's. We may have our reasons for so taking this 'Sam', and we may on occasion be able to state some. On the view of holidays for language, the reasons we could state, if any, would vary with the circumstances of stating them – with such things, perhaps, as which other ways of taking 'Sam' are to be ruled out, or what reasons there are to think that 'Sam' might not mean Goode. On the staring philosopher's view, if 'Sam' does mean Goode, then there are reasons that could be stated for taking 'Sam' to do so, where these reasons are incompatible with 'Sam' not doing so: *wherever* those reasons held true, 'Sam' would mean Goode. Such reasons would be, as it were, constitutive of its being a fact that 'Sam' means Goode. Conversely, if there are no such reasons, then at best there is no fact of the matter as to 'Sam' meaning Goode.

Suppose now that we offer reasons for taking 'Sam' to mean Goode which are not conclusive in the way the staring philosopher demands. So they are compatible with 'Sam' not meaning Goode in the sense that they could hold in some possible situations in which 'Sam' would not do so. Perhaps there is a possible story, for example, on which those reasons hold true but 'Sam' refers to Sam Peckinpah. What does the existence of such stories or possibilities show about the reasons in question and its being a fact that 'Sam' means Goode? Consider the view of 136 as applied to names. Grant that 'Sam' is to be understood to function as a name. So it is to be understood that there is someone 'Sam' is to be understood to mean. Then on the view that there is someone 'Sam' means, such are the facts – unless supposing so proves too stupid or complicated or something of the sort. Does the existence of such possibilities show anything of this sort?

Does it show either that it is unreasonable to take 'Sam' to mean Goode given that 'Sam' means someone, or that it is unreasonable to take it, as on the proper understanding of 'Sam', that there is someone 'Sam' means? If there is someone 'Sam' is most reasonably taken to mean, supposing it to mean someone, then, in the sense of 136, it is not too stupid or complicated to suppose 'Sam' to mean someone. So, on this view, it is only the former question that needs considering.

Whether a possibility for 'Sam' not to mean Goode convinces us that it is not reasonably taken to do so depends, of course, on the possibility in question and the circumstances under which the convincing is to be done. Some possibilities might sometimes convince us of such things. But the mere fact that there *are* such possibilities for 'Sam' shows nothing of the kind, as our actual understandings of names ought to convince us. Not just any story on which 'Sam' means Peckinpah would convince us that perhaps, after all, it might do so, even in the absence of reasons which positively rule it out. Some stories, at least, ask for reason to suppose they might be true. In present terms, not every possibility for 'Sam' not to mean Goode would show that we were being stupid or unreasonable in supposing it to do so. It might, on the contrary, be unreasonable to cease to suppose this merely in virtue of the story. Not every such story could show that we did not know that 'Sam' meant Goode, or that a given explanation did not explain why it did. But if we do know that 'Sam' means Goode, or there is an explanation why, then trivially 'Sam' does mean Goode.

The above are remarks on what we find stupid or uninteresting, sensible or pointful, and so on, or what we do when being reasonable. But the view of 136 applied to names has it that it is exactly out of these phenomena that facts about what 'Sam' means are constituted. If there are no reasons which are conclusive in the way the staring philosopher requires, still, as long as the stories that can be told on which 'Sam' would not mean Goode do not make it too stupid or whatever to take it to do so, given the reasons there are for doing so, the fact will be, on the present view, that 'Sam' means Goode.

The point is not, of course, that possibilities of 'Sam' not meaning Goode are irrelevant *per se*. Our reasons for taking 'Sam' to do so may or may not be good ones. If they are not good, then presumably they are not because for all that they say to be so, 'Sam' might, or might just as well not, mean Goode. And such is to be shown, presumably, by *some* stories on which the reasons hold true but 'Sam' does not mean Goode. So, for a given claim that 'Sam' means Goode, there are possibilities which might impeach it and possibilities which would not. This idea of different sorts of possibilities is of fundamental importance for Wittgenstein and a recurrent theme in the *Investigations*. It is developed, for example, in 84 as a general epistemological point, to be applied in a discussion, from about 84 to 87, of the existence of facts about correct novel applications of words to things, of rules, directions and so on. There the point is put in terms of doubts. For a given proposition P, we may take a doubt with respect to P simply to be some way in which what P says to be so would not be so. In 84, Wittgenstein distinguishes between 'real' doubts and 'merely imaginable' ones. For a given claim that someone knows that P, a real doubt would be one that shows the claim to be correct, if compatible with all the person's information with respect to P (leaving aside the information that P). With respect to that claim, any other doubt is a merely imaginable one.

One point of 84, is that for a given claim to know P, the class of merely imaginable doubts is non-empty. In present terms, not just any way in which we could conceive of P not being true given the information we have would show it to be stupid or unreasonable or wrong to continue to take it that *P*. Hence not just any doubt would show that we did not know that *P*. But in 85 and succeeding sections, another point emerges. Suppose we consider a given proposition – say, that my aunt's pen is on the dresser. Suppose we ask which doubts are real and which doubts are not with respect to a claim to know this. Then we have another case of language on holiday. For a given doubt may sometimes be real and sometimes not, for different considerings whether a given person knows where my aunt's pen is. If we suppose that doubts are real or not *tout court*, then a doubt which is sometimes real must be classified as always real. For 'always real' and 'always not' are the only classifications there are. On the other hand, a doubt as to whether *P* may make it unreasonable to judge that *P* for some judgings of the matter, while for others it does not do so. Where a doubt does not count against judging that *P*, it does not count against knowing it. From which it follows that there are a variety of distinct things to be said in claiming a given person *A* to know that *P*.

Suppose now that *P* is the proposition that 'Sam' means Goode. Consider given reasons for taking it that that is what 'Sam' does. Given those reasons, one ought to take it that 'Sam' means Goode if they leave no real doubt that that is what 'Sam' does. If they do not, and there are no better reasons for taking 'Sam' in some other way, then those reasons make it the case that 'Sam' is to be taken to mean Goode. In which case, on the view of 136 applied, that is what it does. But, given the point just developed, a doubt which is not reasonable for some considerations of what 'Sam' means may be reasonable for others. In which case, reasons which sometimes make it the case that 'Sam' is to be taken to mean Goode may at other times fail to do so. The staring philosopher supposed that reasons which make it the case that 'Sam' is (or is not) to be taken to mean Goode must do so *tout court*, and there must be reasons which make this the case if there is a fact of the matter at all as to who 'Sam' means. But, in so supposing, he wrongly construes the role of doubts, at least on the above view of them. It is this thought that gives the doctrine of holidays for language its point in the context of 38.

The truth of a claim that *X* knows that *F* requires that there be no *real* doubts with respect to it which are consistent with *X*'s information as to whether F – doubts such that, if they obtained, X would have the same reason he now has to take it that F, even though not F. It requires also, of course, that F in fact obtain. On a standard conception we think of these as two distinct requirements, either of which might be satisfied while the other is not. Where the mere existence of a possibility for F not to obtain would not refute a knowledge claim, still, the actual obtaining of that possibility would. So we may have every reason to take it that the pen is on the dresser, and there may be no real doubt about this. But it is conceivable that all that is so, while the fact is that the pen is not on the dresser. As long as such is conceivable, the fact that the pen is on the dresser cannot consist in the fact that our reasons for taking it to be there hold. So whatever constitutes that fact, it must be something other than those reasons. It is along such lines that the staring philosopher appears to be conceiving of facts such as the fact that 'Sam' means Goode. Whatever the reasons for *taking* 'Sam' to do that, if they are not conclusive in the way he demands, then they can be at best no more than indications of that fact. The fact itself must, for him, consist in something else, where that cannot merely be the fact that 'Sam' means Goode.

Wherever the idea of 136 applies, at least, there is a more intimate connection between the reasons for taking a fact to obtain and its actually obtaining than the above model suggests. Nor are the above two requirements on knowledge quite so independent as they seem in the case of my aunt's pen. Suppose there are reasons for taking 'Sam' to mean Goode which, for given judgings of the matter, leave no real doubt as to whether that is what 'Sam' does, where those reasons are non-conclusive in the present sense. We may still conceive of the following gap between the obtaining of those reasons and 'Sam' meaning Goode: there may be further non-conclusive reasons for taking 'Sam' in some other way (for example, as meaning Peckinpah) where these reasons make it more reasonable to take 'Sam' in that way, even given the first-mentioned ones. Conceivably we may have no reason to suspect that such reasons exist; some facts about Hugo's speaking may have simply escaped us. But where there are no such further reasons, where all relevant non-conclusive facts about a speaking have been given their due, there is no further possibility for the

Truth bearing and content

non-obtaining of the fact that 'Sam' means Goode. There is then no *further* thing for that fact to consist in. This might be put by saying: the fact that 'Sam' means Goode does consist in the obtaining of the reasons there are for taking it to do so, in particular circumstances where those reasons leave no further question about the matter. This is not to say that those reasons would always constitute such a fact, or that this fact might not at other times be constituted by something else. One might speak of a family of situations which count as the obtaining of the fact that 'Sam' means Goode. Even if some one thing could be found which united all members of this family, like the extra ingredient that the staring philosopher sought, it would not be that ingredient which makes the facts about naming what they are.

The staring philosopher was looking for something incompatible with N's not naming T (if naming T is what N does.) Failing to find such a thing, some philosophers have been inclined to conclude that all facts, other than the fact, if it is one, that N names T, might be just what they were both where N named T and where it did not, or that all such other facts are compatible, perhaps equally so, with N's doing either. So, for example, all facts at some other level – say, about linguistic behaviour, or about movements of particles in the universe – might be just what they are, compatible with N's meaning T or not. But such is the wrong conclusion to draw from the philosopher's failure. For that failure came to this. Suppose the philosopher cited F as making N mean T. Then there are possible situations in which F obtains but N does not mean T. And such would remain true no matter what F the philosopher chose. But a situation in which F obtains and N does not mean T need not be like the actual one in all other respects. It might be one in which there are other facts which do not obtain as things are, and which make F non-decisive in that situation. What shows 'Sam' to mean Goode might not do so if Goode had a double, for example. But as things are, he does not. On the present view, such an other situation would have to differ from the actual one in some such respect. For further facts of some sort would be required to make what is now reasonable pointless or stupid or the like. It is sometimes said that other facts underdetermine facts about proper understandings of words. But if determination may proceed according to the Wittgensteinian idea sketched above, then at least in the case of names there is no reason to believe this.

There are interpretations in the literature on which Wittgenstein questioned the objectivity of meaning, or at least the existence of facts about the correctness of novel applications of words to things. The alleged grounds for the question are that all meaning fixing facts about a word – facts about its prior uses, the mental states of its users and so on – are consistent with various hypotheses about which novel uses are correct.[5] We have now developed two reasons why such interpretations must be incorrect. First, on them, Wittgenstein offers an argument to prove that certain forms of words could not be truth bearers – for example, '"pen" does not describe this truly'. But on the view of 136, there could be no such proof. Nothing about the words in question could make it impossible to treat them as truth bearers. If that is how we do treat them, and doing so runs smoothly enough, then, on Wittgenstein's view, that is what they are. Second, given Wittgenstein's general epistemological principles, and the connection he saw between these principles and the obtaining of facts of the sort here in question, it could not have been his view that the obtaining of facts about to what words would apply truly requires the obtaining of further facts inconsistent with such facts about meaning not obtaining. We can, perhaps, imagine circumstances in which 'blue' is properly construed so as to apply truly to the tree outside my window. On Wittgenstein's view, that does nothing towards showing us not to know that those are not the circumstances we are in.

CONTENT

Our original aim was to say something about facts about content and what it requires. Having applied Wittgenstein's idea about truth in one other area, we can now try applying it here as well. The application can be made in two parts. The first part concerns

---

5 See Saul A. Kripke, *Wittgenstein on Rules and Private Language*, Basil Blackwell, Oxford, 1982.

what is required for there to be facts about content. For there to be facts of a given sort about the content of words W, two conditions must be met. First, it must be part of a proper understanding of W that there are to be understood to be facts of that sort. Second, supposing there to be facts of this sort must run smoothly; working out what these facts are, in so far as such is called for, must not be too stupid or complicated or whatever. The second part might be put by saying that facts about content are autonomous. Aside from the requirements just mentioned, no other facts about words could guarantee that there were facts of a given sort about content, or that there were not.

The first part of this application may seem circular. For it to be taken to be understood about W that there are facts of a given sort about its content, is already for there to be some facts about its content. But when would *that* be the case? Once again it will help to consider an example. Consider my words, 'My suit is brown'. Suppose we are now confronted with a suit, and with the issue of whether the words are true of that. A natural view is that there is something that the content of the words requires for them to be true of that suit. So either it is a fact that they have a content such as to be true of it, or it is a fact that they have a content such as not to be true of it. (Let us ignore for now the possibility of borderline cases.) Is the natural view right? On the present account, it is just in case the words were to be understood to have a content of that sort (and the second requirement is met). But were they? One consequence of the view is that there are two distinct ways in which words may be taken to be understood: as having such a content, or as not. We can then pose the problem: given these alternatives, which sort of content are these words most reasonably taken to have? The usual standards for solving such problems apply. And of course there is also the possibility that the problem has no solution: it would be too stupid or whatever to maintain that the words had either sort of content rather than the other. But of course it *might* also be too stupid or whatever to maintain *that*.

We need not prejudge the issue of what the correct solution to the above problem is. But it could be such that on it there are to be understood to be facts about the content of my words of the sort that the natural view supposes. The question then arises as to which sort of content my words had – one such as to be true of the words in question, or one such as not to be. Again, this question may have no positive answer. Every reason for assigning my words a content of the one sort may be counterbalanced by a reason for assigning them a content of the other. Or the problem may lie with the suit: every reason for finding it as said to be in my words may be counterbalanced by a reason for finding it otherwise. But unless we find that it is in general too stupid or whatever to treat words as having content of the kind in question, we may be guided by the fact that such outcomes are exceptions rather than rule. And if there *is* a most reasonable positive answer to the question posed, then, on the account now on offer, the fact is that my words have the content that that answer assigns to them.

The above ought not to suggest that issues about content are simple. But if there are hard issues about content, then, on this view, these will not be over whether there are facts about content or not, but rather over precisely what sorts of content there are to be understood to be for given words and what sorts it is supportable to take them to have. For example, take my words 'is brown'. It seems easy to suppose of them, or even of the English words 'is brown', that they have a content which permits the following: we could now, or any time we liked, take any arbitrary set of objects and sort them into those the words are true of and those the words are not. That is, the fact is that the content of the words is such as to impose a requirement for being true of something which arbitrary objects either satisfy or do not, *tout court*. But the facts of our use of such words make it obvious neither that the words are to be understood to have that sort of content, nor that taking them to do so is a supportable undertaking. If anything is obvious, it is merely that on (most) occasions where we are called on to judge whether, for example, my words are true of a given suit, we can find reasons for taking the words to have a content such as to make them true of that or a content such as to make them untrue of it. Finding the right morals to draw from what we actually do with words, or even the right descriptions of what that is, is a long, arduous and far from obvious task. Thus, a philosopher who challenges the existence of particular sorts of facts about content need not be challenging the Wittgensteinian view outlined above.

He may merely be challenging the interpretation assigned to certain facts about proper understandings by some other philosopher.

The interest of the present Wittgensteinian view is most likely to lie in its implications for a sceptic about facts about content. And in so far as this is so, it may be of some interest to note that it *is* a Wittgensteinian view. The sceptic about content, like the philosopher who stares at a thing and repeats a name, is someone who seeks some *other* sort of fact which would guarantee that a given sort of fact about content held – that is, which was incompatible with its not holding. The fact about content might be, for example, that my words had a content such as to be true of such-and-such a suit. And the other sorts of facts might be, for example, facts about other prior uses of those words, or about my mental states at the time of my speaking. Failing to find any other facts incompatible with my words having the sort of content just described, the sceptic, being a sceptic, would conclude that it is not a fact that they do have such a content. For this sort of manoeuvre, there are clear morals in the Wittgensteinian view. First, it was to be predicted in advance that the sceptic would not find any 'content-making' ingredient of the kind he sought, since facts about content are autonomous from other facts, in the same way that being a truth bearer or being a name is autonomous from other facts. Second, for the same sorts of reasons that no such ingredient is required for it to be a fact that a name N names a thing T, no such ingredient is required for it to be a fact that my words, 'My suit is brown', have a content of the sort under discussion. Of course, nothing in these Wittgensteinian morals entails that those words do have such a content. But for deciding whether they do or not, the sceptic is simply looking in the wrong place.

FACTS

The story thus far seems to have a moral for anti-realism, which I shall now try to draw. Let us take anti-realism for words W to be the view that there is no fact which might obtain or not such that that is the fact W states; thus, that there is nothing which W says to be so which, by being so or not, would make *W* either true or false. This view of *W* is to be distinguished from one on which the fact that *W* states neither obtains nor fails to (but perhaps might under other circumstances). For example, the latter might be one view of some semantic paradoxes – say, those that may arise for words, 'What I last said is true.' Though some of what will be said here may apply to the latter view as well, it is only the former that is under discussion. One may be an anti-realist with respect to a wide class of words, for example causal statements, holding with Hume that there are no facts about what caused what, or ethical claims, or descriptions of the content of words, or ascriptions of propositional attitudes. Or one may be anti-realist about isolated or singular words, such as historical claims for which there could be no evidence, or mathematical claims for which there is no proof. Or one may be not quite an anti-realist, holding that the view could never be *proved* for given words *W*, but then nor could it ever be refuted.

There are reasons and reasons for being an anti-realist. For example, one might be anti-realist about ethical statements simply because he holds that, in point of fact, we do not understand these as even purporting to say anything such as to be true or false, or because it would be wrong or stupid to combine such an understanding with our practices in assigning praise, blame, punishment, etc. Or one could be an anti-realist because he is convinced, for whatever reason, of what it would be for a particular sort of fact to obtain – for example, that for a mathematical fact to obtain is for there to be a proof of it, or with Hume, that what it would be for a causal fact to obtain would be for it to be observable as a remainder after a presumably exhaustive description of a situation had been subtracted. Sometimes, again, someone is an anti-realist because of views about limitations on our mental powers. The idea seems to be roughly this. If there is a fact *F* which *W* states, then in understanding *W* one must know what it would be like for *F* to obtain, or have an adequate conception of this. If *W* are words that we can understand, then we must be capable of having such a conception. But it might then be claimed for any of a variety of reasons that we could not have such a conception – for example because, given the sort of fact *W* would have to state if it stated any, nothing we could ever know could put us in a position to know that such a fact obtained.

The moral to be drawn here does not concern the correctness of any particular anti-realist view. It would be heroic in the extreme to maintain that there were absolutely no words whatsoever which were neither true nor false, nor which did not state facts (e.g. 'What time is it?'), though here philosophy has known its heroes. Sorting out words which are fact stating from those which are not is undoubtedly an intricate and sometimes tedious business, not ended simply by giving an account of what it is for something to be a truth bearer, or to be fact stating. Such an account may have consequences, however, for the sorts of reasons there might be for or against anti-realism in any particular case.

On the present account, for there to be a fact F which is the fact W states, two things are required. First, W must be to be understood to be stating a fact. Second, treating it as doing so must be neither too stupid nor complicated nor whatever. Such is merely our account of being a truth bearer put in terms of facts. If these two conditions are met, then, on this account, no further facts could show that there 'really' was no fact which W stated. So, for example, the ethical anti-realist described above clearly and directly addresses the right issues. If ethical claims are not in fact to be understood to be stating facts, then they do not do so. Similarly, if treating them as stating facts is too stupid given our other practices, then we ought not so to treat them. All of which is not to endorse the ethical anti-realist's conclusions.

What is much more doubtful, however, is that the other sorts of reasons mentioned above ought to be taken as persuasive. Consider causation, for example. Suppose we are convinced that, on the assumption that there are facts which causal statements say to obtain, it is clear enough which would state what is a fact and which would not. Not that we could tell this all the time. But there would be little enough real doubt about what to say enough of the time for the practice of making such judgements not to be unacceptably stupid. Then, given that causal statements are naturally understood as stating facts, we may conclude that that is what they do. And we ought to be utterly unimpressed by arguments about not being able to observe, in addition to the events involved, the causing that the one event does to the other. Such sorts of observation might just be beside the point. In fact, we might even use the fact that causal statements state facts to generate an anti-Humean argument: since we can sometimes see that what a causal statement says to be so is so, we can sometimes see that A caused B. Where we can see something happening that would make a causal statement true, we can say that we see A causing B (as we might see Hugo making Odile angry). Nothing is required for seeing this over and above what we do see when we see A and B in a situation where A causes B. For what we then see is the obtaining of the fact that a given causal statement states. Similar remarks apply to arguments about limitations on our mental powers. If we are convinced that statements about the past, or mathematical propositions, are to be understood to be stating facts, and that so treating them is neither too stupid nor whatever, then we ought to conclude that that is what they do. If all that is so, then additional facts about our mental powers – for example, that we could never be in a position to know some such fact to obtain – are beside the point. Perhaps, for example, understanding W does not after all require knowing what it would be like for the fact it states to obtain. Perhaps we might rest content with something else, such as our confidence that we could recognize what this would be like if the right situation ever came along. Or perhaps we should hold that we *do* know what it would be like for such a fact to obtain. For this would simply be for what W says to be so to be so. And we do, after all, know what W says.

This way of casting issues is, in a way, unfair to the anti-realist of the sort just described. For he may claim, sometimes with some justice, that in, for example, pointing to limitations on our mental powers in the way he does, he is precisely speaking to our second requirement on fact stating. That is, he is showing why it is too stupid or complicated or whatever to regard the discourse in question as fact stating. In this vein, it might be claimed, for example, that it is pointless to regard statements as either true or false if we could never tell which they were. Or Hume might be seen as claiming that it is really too stupid to try to determine which of the facts that causal statements state obtain, on the assumption that they state such. Our agreement on cases may have fooled us into thinking that this was not stupid. But when we look closer at the reasons for that agreement (habit, prejudice and the like), we will become convinced that we were wrong to think this.

Arguments for anti-realism can, perhaps, regularly be recast in this way. But if we are right about where such arguments get their force from, then the recasting is important. For we can then see when to be persuaded by them, when to be unpersuaded, and when to be in doubt, according to what we find reasonable and pointful or not when it comes to speaking of facts. The independence of an axiom or proposition from others which characterize a system, such as set theory or geometry, may well convince us that it is pointless to regard it nevertheless as stating a fact which either obtains or doesn't. For it may be that we can find no further use for that way of regarding things. On the other hand, where, as with geometry, the system has applications, these may provide sufficient point to regarding the proposition in question as fact stating after all – as some have found with the Euclidean parallel postulate. Nor is it easy to predict when systems may gain applications which we may come to regard as partly constitutive of their subject matter. Similarly, the fact that we could never be in a position to know whether given words were either true or false – as in the case of some words about the past – certainly takes away *some* of the point of regarding them as being really the one or the other. But, as is well known, there is still some point left. Nor ought we to suppose that there is always a clear answer to the question of whether the point that remains is enough to make it neither too stupid nor pointless nor whatever to regard the words as fact stating. Viewed in this light, hard cases for anti-realism (or realism) may well often turn out to be borderline cases.

If this account provides any new tool with which realism might be defended, it is not likely to be one that would gladden a realist's heart. For the realist idea did not seem to be that there are facts of the matter where we take there to be and where doing so is supportable. But if neither realist nor anti-realist is satisfied with the results here, there is some reason to think that that is just the outcome Wittgenstein thought most philosophical disputes ought to have.[6]

---

6 The shortcomings of this paper have survived help from numerous quarters. I would particularly like to thank Crispin Wright, John McDowell, John Campbell and Samuel Guttenplan both for inspiration and for proddings in the direction of clarity.

10
Rule following, meaning and constructivism
Crispin Wright

INTRODUCTION

John McDowell writes:[1]

> We find it natural to think of meaning and understanding in, as it were, contractual terms. Our idea is that to learn the meaning of a word is to acquire an understanding that obliges us subsequently – if we have occasion to deploy the concept in question – to judge and speak in certain determinate ways, on pain of failure to obey the dictates of the meaning we have grasped; that we are 'committed to certain patterns of linguistic usage by the meanings we attach to expressions'.[2] According to Crispin Wright, the burden of Wittgenstein's reflections on following a rule, in his later work, is that these natural ideas lack the substance we are inclined to credit them with:

This chapter expands some of the material which I presented at the conference on 'The psychological content of logic' at the University of Tilburg in October 1982, and at the Thyssen conference on 'Constructivism' at Lyme Regis in March 1983. I am grateful to the participants on those occasions for their helpful comments; to the audiences at seminars held at the Universities of Manchester, Belfast, Pennsylvania, Harvard and Stirling at which I presented ancestors of this essay; and to Leslie Stevenson, John Skorupski and Charles Travis for criticisms of an earlier draft.

1 John McDowell, 'Following a rule', *Synthese* 58 (1984), p. 325.
2 C. Wright, *Wittgenstein on the Foundations of Mathematics* (Duckworth, London, 1981), chapter 2, p. 21.

'There is in our understanding of a concept no rigid, advance determination of what is to count as its correct application.'³

If Wittgenstein's conclusion, as Wright interprets it, is allowed to stand, the most striking casualty is a familiar intuitive notion of objectivity. The idea at risk is the idea of things being thus and so anyway, whether or not we choose to investigate the matter in question, and whatever be the outcome of any such investigation. That idea requires the conception of how things could correctly be said to be anyway – whatever, if anything, we in fact go on to say about the matter; and this notion of correctness can only be the notion of how the pattern of application that we grasp, when we come to understand the concept in question, extends, independently of the actual outcome of any investigation, to the relevant case. So if the notion of investigation-independent patterns of application is to be discarded, then so is the idea that things are, at least sometimes, thus and so anyway, independently of our ratifying the judgement that this is how they are. It seems fair to describe this extremely radical consequence as a kind of idealism.

My purpose in this chapter is not to try to meet McDowell's criticisms of this interpretation of Wittgenstein, but to attempt to provide a fuller perspective upon the kind of considerations⁴ which suggest the 'extremely radical consequence'. Whether Wittgenstein actually ever had exactly these, or similar, considerations in mind is a question of much less interest than what force attaches to them. The exegetical issue between myself and McDowell is, I suggest, best viewed as concerning whether Wittgenstein, as McDowell interprets him, has any proper recourse to the constructivist imagery which is so prominent in the *Remarks on the Foundations of Mathematics*. I reserve pursuit of that issue to another occasion.

3 Ibid.
4 The account suggested here differs from *Wittgenstein on the Foundations of Mathematics* primarily in dissociating the argument from reliance on general 'anti-realist' premises. It is important, I think, to recognize that, as was argued in chapters 11 and 12 of that book, the sort of anti-realism about meaning developed by Dummett does command suspicion of the contractual conception of understanding illustrated by the above quotation from McDowell; but equally important that grounds exist for discontent with the contractual conception which depend not upon general anti-realist sympathies but only on principles which could hope to pass as platitudes.

PRELIMINARIES

Three preliminary sets of remarks may assist the evaluation of what follows.

First, 'idealism' does not entirely happily characterize the adjustment required if the argument to be presented is sustained. Idealism has traditionally involved the view that human consciousness in some way creates the world; that material objects, for instance, exist only for the mind. The present target, however, is a thesis about meaning. We ordinarily think of the truth value of a statement, whether assessed or not, as depending only upon a *semantic component*, its content, and a *worldly component*, the state of those aspects of the world which it is about. This conception has, indeed, the status of a platitude and is not under challenge in what follows. What is under challenge is a certain idea of determinacy in the first component: the idea that we can, by appropriately rigorous explanations and sufficiently distinctive paradigms, lay down so specific a content for a statement that its truth value is settled, in the manner described by the platitude, quite independently of the result of any investigations which we may carry out to settle it; and any correspondence between the truth value and our findings about it, if we bother to investigate, is utterly contingent on our capacity to keep track of our antecedent semantic obligations. The target – what I shall call *objectivity of meaning* – is the conception that the meaning of an expression stands to the unfolding tapestry of the way it is used in our linguistic practices as a person's character, according to a certain misconception of it, stands to his or her unfolding behaviour. The misconception would have it that character is, as it were, a finished design for a person's life which they usually act out, but which their behaviour may, at any particular stage, somehow betray. This has at least the virtue of explaining, but goes far beyond what is necessary to explain, the use we make of the idea that a person can act 'out of character'. But it is obvious enough that we also conceive of character as determined by behaviour: there are, we would like to say, *conceptual* limits to the extent and variety of ways in which a person can act out of character. A proper account of the relations between character and behaviour would have to display both how the nature of someone's character is a conceptual construct from what is said and done, and how it is nevertheless intelligible and fruitful to allow for the sort of contrast which we describe as 'acting out of character'.

The conclusion of this chapter will be that there is a structurally parallel problem posed by the concepts of meaning and use: that, whatever the proper interpretation of the *normativity* of meaning, and of what it is to use an expression in a way which fails to fit its meaning, it cannot issue from the picture of a semantic contract to which McDowell referred. Rather, the proper interpretation of these notions has to be compatible with the capacity of ongoing use to determine meaning. Our collective ability to misuse an expression – to use it in a way out of accordance with its meaning – is conceptually limited in the same sort of way as is the individual's ability to act out of a character. For the believer in objectivity of meaning, there can be no such limitation.

Idealism, it seems to me, implies that there is, in advance of appropriate human activity, an indeterminacy in the second, worldly component out of which the platitude manufactures truth value. The present thesis, however, entirely concerns the first component. It is that while, in accordance with the platitude, we may regard the truth values of uninvestigated statements as settled by their contents and relevant worldly aspects, we should not also think of those contents as fully settled by over-and-done-with behavioural and intellectual episodes. The positive task, if we accept this negative conclusion, will be to explain exactly how the content of a statement, and hence its truth value, must be seen as shaped by features of our ongoing linguistic behaviour. But that task will not be broached here. We shall be fully occupied with the attempt to articulate one set of grounds for the negative conclusion.

We are now in a position – the second preliminary – to see a contrast between the intended target of the argument with which we shall be concerned and that of a proponent of Kripke's 'sceptical argument', vividly expounded in his *Wittgenstein on Rules and Private Language*.[5] Fundamental to Hume's philo-

---

5 S. Kripke, *Wittgenstein on Rules and Private Language* (Basil Blackwell, Oxford, 1982).

sophical opinions concerning ethics, and causation, is a distinction between genuinely descriptive statements – our assent to which may mark cognition of a real state of affairs – and sentences which, while possessed of the syntax of genuine statements, serve rather to *project* emotions and attitudes of ours on to the world. Now, the conclusion of the 'sceptical argument' which Kripke finds in Wittgenstein is exactly that all talk of meaning and understanding is, in essentially this sense, *projective*: there are no substantial facts concerning meaning and understanding, *a fortiori* none to serve as possible objects of cognition. The route to this conclusion is of no importance to us here. What is clear is that it is a yet more radical contention than any involved in a rejection of objectivity of meaning in the above sense. To be sure, Wittgenstein is not represented by Kripke as recommending, like Quine in places, that we should jettison the concepts of meaning and understanding altogether; projective discourse may, after all, have some socially valid role. (That, in effect, is the tenet of Kripke's attempted 'sceptical solution'.) But there is a grave doubt whether Wittgenstein, as so represented, can be saying anything coherent. The trouble is the platitude above. If the truth value of a statement is a function of its meaning and relevant aspects of the world, then if meaning is nothing *factual*, how can truth value be? (A rough parallel: if whether it is worth going to see a certain show is a function of, *inter alia*, how funny the leading act is, and if we think that judgements about what is funny are projective, *ergo* non-factual, then that non-factuality is going to infect the judgement whether the show is worth seeing.) The result would seem to be that *every* judgement of the truth of a statement, so every statement, becomes non-factual. How then is the contrast between factual and projective statements to be drawn, in terms of which Wittgenstein's position on meaning, as interpreted by Kripke, is to be explained?

Kripke's sceptic must, of course, repudiate objectivity of meaning: if there are no genuine facts about meaning at all, there cannot be facts about what meanings require of us on new occasions. But, at the risk of leaning too heavily upon the analogy, a rejection of the objectivity of meaning should no more entail that there are literally no true statements to be made about meaning than the avoidance of the misconception about character outlined above entails that there are no true statements to be made about somebody's character. This opinion is, of course, quite consistent with holding that the argument which Kripke finds in the *Investigations* is of great independent interest. I merely record my suspicion that nobody can coherently accept its conclusion; that, accordingly, its power can only be that of a paradox. The contrast with my present argument is that the latter, if sustained, can have the status of a result.

Let me indicate, finally, something of the structure of the ensuing argument. There is a certain basic class of judgements which, it is plausible to suppose, are crucially involved in all the judgements we make. It will be argued that the supposition that these *basic* judgements possess objectivity of meaning is at odds with one aspect of standard criteria for their appraisal as correct. Then the manner of the involvement of these judgements in *all* judgement will be argued to impose upon us a choice between abandoning the objectivity of meaning quite generally and falling prey to global scepticism.

BASIC JUDGEMENTS

The concluding remark of what is usually regarded as the 'chapter' on rule following in the *Investigations* is famous: Wittgenstein wrote that not merely agreement in definitions but also agreement in *judgements* is a precondition of the possibility of our language serving for communication.[6] But which judgements precisely? Not, evidently, judgements concerning economic theory, or molecular biology, or the existence of a tenth planet; or any judgements concerning matters theoretical or controversial. Nevertheless Wittgenstein's remark will bear interpretation, I suggest, as concerning a specific class of judgements: those which we make responsively, without articulated reasons, under the causal impact of those aspects of our environment which we can most directly perceive. For it is indeed a plausible precondition of our reciprocal intelligibility that we share a network of certain

---

6 L. Wittgenstein, *Investigations*, §242.

basic concepts, by which we exercise perceptual recognition and in whose application to novel cases we concur (by and large) without collusion and without statable grounds to fall back on if disagreement should arise. The most natural examples would be attributive and relational concepts of form, pattern, colour, loudness, pitch, texture, taste, smell, warmth and cold, temporal precedence, etc. Only, it seems, if we do indeed share such a system of basic concepts, furnishing corresponding basic judgements, will our attempts to negotiate disagreement about judgements of a more sophisticated kind be fruitful. The basis of this insight of Wittgenstein's is the thought, on which we shall dwell below, that basic perceptual judgements are involved in all judgement: that there could not be a common conception of the conditions of justified assent to (and dissent from) judgements of any sort unless certain relevant basic concepts were also held in common. This is not to say that any *particular* basic concepts are necessary, but only that if we do succeed in understanding each other, we will share some basic concepts. Nor are we committed to supposing that any basic concepts have that status absolutely; which concepts are basic for us will be a function of our sensory capabilities, and concepts may be envisaged as shifting their status according as we imagine those capabilities enlarged or restricted in relevant ways. (A judgement of the rough similarity, for example, in the geometrical sense, of a pair of drawn triangles, which the normally sighted are able to make at a glance, may be available to those with extreme 'tunnel vision' only on the basis of a series of measurements and inferences.)

A fuller account is desirable of the nature of concepts of this sort, but providing one is not entirely straightforward. We are concerned with concepts which are characteristically introduced by ostensive means, incapable of definitional paraphrase, and whose applications in at least a large class of cases are directly recognitional. Yet if the intention is to pick out the sort of concepts listed above, more needs to be said. Let us call a *recognition statement* any statement composed purely of demonstratives, predicates, and relations of arbitrary degree, of which a competent use standardly presupposes no more than normal sensory capacities and ostensive teaching. 'That is red', 'That is deeper than that' (said of sounds), 'That is salty', etc., all qualify. So, however, may recognition statements concerning cedar trees, pineapples, Geiger counters, cathode ray tubes, and telephones. We confront the familiar range of difficulties besetting the attempt to elucidate a worthwhile notion of *observation statement*, difficulties which have been the despair of so many foundationalistically inclined epistemologists and philosophers of science. So, whether or not it will involve a contribution to *that* issue, there is more to be said for our present purpose.[7] Let us stipulate that a predicate F, or a relation R, is *basic* just in case it satisfies all the following conditions:

1. F, or R, is capable of featuring in recognition statements.
2. Nobody counts as understanding F, or R, who lacks the capacity – even when perceiving normally in normal circumstances – competently to appraise recognition statements which contain them.

This condition excludes expressions like 'Geiger counter' and 'cathode ray tube'. For their instances, while sensorily recognizable, could in principle take any of indefinitely many various overt forms. It is thus no essential part of understanding such predicates to have the capacity to handle recognition statements involving them; you can know exactly what Geiger counters are without knowing the gross form they conventionally assume.

The corresponding claim about 'pineapple', 'cedar tree', and indeed a whole host of natural kind terms is, however, much less plausible. Intuitively no one fully understands 'pineapple' who has no inkling of the distinctive appearance of pineapples. Here appropriate recognitional capacities do seem necessary for understanding; what distinguishes these expressions from those in the class we seek to characterize is that such capacities are not *sufficient*. We therefore stipulate:

---

7 The following proposals were conceived with the benefit of discussion with Christopher Peacocke and bear analogies to material which he has since published as chapter 4 of his *Sense and Content* (OUP, Oxford, 1983).

3 It is not possible coherently to regard someone both as able to pass all reasonable tests for the ability to recognize demonstrative presentations of Fs, or R-relata, *and* as lacking a full understanding of F, or R.

Conditions 2 and 3 determine that the recognitional capacities which bestow competence with recognition statements involving F, or R, are to be constitutive of an understanding of those expressions. There is to be no possibility of understanding of what it is for such statements to be true without possessing the appropriate recognitional capacities; and no possibility of possessing the appropriate recognitional capacities without understanding what it is for such statements to be true (so no possibility of 'fools' Fs').[8] Finally

4 F, or R, has no analysis in terms of other predicates, or relations, meeting requirements 1, 2 and 3.

The intention of condition 4 is – perhaps unimportantly – to reflect the feeling that the sought-for characterization should be of a class of concepts which are *primitive*.

Some commentary on this characterization is called for. To begin with, it is worth drawing a distinction between basic *statements* and basic *judgements*. A basic judgement is any judgement which could be expressed by a recognition statement involving only basic concepts, and which is made by exercising appropriate recognitional capacities. But the content of a statement which expresses such a judgement does not, obviously, preclude that the very same statement should be made not on the basis of exercise of the appropriate recognitional capacities but as the conclusion, for example, of a chain of inferences. There are thus no sentences which are apt *only* for the expression of basic judgements. We shall understand a *basic statement* to be a particular *historic utterance* of a recognition statement which involves only basic concepts and which, in context, expresses an exercise of the relevant recognitional capacities. In what follows, I shall work with the fiction

---

8 Ibid., pp. 92–3.

that we have the means to coin basic statements apt for expression of any basic judgements which we are actually able to make. This is presumably a substantial idealization: we share a tremendous number of basic concepts, as evinced in various discriminatory abilities which we have, for which we have no direct (non-comparative) means of expression. But the idealization is perfectly in order in the present context: if it can cogently be argued that the vocabulary of English, enriched only by the addition of a fuller range of expressions for basic concepts, cannot serve to construct sentences with objectivity of meaning, then it is quite unclear how English as we presently have it – a fragment of that language – could somehow fare better. The point of the idealization, as the reader will anticipate, is that we shall thereby be enabled to apply our reflections concerning the objectivity of meaning to basic judgements as a class, without the need to attempt to construct some analogous concept which might characterize, or fail to characterize, basic judgements for which we happen to have no means of expression.

Second, on the notion of an *observation statement*. The notion traditional in the philosophy of science – that which Carnap intended by *Protocolsatz*, for example – is that of a statement possessed of a special epistemic security and free of theoretical presupposition. Whether basic statements, as characterized above, have either of these features is a matter for further investigation. *Prima facie*, at least, it is not obvious that they do: the recognitional capacity constitutive of an understanding of a particular basic concept may well, typically will, be a *fallible* capacity; and our conception of some of the conditions under which its fallibility will emerge may well be a 'theoretically conditioned' one. Enough has been said, perhaps, to make it clear that those philosophers who have thought that there is no interesting distinction between theoretical statements and records of observation may be mistaken; but whether the notion of a basic statement gives us the germ of a distinction which will subserve the traditional purposes of foundationalism in epistemology and the philosophy of science will not further be considered here.

There is a further concept of some importance, to be introduced before we tackle the main argument that basic statements lack objectivity of meaning. The most fundamental notion of objectivity is (what I propose to call) the *objectivity of judgement*. To think of a class of statements as apt to express objective judgements is to conceive of them as having a real subject matter, as dealing in genuine matters of fact, as apt to be correct or incorrect in virtue of how matters stand in certain objective states of affairs which may be the objects of human cognition. This is the notion which divides genuine statements from the sort of projective impostors postulated by Hume, and from *quasi-assertions*[9] of other sorts. Clarification of this notion of objectivity is a matter of great importance: there is a long history of philosophical disputes – about morals, aesthetics, theoretical statements in science, pure mathematical statements, etc. – all of which are precisely disputes about whether these types of statements qualify for objectivity of judgement.

What, though, is the hallmark of the genuinely factual? How should we set about deciding whether a given class of statements really do have this kind of objectivity? No doubt the disputes just alluded to would not have been so long lived if there were an easy answer. But one important initial consideration is the following. Cognition is *relational*: it is a matter of arriving at true opinions in a manner *sensitive* to states of affairs whose obtaining is somehow independent of one's so arriving. Moreover, such sensitivity must be conceived as essentially fallible; whatever the details are of the process which induces in a subject a belief that P, it must be conceivable – at least with the simple empirical judgements which basic statements serve to express – that the process should on occasion misfire, that the appropriate sensitivity should be missing. These two considerations – the independence of the objects of knowledge and the fallibility of cognitive capacities – suggest as at least a necessary condition for a class of statements to have a genuinely cognizable, *ergo* factual, subject matter that sense can be made of the possibility of a subject's or a group of subjects' *ignorance* or *error* concerning their truth status.[10]

---

9 M. Dummett, *Frege: Philosophy of Language*, 2nd edn (Duckworth, 1981), pp. 353–60.
10 This thought underlies the doubt about 'private language' voiced by Wittgenstein in *Investigations* §258 (see pp. 295–7 below).

I do not believe that a full account of objectivity of judgement can be anything so simple, only that it must build on the foregoing thought. If a class of statements are to be credited with objectivity of judgement, then, for arbitrarily chosen P in that class, there has to be an appropriate contrast in content between:

(a) X believes that P is true; and
(b) P is true.

Only if (a) may conceivably be denied while (b) may be asserted have we made sense of the possibility of X being ignorant of the status of P; only if (a) may conceivably be asserted while (b) may be denied have we made sense of the possibility of X being mistaken.

Now 'X' may, of course, be taken to range not merely over a single individual but also over groups of individuals including, as a limiting case, an entire community. Even so, there seems no reason to doubt that basic statements can legitimately aspire to meet the condition. Individuals can, of course, be ignorant of or mistaken about the truth status of a basic statement. And most of the explanations why – bad lighting, poor eyesight, tone deafness, not noticing, absence at the relevant time, etc. – would in principle serve equally well for whole communities. Accordingly, to have grounds for thinking that a communal consensus on some basic statement is, or was, mistaken is a remote but real possibility (systematic sorts of misperception, for example, may be induced by disease). Conversely, most of the basic judgements which each of us makes, with perfect justification, are made not merely in ignorance of any communal consensus that there may be about their status but with a strong presupposition that most members of our community will never consider them. So we certainly cannot affirm, even with basic statements, that 'whatever seems right to the community is right', or anything of that sort. At least, we cannot do so without betraying a class of distinctions which, as we think, we are ordinarily able to draw soundly.

At this point, it may seem that we must either sustain the objectivity of meaning of basic statements, thereby entitling ourselves to the sorts of distinction just sketched; or we must embrace some sort of crude 'consensusism' about those statements, forgoing our rights to practise the distinctions in question. Wittgenstein himself rejects the second alternative.[11] The dilemma is, however, a false one. The capacity of a class of statements to satisfy the indicated necessary condition for objectivity of judgement does not depend upon the legitimacy of accrediting them with objectivity of meaning; and the reason why not is best brought out by considering why the latter is in doubt – to which task I now turn.

BASIC STATEMENTS AND OBJECTIVITY OF MEANING AND JUDGEMENT

Let ϕ be some basic concept, and consider a large series of basic statements involving ϕ, about which there is, as it happens, a near universal consensus. If we are to believe in the objectivity of meaning of these statements, there has to be a possibility that this consensus is, in any particular case, misplaced: for belief in objectivity of meaning is exactly the belief that what determines the truth values of these statements is wholly independent of human assessment of them and, at best, contingently correspondent with it. Now there is, of course, a distinction between the claims:

1. For each statement in question, it is possible that our verdict and the truth status diverge.
2. It is possible that, for each statement in question, our verdict and the truth status diverge.

The question is what, if any, reason the believer in objectivity of meaning can give for accepting claim 1 but refusing to accept claim 2. Generally speaking, the transition from $(x) \Diamond : Fx$ to $\Diamond : (x)Fx$ fails just in case F is a predicate the conditions of whose application to any particular individual in the range of quantification are a

---

[11] *Investigations* §241; cf. *Remarks on the Foundations of Mathematics* (3rd edn), VII, 40.

function of relevant characteristics of other members of the range. Thus, familiarly, the transition fails, for example, for Fx = 'x is below average height.' More strikingly for our present purposes, it fails, letting 'x' range over episodes of Jones's behaviour, for Fx = 'x is totally out of character.' The only apparent way of resisting the transition from claim 1 to claim 2 would be to insist that our consensus over so large a class of cases must be regarded as playing some sort of *constitutive* role in determining what counts as correct use of φ, just as Jones's behaviour over a sufficiently large class of cases plays a constitutive role in determining his character. But that is exactly the parallel which the believer in objectivity of meaning must resist. Letting 'x' range over the basic statements in question, and Fx = 'the community's assessment of x is out of accord with the requirements of the meaning of φ', the believer in φ's objective meaning ought to hold that the considerations which determine whether or not φ applies in any particular case will concern nothing other than the relevant facts about it (the 'worldly component' referred to above) and those episodes in the linguistic and intellectual history of the community which constituted the determination of the ('objective') meaning of φ. What is crucial is that we may think of those episodes as having entirely *antedated* the series of statements in question. And in that case, what determines whether or not φ applies in any of the relevant cases is quite independent of the communal response in other cases in that range. We should conclude that believers in objectivity of meaning have no satisfactory ground why, having accepted claim 1, they should not also accept claim 2.

What has been said is already enough to suggest how it is that one who rejected objectivity of meaning for a given class of statements might nevertheless quite consistently reserve the right to endorse objectivity of judgement for them (or at least, to endorse their capacity to pass the test on which, I suggested above, a full account of objectivity of judgement should build). Actually, it is not clear whether belief in objectivity of judgement for a given class of statements really does require that we give sense to the possibility of massive communal *error* about their status (whether it would not be enough to give sense, for example, merely to the possibility of massive communal *ignorance*). But if it does, no more is required, at any rate, than that we substantiate claim 1 above. Belief in objectivity of meaning, in contrast, requires – if the foregoing is correct – that we additionally substantiate claim 2. And crude consensusism would reject both.

Now, what is supposed to be the difficulty with claim 2? What is wrong with the idea that as a bare and no doubt very remote possibility, all or almost all the members of a linguistic community might collectively, but non-collusively, go right off track in their applications of some basic predicate, that the paths of truth and shared opinion over a protracted series of basic statements might radically diverge? The immediate worry has to be, of course, whether the alleged possibility is really intelligible. What would it be to have satisfactory grounds for thinking that it actually obtained? Naturally, no one can be considered competent to criticize a range of statements accepted by others unless there is a reason to think that the critic and the criticized share an understanding of those statements. But with basic concepts, the criterion for such a shared understanding is precisely the disposition to agree in basic judgements involving those concepts. How then, if somebody finds himself out of line with the verdict of his community in a protracted series of cases, can we or anyone else retain the right to think of him as a competent critic? Why is the position not rather that it has emerged that he never succeeded in understanding or no longer understands the basic concepts in question? It would seem to follow that there is no such thing as being in a position reasonably to criticize a sufficiently protracted non-collusive consensus on basic statements; so no such thing as having reason to think that a 'radical divergence' had taken place. 'Anti-realist' constraints would accordingly enjoin that there is no such genuine possibility.

This in essentials was the argument of chapter XI of *Wittgenstein on the Foundations of Mathematics*. However, the conclusion is, at this stage, too swiftly drawn, since it overlooks the possibility that the critic is able to support his charge by evidence that something is interfering with the (physiological basis) of the capacities of his community. Certain sorts of environmental contaminant may, for example, be known adversely to affect people's capacity to apply certain basic concepts, but to do so in a uniform way so that the disposition to consensus is not disrupted. So could there not, in appropriately fantastic circumstances, be reason to think that *everyone* had, perhaps irreversibly, gone astray in their application of certain basic concepts? Yet a little reflection renders it doubtful whether this thought really meets the issue. There seem to be three sorts of basis on which it might be claimed that such a contaminant, or other factor, had produced an episode of radical divergence. First, and most simply, the contaminant might be associated with overt damage to its victims so gross – near-total deafness, for example – that nothing would have to be known about the detailed character of their suspect judgements in order reasonably to hold them in suspicion. Second, the judgements in question might be found to betray an established correlation with some associated physical parameter: measured temperature, for instance, or the frequency of sound waves. Or, third, the contaminant might previously have been recognized to have induced disruption in the relevant recognitional capacities of a previously affected subpopulation – disruption, that is, as evinced by discord with the responses of an unaffected majority. Now, the second and third types of case both turn on the assumed reliability of certain basic judgements outwith the putative episode of radical divergence – those, respectively, by reference to which the association with the relevant physical parameter and the adverse effect of the contaminant on the subpopulation were established. No doubt that might be perfectly reasonable: the judgements in question will be assumed reliable because no consideration of the three kinds adumbrated, or any other, are on hand to call them into question. But can the theorist who accepts objectivity of meaning *explain* why that is a reasonable assumption?

The real difficulty for the theorist is to keep the tiger in the cage – to disclose any reason why the range of possibilities for radical divergence is appropriately constrained by the criteria on which we should actually rely in order to affirm that such a possibility had been realized. Why shouldn't our belief in the reliability of some associated physical parameter itself have been the product of an extended bout of radical divergence? Why shouldn't those communal judgements with which the responses of the contaminated subpopulation were compared themselves have been haywire?

These seem foolish questions. And the reason they seem so, I surmise, goes deep. Suppose a subject sincerely assents to a statement S in circumstances C in which we have adequate reason to believe that each of the following holds:

1. The subject has had a normal teaching in the concepts involved in S and has given every indication of a normal understanding of them.
2. The subject is functioning normally in C – is unaffected by drugs, disease, etc.
3. The perceptual conditions obtaining in C are normal – no funny lighting, tricky mirrors, etc.

Obviously enough, adequate reason to believe the conjunction of 1 – 3 cannot in general constitute adequate reason to believe S, since the current normality of the subject and the perceptual conditions is no special asset if S does not concern what the subject is currently in position to perceive. But if S is a *basic* statement, the position is different: precisely because 2 and 3 constitute conditions which are optimal for the subject's exercise of the relevant recognitional capacities, and because 1 suggests that it is indeed those capacities which the subject is attempting to exercise, adequate reason to believe each of 1 – 3 must be, it appears, adequate reason to believe S.

This conclusion in fact needs a supplementary assumption:

4. S expresses a basic statement *for* the subject, that is his assent to it is based entirely on an exercise of recognitional capacities.

(Otherwise it will be easy to conjure up counter-examples involving the subject's recourse, for whatever reason, to an unreliable secondary source, for example, or a problematic chain of inferences.) But granted that assumption, it is, I suggest, not merely true but *necessarily* true that sufficient reason for each of 1 – 4 confers a (defeasible) warrant to believe S. More specifically, it is impossible to understand how a recipient of adequate grounds for each of 1 – 4 could reasonably doubt S if he possessed no other relevant information.

Intuitively, the case for S is stronger if what is involved is a widespread non-collusive *consensus* of subjects about its truth. That, I surmise, is because the fact of such a consensus would *eo ipso* be grounds against supposing that misunderstanding, or abnormal function – usually an idiosyncratic matter – or certain sorts of tricky perceptual circumstances (misleading perspectival effects, for example) were materially involved. That is, consensus, of that sort, enhances the likelihood, though it does not make it certain, that 1, 2 and 3 hold for each of the participants. Whether or not that is quite the right reason, the following principle has an exceedingly powerful intuitive appeal.

P: If, without any form of collusion occurring, there is widespread agreement about the truth of an S which is basic for each of the judges; and if someone has adequate grounds for supposing that 1, 2 and 3 each hold of each of the judges, but no other relevant information, then he has excellent grounds for regarding S as true.

The appeal of P is, I suggest again, owing to its being analytic of the notion of a basic statement. The salient question, however, is how the principle can so much as hold, let alone how it can hold in necessitated form, if objectivity of meaning is accepted for basic statements. For in that case, what determines the truth or falsity of any S is constituted quite independently and in advance of the judges' response to it. To hold to the principle P (in necessitated form) would then be, accordingly, to hold that there is (necessarily) reason to think that those responses tend by and large to keep in step with the objective pattern of correct use of the concepts involved in S. Presumably, then, we can produce a reason for discounting as a possibility the suggestion that we may be prone, without any external interference either with us or with the conditions of observation, simply to swing collectively away, without any sense of disquiet, from the paths laid down by objective meanings and the wordly facts. If some sceptic suggests that human beings may just be rather bad, in very similar ways, at internalizing the requirements of objective meanings, we presumably have ready to hand a consideration to confound him. What is it?

The proper response, it seems to me, to this train of thought is to reject objectivity of meaning for basic statements. *P* holds good not because objective meanings, in their and our very nature, somehow exert a tug on the responses of people who satisfy its antecedent clauses, but because the relation, for the case of basic statements, between correctness and human response – however difficult to do justice to in detail – is such as to render the principle analytic. It follows that the fantasy of a collective 'radical divergence' over a series of basic statements, where no standard grounds exist for suspicion, is incoherent.

The effect of supposing that *P* can be false is that satisfaction of the conditions expressed in its antecedent need provide no adequate case for regarding the relevant statement as true. Yet the fact is that – at least when the judges include ourselves – we have not the slightest idea what it would be to increase the strength of the case. The result will be that the truth, or falsity, of such statements comes to transcend our strongest standard grounds for affirming them to be one or the other. That is an extreme and unappealing form of realism: it reduces our belief in our competence to use our own language correctly to a matter of faith. There is, however, no need to assail it with the familiar anti-realist arguments of full generality. Anyone who recognizes the fidelity of the principle *P* to their intuitive concept of reasonable belief already has decisive grounds for rejecting it.

To reject objectivity of meaning for basic statements is to come to regard their content, and so their truth status, as ever open to ongoing determination by our linguistic behaviour. The competent use of basic vocabulary, with whatever degree of confidence, should not be viewed as reflecting cognition of the requirements of objective meanings. Rather, we should view it as an expression of certain basic reactive propensities, primitive classificatory dispositions – a common human (or at least cultural) heritage without which our language would fail. We must endeavour to see the content of basic statements as plastic in response to speakers' continuing performance with the basic vocabulary which they involve. Such metaphors are, of course, unsatisfactory and are no substitute for a sharp account of the sort of supervenience relation which we now seem obliged to decry. But it is at least clear that we can no longer think of the truth conditions of basic statements as fixed quite independently of responses of ours, yet to be elicited from us, involving the relevant basic concepts. It is this *openness* in the content of basic statements which is critical in what follows.

THE UBIQUITY OF BASIC JUDGEMENT

There is no immediate generalization of these considerations to non-basic statements since, as noted, P holds only for basic statements. Nevertheless, the argument ought to generalize. The suggestive thought is that exercise of basic concepts seems to be involved in the formation of judgements of all kinds. Think, for example, of the judgements of shape and colour which may be involved in recognizing a cedar tree outside the window; the judgements of temporal precedence involved in competently running a scientific experiment; or the judgements of congruity of pattern involved in recognizing a formal proof. But the mode of involvement is not usually, or even often, inferential. Basic judgements appear to form a foundation for judgement in general, not in the sense that they supply premises from which other judgements are derived, but in the sense that getting them right is a necessary condition, in context, for arriving at any other judgement *soundly*, for having a well-founded reason for thinking that judgement true. One's warrant to make a judgement of any kind, however sophisticated the context, will, it seems, always be *defeasible* by considerations which suggest that one misapplied certain basic concepts in coming to that judgement.

Let us try to amplify this claim a little. Defeasibility comes in several kinds. One way of defeating evidence for a particular belief is to bring to bear other evidence, stronger or equally strong, that the belief is false. Another is to show that there is an alternative equally plausible account of why the original evidence is available. A third mode of defeat is to fault the *pedigree* of the evidence in some way, to call attention to some feature of the evidence gathering (or gatherer) which disqualifies it. Examples would be the disclosure of pressure leaks in the apparatus, drunkenness in the observer, or a powerful magnetic field which may have affected the gauges. Defeat of either of the first two sorts admits the data but disputes their capacity to warrant the belief in question; defeat of the third sort undermines the validity of the data. I shall say that a case for a particular belief is *impeccable* if it is immune to defeat of the third sort; and that it constitutes a *genuine warrant* for that belief if it is both impeccable and will not be defeated in either of the first two ways no matter what the additions to our knowledge. To have a genuine warrant is thus to have a case for a particular belief which both possesses a faultless pedigree and will retain its supportive character through arbitrarily extensive improvements in our state of information.

One way of expressing the involvement of basic judgements in all judgement is now to say that in order to possess a genuine warrant for a particular belief, it is necessary that a large class of relevant basic judgements, pertaining to the process whereby the belief was acquired, be true; failing their truth, the process will lack the requisite impeccability. This is not to say that the relevant basic judgements need actually have been consciously entertained by a subject in the course of his arriving at the belief; but rather that if, having arrived at that belief, the subject were to be persuaded that any of them were false, he would be rationally constrained to consider the belief unjustified. In the presence of our earlier assumption that the language contain means for the expression of all the basic judgements which its practitioners can make, we may summarize the proposal as follows:

T: For any context C, agent X, and statement S: if X acquires the belief that S in C, then there will be certain basic statements relating to the circumstances and process whereby X's belief was acquired such that (1) if he did not actually do so, X *could* have assessed any of these statements in the course of arriving at his belief that S; and (2) X has acquired impeccable, *a fortiori* genuine warrant for his belief that S only if each such statement is true.

I don't know how to support this principle beyond inviting a reader who is sceptical about it to try to come up with a counter-example: a case, in effect, of reasonable belief, acquired via some process with which no basic statements are so associated that evidence of their falsity would constitute defeat of the third kind. In any event, there seems no reason to doubt that T holds in a very wide class of cases. A reader sceptical whether it holds universally may simply restrict the scope of the argument which follows to the cases where it does hold.

NON-BASIC STATEMENTS AND OBJECTIVITY OF MEANING

We now introduce a further seemingly platitudinous principle:

P^*: Necessarily: if X has acquired, in context C, a genuine warrant for believing S, then it is reasonable for X to believe S to be true.

At any rate, this principle ought to seem platitudinous since a genuine warrant is *more* than is required for reasonable belief: beliefs may reasonably be held on what are, in fact, defeasible grounds. However, if we try to retain, along with the lemma that basic statements lack objective meaning and thesis T, the view that the truth and falsity of non-basic statements *is* subject to determination by objective meanings, then it becomes unclear whether, so far from being platitudinous, P^* has so much as a plausible claim to truth. This is the crux of the argument.

Let S be a non-basic statement and consider:

1 We have, in context C, genuine warrant for believing S; and
2 S is true.

If objectivity of meaning continues to be assumed for non-basic statements, an asymmetry now emerges in the types of states of affairs apt to confer truth on 1 and 2 respectively. The question of whether 2 is true is a *closed* question: it is settled by the state of the world in relevant respects and the objective meaning of S, which in turn is settled by past episodes in the linguistic and intellectual life of the community. But the question of whether 1 is true is, in the sense canvassed on pages 289–90, *open*. For a necessary condition for the truth of 1 will be – given T – that certain basic statements are true; and the truth of those statements, in so far as it depends upon their content, has to be conceived – in the presence of the lemma – as a function of, *inter alia*, future and counterfactual responses, involving the relevant basic concepts, of members of the linguistic community. Rejection of objectivity of meaning for basic statements led us to the view that what it is true to say about the meaning of any basic expression, and hence the nature of that meaning, is indefinitely open to further determination by ongoing responses of members of the linguistic community, rather as what it is true to say about someone's character, and hence the nature of his character, is indefinitely open to further determination by what he says and does. In the presence of T, this feature of basic statements flows upwards, as it were, to affect all judgements of the sort typified by 1: their truth depends on the truth of basic statements; which depends on their content; which depends on things we have not but would have done, or will or would do.

Why does this consideration pose a threat to P^*? Because in order for P^* to hold, it is necessary that the sorts of circumstance which go to make up a genuine warrant for S be a *reliable indication* of the sorts of circumstance which constitute S's truth; that pursuit of the policy, as it were, of aiming at genuine warrants for one's beliefs will enhance the chances of selecting true beliefs. For the believer in objectivity of meaning, however, the claim that S is true is a claim about the deliverance of objective meanings. The result is that, in view of the noted asymmetry, the question of the reliability of genuine warrants for statements in S's class becomes imponderable. For to believe in their reliability is to believe that the obtaining of the ingredients involved in a genuine warrant, including certain non-actual but elicitable primitive linguistic responses involving basic vocabulary *which may not even feature in the non-basic statement at issue*, is a reliable indication of that statement's truth. And that demands reason to believe in what seems to be a most mysterious *felicity* in our basic conceptual responses. In order for genuine warrants and truth to tend to go in step, it has to have been contrived that our primitive dispositions with basic vocabulary somehow follow suit after the requirements of the objective meanings of non-basic vocabulary, engineering a sufficient measure of covariance, among statements in general, between truth and the availability of genuine warrants to give point to the practice of trying to secure genuine warrants as, wherever practicable, a precondition of belief. The asymmetry thus brings it about that P^*, so far from having the status of a platitude, emerges in the role of postulate of an odd sort of pre-established harmony.

Naturally it is quite unclear how it could be *necessary* that such harmony obtained. The attractiveness of P^* is merely that of a principle that is analytic of our ordinary concepts of truth and evidence. But in that case, the only way of retaining a belief in objectivity of meaning for non-basic statements while acknowledging the force of the above argument is to see it as a demonstration that the conditions for reasonable belief in the truth of non-basic statements are never satisfied. The best we can aim at is genuine warrant; and the probability that we shall thereby tend to believe more truths is inscrutable. Perhaps this outcome is only to be expected. The penalty which we risk by endorsing the kind of semantic autonomy with which objective meanings would infuse our language is that we shall find ourselves hard pressed to explain with what right we consider ourselves in any way sensitive to the course taken by the semantic tracks thereby laid down. The burden of the argument has been that, first at the level of basic statements and then with all the rest, this penalty cannot be avoided. The price of objective meaning is an absolute conception of truth: a conception absolved from all practical controls. This is not the notion we actually have, if P^* is true. It is not a notion we should want, if our cognitive endeavours are to fare better than cannon-fodder for the sceptic's artillery.

CONSTRUCTIVISM

It was suggested earlier that 'idealism' was not a happy label for the view which repudiates objectivity of meaning. The label of 'constructivism' is another matter. There really is a point, if the argument of this chapter is sustained, in seeing ourselves as the perennial creators of our concepts, not in the style of conscious architects but just by doing what comes naturally. Thereby we contribute towards the creation not of extra-linguistic facts, but of true sentences. It is, however, another question whether this shift in perspective must engender revision in the classical 'non-constructive' techniques and concepts of mathematics and logic against which the twentieth-century schools of constructivism in the philosophies of logic and mathematics have rebelled. Certainly from one point of view it seems that radical methodological revisions may have to be involved. If, for example, the mathematical intuitionists' willingness to accept the law of the excluded middle for all quantifier-free statements in number theory had to be taken as evincing a belief in the validity of the principle of bivalence for those statements, then it is hard to see that that practice could now be justified. What could sustain the idea that finitely decidable, but in practice hopelessly undecidable, number-theoretic statements are in every case *determinately* true or false, except the conception that they have objective meanings capable of settling their truth values without any further contribution from us? It is, however, unobvious that the intuitionists' willingness to accept excluded middle in such cases has to be interpreted in that light.[12] And the issue is, in any case, overshadowed by very delicate and unresolved questions concerning revisionism in the philosophy of logic – including, in particular, the question of what can be made of the notion of *conservativeness* of a set of principles of inference among statements for which objectivity of meaning has been rejected – which cannot be broached here.

Finally, if we take it that the target of Wittgenstein's reflections on following a rule *is* objectivity of meaning quite generally (whatever the relation of the preceding argument to the detail of his own thought), where does that leave the relation between the 'rule-following considerations' and the polemic against 'private language' which, *pace* Kripke, begins at *Investigations* §243? In §258 Wittgenstein urges, famously, that the would-be private linguist ought to be disquieted by his inability to make anything of the distinction between uses of his private language which seem right to him and uses which really are. (Those of Cartesian sympathies are apt to see no force at all in the consideration,

---

12 Wright, *Wittgenstein*, chapter 11, §§4 – 6.

precisely because they aspire to regard one's impressions of one's own mental contents as especially sure. They entirely miss Wittgenstein's point.) Now one thing which is clear is that if expressions in a private language could have objective meaning, then there would *be* a distinction between what seemed right to a practitioner and what was right, even if he could not apply the distinction; that is, what *determined* the rightness of any particular description of his sensations, or whatever the private material was supposed to be, would be independent of the way in which the subject was inclined to describe them. Hence, a general attack on objective meaning would pre-empt one effective rejoinder to Wittgenstein's apparent train of thought at this point. So an extensive discussion of rule following, with objectivity of meaning as its general target, would certainly be intelligible as a *preparation* for the argument against private language. But quite other interpretations of the relations between the two 'chapters' are possible; someone who took the view, for example, that the material on rule following is not directed against objectivity of meaning, could essay to see Wittgenstein's remarks about private ostensive definition as expressing the view that, in contrast to a situation in a public language, the private linguist cannot establish any objective meanings for himself. Fare that approach as it may, it is evident that a quite general assault on objectivity of meaning cannot of itself establish any *special* problem for private language.

The rule-following considerations have been fairly intensively discussed in philosophical circles for a number of years now and the impression is, I think, prevalent that while Wittgenstein may have achieved certain destructive insights into widespread lay-philosophical notions of meaning, confusion has overtaken him when he thinks that private language somehow fares especially badly.[13] (Admittedly a Cartesian, if confronted with the issue in these terms, might well wish to invest his private language with objective meanings; so Wittgenstein could still be credited with an anti-Cartesian point.) The truth seems to me to be different. Wittgenstein does have a special query to raise about private

---

13 See especially Simon Blackburn's 'The individual strikes back', *Synthese* 58 (1984), pp. 281–301.

language, even if we suppose that a successful general attack has been mounted against objectivity of meaning. The query is, precisely, whether the would-be statements of the private linguist can have *objectivity of judgement*, whether they can be so much as factual. But corroboration of that claim I must defer to another occasion.[14]

---

14 C. Wright, 'Does *Investigations* §§258 – 60 suggest a cogent argument against private language', in *Subject, Thought and Context*, eds J. McDowell and P. Pettit (Oxford, 1986).

Index

action 163
Adams, E. W. 210, 212–15, 220, 223
Adams Commitments 211, 213–15, 222–3, 225, 228, 229
ambiguity 30, 43, 77–82, 99, 102
  lexical 82
  truth-conditional test of 78, 80–2, 88
analytical philosophy 159
anaphora 98–101
anaphoric relations 105
  of quantifiers 105, 113
Anscombe, E. 234
Anscombe, J. 94
anti-realism 178–80, 182–4, 186–94, 196–200, 204–10, 233, 265–9, 272n, 285, 289
anti-realist semantics 180, 183–7, 190, 193, 195, 199
Appiah, A. 215, 232
Armstrong, D. 207
ASSENT 219, 226, 229
assertability conditions 208–22, 229, 230
  see also assertability conditions
assertability conditions 186–9, 195, 196, 201, 208
  conclusive 186–95, 197
  defeasible 194–9

assertability, warranted 178, 179, 183, 184, 195
assumption, implicated 59, 61, 62, 65–6, 69, 73–4
assumption, passing 209
attitudes
  cognitive 204–5, 207–8, 232
  propositional 140–6, 166–7, 171, 172, 174, 188, 266
Austin, J. 9

Bach, K. 48, 62
background
  assumptions 49, 54
  knowledge 8, 49, 101, 129
Baker, G. P. 134, 195
Bayes 211, 226
de Beaugrande, R. 45
behaviour 274, 284
  linguistic 289
beliefs 28, 42–3, 131, 140–6, 158, 201–5, 208, 226
  ascription of 203
  evidence for 290–4
  see also propositional attitudes
Bell, J. L. 106
bivalence, principle of 184–6, 191, 204, 295
Blackburn, S. 135, 137–8, 152, 154–5, 158, 201, 206, 296

Bohnert, H. 114
Boolus, G. 106
Borkin, A. 20
Bouvresse, G. 183
boxology, functional 140
bridging 68
   cross-reference 100n
   implicature 68–9
Brockway, D. 93
Brown, G. 45, 48
Butterfield, J. 158

C-resistant conditional 222
calculability requirement 46
Campbell, J. v, 3, 142, 159, 269
Carlstrom, I. F. 215
Carroll, L. 202
Carston, R. 87
causal order, sense of 162
causality 206–7, 267, 275
character 273, 275–6, 285, 293
Chastain, C. 114
Chomsky, N. 137, 140–2
   on realism 137
clarity, maxim of 46, 47
Clark, H. H. 68–9
Clossman, G. 33
cognition, theory of 204
Cole, P. 46, 47, 77
Coltheart, M. 140, 158
commitments 201–5, 207–9, 218, 220–3, 229–30, 232
   thick theory of 204
   thin theory of 209
common partial causal explanation 136
common-sense metaphysics 120, 122
communication 160–1, 164
   account of 160
   concept of 164
   precondition of 276
communicative intention 53–4, 75
competence 2, 4, 194
composition 4, 127–8, 130
   see also construction, structure
concept 2, 142–3, 153, 156, 159–60, 165–7, 169, 171, 173–4, 202, 234, 244, 249–52, 274–5
   attributive 277
   basic 277, 280, 283, 285, 286, 290
   general 249–51
   individual 249–52
   of meaning 234, 244, 274–5
   possession of 142–3, 153, 156, 159–60, 165, 167, 169, 171, 272, 275
   primitive 279
   relational 277
   of use 274
conceptual structure, grasp of 160–1, 164–9, 171, 173–4
conclusion, implicated 56, 59, 61–2, 66, 73, 74
COND 218–21, 223, 226, 230
conditionals 188–92, 193, 200, 203–15, 221–7, 229, 230–2
   anti-realist grasp of 193
   dispositional theory of 201, 212
conditional probability 210–11, 213, 215–20, 225–8, 231
   paradox of 227
confirmation
   theory of 64
   values 66–71
connecting paths 36–9
connections 19–21, 23, 30, 31, 36, 41, 43
   distinct from domains 31
   see also links
connective, probabilistic 215–16, 218
consensusism 282–6, 288
consequences, accessible 42n
constraints 8, 9, 19, 78, 98, 102, 130, 186
   conceptual 169, 170–2
   see also requirements, restrictions

Index

construction, semantic 20–2, 27–8, 30, 38, 42
  see also structure
constructivism 42, 205, 271–2, 294–5
content 10, 11, 15, 48, 79, 84, 87–8, 98–100, 129, 172, 233–4, 241, 262–5, 273–5, 283, 295
  ascription of 172
  explicit 129
  implicit 129
  non-conceptual 172
  occasion-variability of 10, 11
  propositional 79, 84, 87, 88, 98–100
context 10, 27–30, 35, 43, 56–8, 60–1, 64–5, 78, 90, 108, 128–9
  concept of 90
  construction of 78, 93, 95, 98, 102
contextual assumption 54, 56, 58–9, 61, 67, 70–1, 73
conversation, maxims of 46–7, 53–4, 70, 72
Cooper, R. 99
Co-Operative Principle 60
Copi, I. 227
Cormack, A. 78, 96
counterfactuals 27–8, 42, 209–10, 293
counterparts 23–5, 27, 29, 30–1, 35, 37, 40
creativity, conceptual 167–9
criteria 195, 198, 251–2

data, linguistic 27, 20
Davidson, D. 157, 159–61, 173–4
Davies, M. I. 127, 132, 136
decomposition, of thought 168–9
degenerate cases 30
demonstrative thought 163–4, 171
dependency, E-type 99–100
disambiguation 46, 53
  see also ambiguity
discourse 24, 27, 106, 109–14, 116–24
  domains of 25, 27, 106, 109–14, 116–24; change of 111; identity of 106; metaphysical 28; quantifiers 110–12, 124
discourse presuppositions 117
dispositions 202–3, 210–13, 221–5, 231
distinctions
  referential/attributive 33
  semantics/pragmatics 78, 89, 102
  sense/force 181
divergence, radical 286
domain, distinct from connections 31
domains
  of space 27–8, 31, 33, 34, 40–3
  of time 21
domain predicate 113–15, 118
domain selection 91–3, 96
double negation, law of 184
doubts 258–60
Dressler, W. 45
Ducrot, O. 94
Dudman, V. 210, 212
Dummett, M. 159, 168, 173, 178–80, 182, 183–6, 190–2, 195, 272, 281

Edgington, D. 186, 213–15, 232
Eikmeyer, H. 77
elementary logic, model theory of 106–9
embedding 225–6, 228–9, 231
emotivist 201
epistemology 198, 202
equivalence thesis, the 183, 187, 189
essential linguistic structure, doctrine of 147, 149, 151–2, 154–5, 158
essentialism 207n

Evans, G. 99–100, 136, 137, 142–6, 165, 178, 186, 210
excluded middle, law of 184–5, 295
existence, unperceived 161
explanation
  inference to the best 166–72
  inference to plausible 48
  semantic 42
expressions
  complex 2
  grasp of 4
  meaning of 2, 3, 4, 6, 8, 10, 77–9, 94–5, 98, 100, 103
  of thought 5, 6, 7, 8, 9

facts 202, 233, 242–5, 247, 256, 258, 260–7, 269, 281–95
  about content 233–4, 262–5
fallibility 281–2
falsity
  of sentences 9, 11
  of thought 5, 6
Fauconnier, G. 8, 9, 19, 20, 26
figurative language, interpretation of 46
de Finetti, B. 211
focus 82
Fodor, J. A. 50–2, 75, 137, 143, 158
Forbes, G. 214
force 181, 237–8
force/sense distinction 181
foundationalism 280
Frege, G. 159, 168, 221, 281
French, P. A. 134, 206
Freund, J. 227
Fricker, E. 148–50

Gardenfors, P. 124
Gazdar, G. 60, 81, 103, 110
Geach, P. 221
generality constraint 144–6, 156, 158, 165–6
  see also permutation constraint
generative theory, 20n, 21
Gibbard, A. 232

Gilchrist, T. 20
global processes of hypothesis formation 57, 75
global rationality 172
Goquem, J. 214
grammar
  formal properties of 102
  pragmatic 102
  task of 100
  theory of 78, 88, 89, 101
Grandy, R. 52
Grice, H. P. 46–9, 52, 54, 60, 70–2, 77, 91
Gricean theory 91
Guenther, K. 114
Gundersen, K. 114
Guttenplan, S. 14, 177, 178, 269

Hacker, P. M. S. 134
Harman, G. 157
Harper, W. 215, 220, 232
Hausser, R. 99
Hellman, G. 232
Heny, F. 99
hierarchy of roles 34
Higginbottom, J. 99–100
Hill, C. S. 215
Hofstader, D. 33
holism, local 143
Holtzman, S. H. 136
Hooker, C. 215, 220
Horn, L. 80–1, 83–4, 86–7
Hornish, R. M. 48, 52
Hume, D. 206–7, 266, 268, 274, 275, 281
Hunter, G. 183
hypothesis
  confirmation of 50–2, 74–5
  formation of 50–4, 74–5
  local processes of 51, 75
  psychology of 50–2

idealism 272–4, 294
identification
  across domains 25

of thoughts 173
across worlds 25
identification principle 23, 25, 27–9, 31, 35–6, 38–9
identity 33, 34
illocutionary force 46
implicature 45–6, 48–50, 52, 54, 58, 60–2, 66, 68, 70–2, 74
  categorical 70, 71
  contextual 45–7, 59, 61–3, 64–6, 69, 71, 73, 78, 90–2, 94–5, 97, 98
  conventional 46, 77, 78, 93
  conversational 46–7, 49, 60, 84, 129
  indeterminacy of 60, 61, 62
  probabilistic nature of 52, 53, 62
  scalar 77, 78, 80, 81, 95, 96
implicit content 129
independence thesis, the 237–9, 240–1
indeterminacy 60–1
indexicals 128, 299
individuation
  of thoughts 5, 6, 173
  of words 5
inference
  to best explanation 166, 172
  core pattern of 169, 170
  deductive 91, 166–8, 172
  non-demonstrative processes of 46–8, 50, 52
  to plausible explanations 48
  rules of 203
inferential insulation 142–3
inferential integration 142–3
information
  encapsulated and unencapsulated systems 143
  processing 51, 55, 59
  relevant 57–9, 69–70, 71, 72
  storage 56
informational sub-systems 172
informativeness, maxim of 46–7, 53, 72

instrumentalism 201
intentions, propositional 90, 95
interpretation
  radical 149–52, 155, 160, 174
  of sentences 77
  of tense 96
intuitionism 186–7, 191, 295
intuitive physics 162–4, 170, 171

Jackson, F. 215, 232
Jeffrey, R. C. 106, 210
Johnson-Laird, P. 68, 81
judgement 213, 231–2, 267–79, 282, 285, 271, 293, 294
  basic 267–77, 279, 280, 282, 285–91, 293
  demonstrative 277–8
  non-basic 290, 292, 294
  objectivity of 281
  probability 213, 231–2

Kamp, H. 77, 89
Kaplan, D. 77
Kartunnen, L. 110
Kempson, R. 77, 96, 101, 127
knowledge, 2, 14, 127, 131, 134–7, 139–41, 146, 147, 182, 194
  manifestation of 182, 194
  of speaker 182
  speaker's 182
  tacit 127, 131, 134–7, 139–41, 146, 147
Kolmogarov 211
Korner, S. 122
Kratzer, A. 77
Kripke, S. 114, 201, 262, 274, 275, 276, 295

Lacy, R. 20
Lakoff, G. 28, 42
Landman, F. 77
language
  game 235, 237, 247
  on holiday 253–6, 259

natural semantics of 127, 129, 130
philosophy of 19, 20
private 295–7
structure of 127, 130–1, 146–8, 149, 155, 158, 173
theory of 159–65, 173
use of 19, 28, 271, 274, 284–5
Lasnik, H. 99
Leech, G. N. 48, 60
Leibniz 5, 249, 250–1
Leibniz's law 5
Leich, C. M. 136
Levin, M. 134
Levinson, S. C. 48, 50
Lewis, D. 215, 219, 220, 223, 230
liar paradox 246
linguistics 19, 102
  ability 140, 147–52
  see also competence and speaker's competence
links
  multiple 25, 33
  salient 20–7, 30, 33, 36–7, 39–40, 42
  see also connections
logic, classical 184–6, 204, 208
  propositional 208
  quantificational 208
  second-order 115–17, 121
Lowenheim-Skolem theorem 107
Lucas, J. 214

McDowell, J. 178, 183, 185, 186, 198–9, 200, 269, 271–2, 274, 292
Maclaran, R. 45
manifestation argument 183, 191
Marin, O. S. M. 140
Marton, A. v, 105
Mates, B. 106
maxims, of conversation 46–7, 53–4, 70–2
meaning 1–6, 8, 11–14, 43, 48, 130–6, 138, 178, 180, 186, 195, 197, 199, 271–5, 296
  central notion of 181, 186, 195, 197, 199
  conception of 5, 181, 199
  construction from parts, 2, 3, 4
  core 80
  determining truth conditions 11, 12, 13
  of expressions 2, 3, 4,6, 8, 10, 128, 129, 131, 148–55
  knowledge of 2, 14
  objectivity of 262, 273–6
  speaker's 48
  specification of 1, 2, 3, 4, 6; derivation of 130–6, 138
  structure of 2, 3
  theory of 178–80, 190, 191, 197; constraints on 178, 182, 184; language specific 181–2; truth-conditional 179–80, 191, 194
  of words 1, 3, 8, 11–14
Mellor, H. 177
mental
  emotivist theories of the 201
  spaces 27, 28, 31, 42
mental map 163–4, 170–1
Meredith, M. 33
metalinguistic negation 83–8
metaphysics 177–80, 184, 186, 190–1, 195, 197, 199–200, 202, 208–9
metonymy 20, 20n, 21, 23, 31
Millar, G. 81
modality, projective theory of 207–8
modular structure of mind 145–6
de Moivre 211
Morgan, J. 46, 77

names and naming 247–57, 261–2
  concept of 254
naming game, the 153
necessity 206, 207
negation operator

descriptive 87–8
pragmatic 83–5
neurophysiology 135, 137–8
Nietzsche 207
number theory 295
Nunberg, G. 20, 23

objectivity
  concept of 160, 161, 169
  intersubjective 160
  of judgement 281–4, 297
  of meaning 272, 273, 281–6, 288–9, 292–7
  of truth 160–1, 164–5, 169
objects
  arbitrary 264
  baptism of 253
  thoughts of 163–4, 166, 170, 171
observation statements 278, 280
Orde, S. 124
order, temporal 161–4, 170
ostension 23n
other minds 194

paradoxes 213–14, 227, 243, 246, 266
Parratt, H. 93, 183
Partee, B. 77, 124
PASS 209–10, 214, 219, 231
passing assumptions 209
past-tense sentences 192, 194, 196, 268
Peacocke, C. 103, 278
Pearce, G. 232
perception 162–4, 170
  time-lags in 102
perspectives 161, 162, 164, 170
Pettit, P. 297
phonology 19
  rules of 28
physics, intuitive 162–4, 170–1
  correction of 164, 170
Posner, M. 140
pragmatics 19, 88, 89, 129
  of discourse 117
  lexical 117

predicates, vague 214
presupposition 109–10, 115–17, 119–20, 122
  theory of 48, 51, 52, 53, 89, 98
Price, H. 228
principles, pragmatic 78, 80, 82–3, 86–8, 99
pro-predicates 114–15
probability
  degrees of 213
  subjective 228
properties, relativity of 21–2, 27, 43
propositions 9–11, 65–6, 72, 205–8, 223–5, 232–5, 258–9
  content of 48, 77–9, 89, 98–103
  context set of 90, 91, 93
propositional attitudes 140–6, 166–7, 171, 172, 174, 188
  ascription of 266
  see also beliefs
psychology, speaker's 4, 30, 33
Putnam, H. 124

quantification
  domains of 110–12, 124
  second order 106, 120
quantifiers 105, 107–12, 114
  anaphora of 105, 113
  relativization of 113
quasi-assertion 281
quasi-realism 205, 208–9, 214, 218
Quine 137, 206, 207, 275

rational reconstruction 134
realism 177–80, 182–5, 190–1, 197, 199, 200, 203, 205–7, 210, 221, 230, 269, 289
  moral 203, 221
realist conception of truth 178–80, 182, 190, 194, 197
reasoning
  analogical 51
  deductive 45–6, 48–54, 64, 73, 74, 169, 171, 172

recognition statement 277–9
recognitional capacity 278–9, 286–7
recursive devices 3
redundancy theory 183, 184, 204
reference assignment 46, 68–9
Reinhart, T. 99, 100
relations
　inferential between thoughts 166–9
　between name and object 253–4
relevance
　degrees of 54, 66
　maxims of 46, 47, 53, 70
　principle of 54–5, 56–62, 66–74, 78, 89–93, 95, 97–8, 101–2, 129
　theory of 53, 54, 57–9, 66, 67, 73, 94, 101
requirements
　of correct use 11
　structured 2, 3, 4
　see also constraints
Reser, H. 77
restrictions, contextually imposed 108–9
roles 19, 31–8, 40
　distinct from values 31
　hierarchy of 34
　super- 34, 38
rules 19, 203, 204
　construction, account of 8
　conversational 121; see also maxims
　following 271, 276, 295–6
　non-demonstrative inference 50, 64, 203
　semantic 137, 140, 147–8
　syntactic 137, 140, 147
Russell, B. 212, 251–4

Sainsbury, M. 155
Sätze 11, 234
sayings, distinct from meaning 5, 8–9, 12

scepticism 274–5
　global 276
Schmidt, S. 77
Schnelle, H. 99
semantics
　anti-realist 180
　formal 77–9, 88, 89, 95, 98, 102
sentences 2, 4–6, 8–12
　declarative 4, 5, 6, 11
　meaning of 5, 30, 148–55
　novel 2
　truth/falsity of 9, 11
　verification transcendent 182–3, 185–7
Shafer, G. 211, 226–7, 232
Shanker, S. 134
Skorupski 271
Slomson, A. B. 106
Smith, N. V. 52, 54
space 27, 28, 31, 33–4, 44–3, 163, 202
speaker's 132–5, 137–8, 140, 147–9
　competence 4, 6
　meaning 48
　psychology 4, 30, 33
speakings 6, 7, 8, 9
Sperber, D. 45–6, 52, 54, 62, 89, 96, 127–8
Stalnaker, R. 110, 210–11, 220, 230, 232
stance 201–6
　see also belief
statements
　basic 292–3
　causal 266–8
　descriptive 279
　emotive 275
　ethical 366
　factual 275
　past-tense 192–4, 196, 268
　projective 275
Stevenson, L. 271
Stich, S. 141–2
Strawson, P. F. 109–10, 153, 177, 197, 199, 210

structure 2, 3, 4, 20, 168, 169
  abstract 132, 134
  causal-exaplanatory 132–3,
    135–6, 138, 146–7, 151
  neurogeographical 139–46
  psychology of 131–3, 134–5,
    139–40, 146, 147
  requirement of 3, 4
  semantic 131, 132–4, 138, 146–7,
    150–4
  syntactic 3, 4
  of thought, 3, 127, 131, 146,
    155–8
  understanding of 2, 3
Stump, G. 77
sub-doxastic states 140–6, 158
subject/predicate contrast 109
subjective probability 228
super-role 34, 38
supervaluation 185
supposition 224–6
syntax 19
  derivations of 28

target 20, 28, 29–30, 36, 40
Teller, P. 226
tense, interpretation of 193
theory
  expectations of 1, 2, 3, 4; see also
    constraints; restrictions
  formal 1, 3, 4
  semantic 1–4, 6, 8–9, 11, 14–15
  substantive 1, 4
  of truth 212–13, 215–17, 232,
    273–5, 283, 295
thought
  account of 159, 161, 164, 166–7,
    169, 173; constraints on
    166, 167, 169, 172
  analysis of 168, 169
  ascription of 105, 107, 171–2
  decomposition of 168, 169
  expression of 5–9
  grasp of 165–6, 168–9, 171, 174
  individuation of 5, 6

spatial conditions of 161, 162
structure of 3, 127, 131, 146,
  155–8, 254–5
truth conditions of 5, 6, 7, 11
see also beliefs, propositional
  attitudes,
tightness constraint 153n
time 202
Travis, C. vii, 1, 27, 43, 78, 158,
  232–2, 271
trigger 20, 28–9, 35–9
triviality proof, Lewis's 218–20,
  223, 225, 230, 231
truth
  –bearers 12, 233–4, 236, 237,
    238–41, 243–5, 247, 262, 267
  concept of 160–1, 169, 177–8,
    180, 184, 187, 191, 193,
    200, 203, 205, 209, 218,
    234, 244
  conditions 5, 6, 7–11, 13, 42–3,
    77–9, 88, 127–8, 130, 183,
    184, 201–3, 205, 209, 214,
    232, 254; grasp of 159–61,
    165–9, 171, 173, 174
  degrees of 213, 214
  moral 218
  objective 160–1, 164–5, 169
  predicate, the 177–9, 182–5, 190,
    197
  realist 178–82, 190, 194, 197
  theory, thin 204, 209, 218;
    Tarskian 9
  transcendent notion of 179
  value 1, 59, 201, 206, 208–10,
    212–13, 215–17, 232,
    234–44, 246–7, 266–9,
    273–5, 283, 295; links
    191–3, 195–6, 198, 200

Uehling, T. 134, 206
understanding 2–4, 10, 12–14,
  27–30, 234–8, 240–1, 243,
  246–51, 257, 261, 263, 265,
  271–2, 275, 279, 285

idealized 4
structure 2, 3
theory of 207
of words 10, 13
utterances
 content of 49, 69, 71–4
 interpretation of 45–6, 50, 52–3, 58, 61, 67–9, 74–5, 77–8, 89–91, 93, 95–6, 98, 101, 103
 moral 203
 referential context of 69
 relevance of 59, 63, 72, 73

value 31–40
 identification of 31
 realist 245
 role, distinct from 31
Van Fraasen, B. 215, 220, 230
Van Straaten 2, 177, 210
Veltman, F. 77
Verstehen 171–2
visual processing, theory of 144
vocabulary
 basic 93
 modal 206
 non-basic 93

Wason, P. C. 68
Werth, P. 54
Wettstein, H. 206
Wiggins, D. 177
Williams, C. 124
Wilson, D. 45–6, 52, 54, 62, 87, 89, 96, 127–8
Wittgenstein, L. 10–12, 165, 195, 201, 233–6, 243, 245, 248–9, 251–4, 258, 262, 264–5, 269, 271, 272, 274–7, 281, 283, 285, 295, 296
words 10, 11, 12–14
 individuation of 5
 meaning of 1, 3, 8, 11, 13
 understanding of 10, 13
 use of 11, 12, 14
Wright, C. 14, 134, 136, 142, 158, 177–8, 188, 195, 269, 271–2, 295, 297

Yule, G. 45, 48